CULT MEDIA, FANDOM, AND TEXTILES

CULT MEDIA, FANDOM, AND TEXTILES

Handicrafting as Fan Art

BRIGID CHERRY

Bloomsbury Academic
An imprint of Bloomsbury Publishing Plc

B L O O M S B U R Y
LONDON · OXFORD · NEW YORK · NEW DELHI · SYDNEY

Bloomsbury Academic

An imprint of Bloomsbury Publishing Plc

50 Bedford Square
London
WC1B 3DP
UK

1385 Broadway
New York
NY 10018
USA

www.bloomsbury.com

BLOOMSBURY and the Diana logo are trademarks of Bloomsbury Publishing Plc

First published 2016

British Library Cataloguing-in-Publication Data
A catalogue record for this book is available from the British Library.

ISBN: HB: 978-1-4742-1515-2
ePDF: 978-1-4742-1516-9
ePub: 978-1-4742-1517-6

Library of Congress Cataloging-in-Publication Data
Names: Cherry, Brigid, 1957- author.
Title: Cult media, fandom and textiles : handicrafting as fan art / Brigid Cherry.
Description: New York : Bloomsbury Academic, 2016.
Identifiers: LCCN 2016025273 | ISBN 9781474215152 (hardback) | ISBN 9781474215176 (epub)
Subjects: LCSH: Textile crafts and popular culture. | Textile crafts–Social aspects. |
Fans (Persons)–Psychology. | BISAC: DESIGN / Textile & Costume. |
SOCIAL SCIENCE / Media Studies. | CRAFTS & HOBBIES / Needlework / Knitting.
Classification: LCC TT699 .C525 2016 | DDC 745.5–dc23 LC record
available at https://lccn.loc.gov/2016025273

Cover design: Catherine Wood
Cover image credits:
Dr Who: Photo by Anwar Hussein/Getty Images
Steampunk enthusiasts: Photo by Adam Berry/Getty Images
Steampunk top hat: Photo by Christopher Furlong/Getty Images
Harry Potter scarf: David Livingston/Stringer
True Blood (US TV series): HBO/THE KOBAL COLLECTION
Textile images: Shutterstock

Typeset by Integra Software Services Pvt. Ltd.
Printed and bound in Great Britain

CONTENTS

LIST OF ILLUSTRATIONS

Table

ACKNOWLEDGMENTS

I would like to acknowledge the many people who have participated in this study and encouraged me along the way. Thanks go to Helen, without whom I might not have joined Ravelry, and to Dr. Jenny Barrett who encouraged me to think about fan handicrafting as a research project. I would also like to thank Dr. Stacey Abbott for her support. Many thanks are also due to the many members of the Ravelry community who participated in this study; they are too many to mention individually, but they all have my gratitude. Special thanks go to Kirsty and Hanka for their enthusiasm for fan handicrafting, to Julie for allowing me to test knit her *Game of Thrones* patterns and for mentoring me as I learned to spin during Tour de Fleece, and to Heatherly and Shannen for giving me the opportunity to design socks for Super Sock Scare Fest. Finally, very special thanks go to my husband Brian for his unwavering support and endless patience.

DISCLAIMER

All photographs of fan art used in this academic work have been reproduced with the permission of their creators. Where fan art includes elements of characters or objects from popular television programs and/or films, which is third-party copyright and/or trademark materials, such use (a) is regarded by the author and publishers as fair dealing and/or fair for the purposes of criticism and review only; and (b) does not imply any form of endorsement, sponsorship, or approval on the part of third-party brand owners.

INTRODUCTION:
CULT MEDIA
AND HANDICRAFTING

In the *Doctor Who* episode "The Impossible Astronaut" (2011), the Doctor tells his companions: "Home! Well, you two are. Off you pop and make babies. Dr Song, back to prison. Me, I'm late for a biplane lesson in 1911, or it could be knitting. Knitting or biplanes, one or the other." The Doctor revealing himself to be interested in knitting delighted one segment of the *Doctor Who* fan community—not only mentioning his (possible) knitting lesson in this instance, but also being shown reading *Knitting for Girls* magazine in "The Wedding of River Song" (2011) and in the webisode "The Night of the Doctor" (2013) saying, "Bring me knitting!" (among other impossibly time-consuming things) when asked how he might fill the last four minutes of life. It was a significant revelation about the Doctor's interests because these particular fans belong to a community that practices the fiber arts and are primarily knitters. They share a hobby with the Doctor, and this makes a character they already love even more appealing. *Doctor Who* has, of course, been linked to knitting since the 1970s, thanks to the excessively long, multicolored scarf that remained—in various forms—a part of his costume for the seven years that Tom Baker played the Doctor (1974–1981). Nor is *Doctor Who* the only TV, film, or fiction series to have an inbuilt connection to knitting and other forms of handicrafting.

In fact, popular culture is full of characters knitting and occasionally crocheting, and many examples of iconic instances of knitwear and knitted items come from media texts in cult genres (such as science fiction, fantasy, and horror) with active fan followings.[1] Such examples of handicrafting in cult media fall into firstly, the category of representations of knitters, and, secondly, knitted accessories worn by characters or displayed as set dressing and props. The *Doctor Who* example is perhaps a special case, forming an instance of the first category only as an intent to learn; we never actually see the Doctor knit. Other examples of the first category are more overt, offering the handicrafter in the audience a strong point of identification. The *Harry Potter* novels (Rowling 1997–2007) and films (2001–2011), for instance, are highly significant, with needlework in general being a popular pastime in the storyworld. A wide range of characters, including Hagrid, Dobby the House Elf, Hermione, Molly Weasley, and Sybil Trelawney, all knit,[2] and a knitting charm makes needles knit by themselves. In the films, knitting provides a colorful source of inspiration for the viewers who handicraft: for example, Molly Weasley's ubiquitous Christmas jumpers and her multicolored crochet cardigan from the *Harry Potter and the Chamber of Secrets* film (2002) and Hagrid knitting his "yellow circus tent" on the train in *Harry Potter and the Philosopher's Stone* (2001). Further examples include the private investigator Emerson Cod in the TV series *Pushing Daisies* (2007–2009), who reads *Knitwit* magazine and knits when he is upset, and Maggie in series 5 of *Misfits* (2013), who has the power of "precognitive crafting" (she knits pictures of future events into jumpers). In the second category, the iconic knitted item might be given a diegetic history identifying the knitter behind the object: in the *Doctor Who* story "The Ark in Space" (1975), the Doctor tells his companion Harry that his scarf was made for him by Madame Nostradamus, "a witty little knitter," and in the *Firefly* (2002–2003) episode "The Message" Jayne receives a gift from his mother of a hand-knitted red, yellow, and orange earflap hat with pom-pom which he wears with pride. More commonly, knitted garments simply represent a character's taste in clothing, fashion trends, or a cultural identity. For example, Sarah Lund's Faroese jumpers in *Forbrydelsen/The Killing* (2007–2012) are a signifier of Danishness. David Starsky's belted, Aztec-patterned cardigan from *Starsky and Hutch* (1975–1979) is a symbol of the character's sexual appeal (Turney 2009: 38). Many of these examples, as well, perhaps, as those from a third, though minor, category of knitted puppets, which would include *The Clangers* (1969–1974) and the ventriloquist Shari Lewis's Lambchop, have all become iconic images instantly connecting to their respective texts. But more importantly, to any fans who knit, such items are easily recreatable, meaning that they have the potential to become handcrafted material objects incorporated into the lived fandom, if not the life, of the maker.

Knitting and popular culture

Why is this important? Such interest in knitwear and other examples of handcrafting might be considered a trivial or minor response to a TV program or other text; the vast majority of viewers will own and wear knitwear on a regular basis, albeit probably mass produced, but the practice of handicrafting is not something they might notice in particular. While representations of the fiber arts and handicrafts may play a very minor part in popular culture overall, it is the fact that they are significant to members of the handicrafting community that watch films or programs with active fan communities that is the relevant point here. We might, of course, pick out any art or craft on display in popular culture—jewellery, soft furnishings, paintings, fashion designs—but handicrafts, especially knitting, hold prominence for many viewers simply because such skills are a very common pastime, hobby, or activity practiced everyday by very large numbers of people (research carried out in 2005 for the Craft Yarn Council of America states that 53 million women in the USA know how to knit or crochet[3]). It is difficult to estimate the total number of practicing knitters and other handicrafters worldwide, but the primary online community for knitters and crocheters Ravelry has over 5 million members.[4] The total number might well be much higher since not all practicing handicrafters will join Ravelry. Regardless of an accurate figure, though, a significant proportion of any audience—and therefore of a fan community—may well have more than a passing interest in examples of handicrafting or handcrafted items in their favorite films, novels, and TV series.

What I would like to suggest here is that since handcrafting is depicted in a wide range of popular culture texts ranging from *Call the Midwife* (2012–)—which infamously, among crafting circles at least, showed a character wrongly "knitting" a crochet blanket with needles rather than a hook, though many other instances of knitting correctly occur—to *Monty Python's Flying Circus* (1969–1974)— where Eric Idle's and Terry Jones's Pepperpots[5] appear to be able knitters in several sketches (though Michael Palin clearly fakes it)—even relatively minor instances of handicrafting or handcrafted items resonate with members of the audience. This can lead to the creation of iconic instances of knitting or knitwear that take on life beyond the text and become fixed in the wider culture where they become recognizable in their own right—the *Doctor Who* scarf being a case in point. But more importantly, any and all representations of handicrafting in popular culture take on significance when closely observed by handicrafters (although they may never become iconic). What makes this interesting is that this audience segment take note of and share the representations of their pastime that they have seen on film and TV in communities online. For example, on the Ravelry forum, there is an ongoing Needlework on the Net discussion thread for "My favourite movie knitting reference," and a group "As seen in the movies" to discuss knitwear seen on screen.

In this context, how do the pleasures of viewing and of handicrafting intersect? How fan audiences respond to popular culture is important here. Audiences are not only active users of media but also, and particularly in the context of media fandom and fan cultures, producers of additions to the text. Discussing the fact that "our interactions with media texts today rarely have any clear boundaries," John L. Sullivan (2013: 191) points out that "media audiences use their interpretive power to actively subvert, distort, and even reimagine mainstream media content to suit their own needs and desires." This can take the form of audiences (or more specifically fans, which is the audience segment I am most interested in) writing their own stories, remixing video or still images, and making their own art and films that take place in the storyworlds created by popular culture. The recent resurgence of interest in do-it-yourself (DIY) crafting makes it important to consider how such activities relate to media content in terms of fans as producers.

Handicrafters in the audience are already catered for to some extent by the yarn industry. Commercial patterns have been inspired by popular culture for decades. This is demonstrated by the Sirdar pattern leaflet 5753 for a Starsky-style cardigan as discussed by Joanne Turney in *The Culture of Knitting* (2009: 38–39). The knitted toy designer Alan Dart has produced toys for *Shaun the Sheep* (2007–2014) and Wallace and Gromit (*A Grand Day Out* 1990) for Patons, *Bob the Builder* (1998–2005) for *Woman's Weekly*, and a set of patterns for *Magic Roundabout* (1964–1971) characters. More recently, in the year when *Doctor Who* celebrated its 50th anniversary, the yarn company Rowan published its Time Traveller's Scarf pattern[6] based on the *Doctor Who* scarf. The same year, the company also incorporated *Doctor Who* scarf colors into its Pure Wool range. In other cases, patterns have been provided by the culture industry itself, as seen with the free Make a Clanger worksheet sent out to viewers who wrote in to the BBC in the 1960s[7] and recently updated with a downloadable pattern on the CBeebies website in conjunction with the launch of new version of the program in 2015.[8] However, these examples are aimed at the general crafting market, and not specifically at fans. Dart is clearly catering to knitters making toys for the children in their lives.

As these examples illustrate, though, there is a long history of the ways in which handicrafting links to popular culture. The examples of knitting patterns tied to film and television programs suggest that fan interests have been commodified by both the culture industries and yarn companies. In recent years, the culture industries have marketed officially approved knitwear: Fox endorsed a Jayne hat sold by ThinkGeek[9] and an official BBC *Doctor Who* scarf is sold through the BBC Shop.[10] Although mass-produced items such as these are available, they are not aimed specifically at handicrafters and may not be of interest to fans who want to, prefer to, and are able to do-it-themselves (something that is central to fan culture with its emphasis on fan-written fiction and fan-produced media). Commercial patterns, as in those for the Starsky cardigan or Rowan *Doctor Who* scarf (which are also, given the lack of overt references to the programs, presumably unlicensed), may be of some interest to fans, and indeed fans may acquire the patterns and make these designs, but they cannot necessarily be considered fan production in their own right, not least in that such items may be made for other reasons such as gifts for children and others. Furthermore, both the Sirdar *Starsky and Hutch* and the Rowan *Doctor Who* patterns are quite obviously inauthentic, being similar to but not identical to the originals. Fan culture, and therefore fan handicrafting, is distinct in several respects. For example, the BBC's *The Doctor Who Pattern Book* (Gammon 1984) remains an object of cult curiosity for *Doctor Who* fans generally (it contains knitting and sewing patterns for logo jumpers, *Doctor Who* outfits for dolls, and toys). Cult collectors have long been interested in unique, hard to track down, or obscure objects such as this, but it may offer particular appeals to those fans who also have a prior interest in handicrafting. In fact, some fan handicrafters have acquired copies of this out-of-print book and some have made the Peter Davison-era cricket jumper to wear as part of a *Doctor Who* costume, for example. Although various patterns exist for similar cricket jumpers, the fact that the fan handicrafter has used the pattern from a cult object in its own right adds to the pleasures of making and wearing the jumper.

Fan handicrafting

So how exactly does the fan making this cricket jumper, for example, differ from handicrafters inspired by popular culture in general? The most obvious difference is that fan handicrafters do not stop at reproducing knitted or crocheted items from films and TV series. Fan handicrafters are avid transformers of the text, using knitted and crocheted textiles as the medium with which they produce fan art. Props, costumes, portraits, action figures, scenes, and narrative themes can all be remediated via the fiber arts. In this way, fan handicrafting is a form of fan production, and while largely unrecognized even within some fan cultures, it deserves to be understood alongside fan fiction and other forms of fan production.

It may seem strange at first to be linking fandom with handicrafting (at least outwith the examples of knitting and knitwear seen in the films and TV programs discussed earlier), but a crocheted bottle of Tru:Blood, knitted TARDIS, R2-D2 beanie hat, Cthulhu balaclava (the "Cthulhuclava"), and colorwork image of the Serenity ship from *Firefly* are only a few among the many themed projects created by fans. One of the most noticeable differences is that none of these examples were originally knitted or crocheted items in the original text. These conjunctions of handcrafted textiles with glass bottles, monstrous entities, wood and metal objects might seem something of a contradiction, but they indicate that there is a growing interest in material fan production, a fan community and even a micro-economy organized around handicrafting practices across many fandoms. In the thriving world of handicrafting, cult media texts, including *My Little Pony: Friendship is Magic* (2010–), Sherlock Holmes, *Game of Thrones* (2011–), Tolkien, science fiction such as *Star Wars* (1977–), and *Battlestar Galactica* (2004–2009), the vampire and horror genres, and Terry Pratchett novels, among others (in addition to *Harry Potter*, *Doctor Who*, and *Firefly* as evidenced by the examples), are source material for creative and entrepreneurial fans who produce an array of projects, yarns, and patterns that fuel the world of fan handicrafting. In fact, such items can be considered examples of fan art, and fan handicrafting thus considered as a distinct form of fan production in its own right.

This distinction is further illustrated by the example of vampire fandom and handicrafting. Given the genre's prominence with *Buffy the Vampire the Slayer* (1997–2003), *Twilight* (Meyer 2005–2008), and *True Blood* (2008–2014), as well as its status in classic horror cinema, it is not particularly surprising to find patterns for knitted vampires. A commercial example is Alan Dart's Going Batty, published in *Simply Knitting* magazine in 2009. In the same way that the Starsky-style cardigan and the Time Traveller's Scarf, as well as Dart's other patterns mentioned earlier, are driven by popularity, this pattern caters to the Halloween market. Ghosts, monsters, and pumpkins take on the form of knitted and crocheted toys in handicrafting magazines and books, just as recipes for party food and cakes might take on scary horror imagery and characters at the same time of year in cookery and women's magazines. *Simply Knitting* magazine advises that: "No trick, this well-dressed vampire bat will make a brilliant treat for any Halloween-loving child ... or grown up!" These are primarily toys (though not necessarily only for children) and are generic in the sense of being based on the idea of the Gothic figure (with widow's peak, prominent fangs, and dark suit with high-collared cape resembling the image of Universal's and Hammer film's version of Dracula as a supernatural creature that can transform into a bat).

By contrast, vampire handicrafting as an instance of fan art can be seen in the book *Vampire Knits* (Miller 2010). This contains patterns loosely inspired by knitwear and accessories from the *Twilight* movies (2008–2012). Perhaps the most telling evidence of it being a fan production is that the pre-launch marketing for the book was at Comic-Con 2010 in San Diego.[11] It represents a specifically fan project, with patterns written by fans and for fans brought together at the fan convention and in the author's Ravelry group, also named Vampire Knits. These patterns are presented in quite a distinct way from the vampire pattern by Alan Dart—that is, in the context of Dart being a well-known toy designer. Rather, the book highlights that the designers of the *Vampire Knits* patterns are fans who knit or crochet. As Genevieve Miller, author/editor of *Vampire Knits*, writes in her introduction (2010, 8–9):

> I'm a knitter who loves vampires—and I'm not the only one. I started out as your average knitter [... but] it didn't take me long to find a group of knitters and designers who were similarly enthralled by modern day vampire stories. We fans of mysterious, brooding and sexy vampires shared ideas and inspirations with one another, creating patterns inspired by beloved immortal characters. And so the idea for this book was born.

This acknowledgment of the attractiveness and sexual appeal of vampire characters for female fans and of the fan knitter interacting with her fellow fans takes on further significance when considered within the context of the fan reception of texts and of fan culture.

Just as DIY culture, of which handicrafting is a significant component, has become more widespread in recent years, so too has participatory fan culture (i.e., fandom that extends beyond average or even intense consumption into fan production as described by Sullivan [2013]). The Internet has opened up access to fan communities organized around fan production and to the kinds of intense activities that were once the hallmark of specialized fandom. This has created a situation where, to borrow a phrase from Lister et al. (2009: 200), who frame this as a form of Long Tail cultural consumption, "we are all fans now." That a significant number of handicrafters may indeed be active viewers and fan producers is the key point in this respect. They take their interest in a storyworld and its characters further by talking online with other fans who handicraft about the text in general or about the examples of handicrafting they have spotted, going on to devise their own patterns, reproducing crafted items, or drawing inspiration from them. This means that handcrafted projects fall into the same category as one of the most significant activities of a fan community, namely fan production. Parallels with fans' acts of making their own additions to the text can be found in handicrafting communities. While there may not appear to be many obvious correspondences with fan production such as writing fan fiction, editing clips into music videos, or making fan films, handicrafters do undertake remediations of the text to suit their own desires and tastes. Rather than drawing, painting, or digitally manipulating pieces of fan art, knitters and crocheters make their own fan fiber art with yarn and needles or hooks. And, of course, crafts are already involved in the material fan production of costume and prop making. The fact that some fans are using their handicrafting skills and adapting their handicrafting projects to reflect their fan interests is a notable addition to the roster of fan production. The representations of handicrafting in cult media and the wider popular culture, particularly when they occur within texts with large fan followings or dedicated audiences, offer an opportunity for handicrafters to celebrate their fandom through their crafting. But beyond this, fans also incorporate their love for the text into a wide range of other projects not represented in the original text, including projects not ostensibly related to the text. In this way, they extend and even transform the text just as fan fiction writers do. This conjunction of cult media, hobby, and fan production forms the arena for this book.

Background of the research and autoethnographical approaches

At this point it is pertinent to set out how this research project arose, and in particular my own background in relation to handicrafting and fan culture. In late 2008, I applied to join the Ravelry knitting and crochet site. I had been directed there when the Ravelry yarn database was recommended on the forum of a retro fashion site as helpful for finding substitutes for yarn specified in 1940s and 1950s knitting patterns. Ravelry was also mentioned as having a group for discussing the vintage pattern updates in the book *A Stitch in Time* (Crawford and Waller 2008). I had come across this book when I picked up an advertising flyer from Alfies Antique Market in London when I was on the way to Nina's Hair Parlour (a retro hair salon). In fact, my first post on Ravelry was to introduce myself in this group, and my first recorded projects in my Ravelry profile include a 1940s Hollywood-inspired cardigan from a contemporary Rowan pattern and 1930s and 1950s jumper patterns from *A Stitch in Time* (both of the latter completed during knit-alongs organized in the Stitch in Time group). While retro and vintage knitting are not examples of fan knitting per se, they do reflect the incorporation of cultural tastes, fan identity, and subcultural affiliations into crafting practices. My own interest in vintage fashion also incorporates Victorian and Edwardian styles that draw specifically on a taste for vampire and Gothic cinema, steampunk (a form of science fiction rooted in the Victorian era), and an enduring nostalgic love for costumes from the film version of *Mary Poppins* (1964). My Ravelry project page quickly grew to display my tastes in popular culture, mingling retro knitwear with frilly steampunk cuffs, Amelia Earhart-style flying helmet, Gothic-influenced fingerless mittens, and stripy Tim Burton-style socks.

I was not alone on Ravelry in having and sharing these stylistic interests and tastes, the members of the site directing others to sources for patterns and making yarn recommendations, and—most importantly—facilitating social interaction. My fan scholar's interest was piqued by discovering that *Harry Potter* fans had gathered together to invent a game organized around lessons at Hogwarts, that fans of science fiction and steampunk produced podcasts about their joint handicrafting and fan interests, that fans of *True Blood* got together to knit socks and other projects together. Curious to learn more, I joined in, making a pair of My Vampire Boyfriend socks for the group knit-along during season 2 of *True Blood* in 2009 and a pair of Eric socks for Team True Blood in Ravelry's version of the Olympic Games in 2010. Discussing this "find" with academic colleagues, the seed was born to explore the practices of fan handicrafting further, and the idea for this research project was formulated. The research, which primarily employs a participant-observation method, is thus informed and underpinned by autoethnography.

As Henry Jenkins (2013: vii) re-emphasizes in the interview (conducted by Suzanne Scott) that opens the twentieth-anniversary edition of *Textual Poachers*, fan scholars are very much invested in and engaged with the fan communities at the heart of their research. They are—to use the term he is credited with coining—"aca-fans" (or academic-fans). The ethnographic method of aca-fan research is embedded in the autobiographical turn of cultural studies (Jenkins 2013: ix). This entails a commitment to a subjective approach, one that was exemplified by emerging bodies of work in feminist and queer scholarship. Within such autoethnography, it is important that the researcher acknowledges and engages with their own knowledge, motivations, and experiences. As the origin of the research recounted earlier indicates, my own investment as a fan and as a handicrafter is central (though largely these interests—apart from one or two previous attempts at *Doctor Who* costumes—remained separate aspects of my life before joining Ravelry).

I grew up in a family in which handicrafting was a regular domestic activity. My mother, aunt, and grandmother always had knitting projects on the go, and I learnt from this, continuing this habit into my teens, at which time I also taught myself to crochet. My grandmother, before she married and had a family, had also been a dressmaker by trade, doing piecework in the garment industry. She made clothes for me as a child on an old Singer treadle machine, on which I also learnt to make clothing (she also taught me to cut my own patterns from brown wrapping paper). I have continued to handicraft intermittently throughout my adult life. Similarly, I have long identified as a fan, of science fiction in particular, and this too relates back to family. My father was a science fiction fan and as a child and young teenager I read through his extensive library of classic literary science fiction, graduating to those offered by the local library. My own tastes spread into horror and the Gothic, and to include science fiction and fantasy television. It was through a particular liking for *Doctor Who* that I began to think of myself as a fan, becoming active in *Doctor Who* fandom, attending local group meetings and conventions, editing and writing for fanzines, and occasionally making forays into fan filmmaking and music video editing. My experiences in fandom and my intellectual interest in film and television studies became the impetus for my PhD research into the female horror film audience and subsequently into fan audiences more widely.

As my growing awareness of fan-themed handicrafting after joining Ravelry in January 2009 made clear to me, the many fan activities and groups provide an interrelating network of creative, social, and affective experiences for fan handicrafters that to a large extent were reflected in my own. In constructing a participant-observation study of a sample of the fan groups covering a wide range of cult media, I was therefore able to reflect on the fan handicrafting experiences of those I was participating with as well as my own. Data was collected not as an outsider, but as an active participant in the Nerd Wars tournaments in which players "compete" in challenges (playing on *Doctor Who*, horror film, *Game of Thrones*, and steampunk teams) and the Harry Potter Knitting and Crochet House Cup crafting for Hogwarts classes and Quidditch matches (in Ravenclaw and Slytherin Houses). I have also taken part in the Super Sock Scare Fest where players watch a program of horror films while making accompanying sock patterns inspired by the films, and played on Team TARDIS in the Ravellenic Games and Tour de Fleece (a spinning event mirroring the Tour de France). All these activities have provided invaluable access to the fan communities I have drawn data from for this study and put me in contact with a wide range of fans who have been subsequently interviewed for the study. But as a fan myself, I have shared in the many positive (and a few negative) experiences. One of the key approaches in understanding fan handicrafting is its affective nature— crafting can be an exceedingly pleasurable undertaking in its own right, but it also facilitates intense connections to the text and to the social culture that it operates within. During the research, I have therefore focused not only on the material objects produced by these fans (including how these relate to the fan text) but also on how the fan communities within Ravelry operate as affective spaces.

Casting on: An account of handicrafting as fan art

The topic of this book, then, is handicrafting in relation to popular culture, specifically in respect of fan cultures associated with cult media. It is not a dedicated account of representations of handicrafting in popular culture, nor is it one about handcrafted textiles depicted in popular culture texts (though both of these aspects often underlie the discussion). Rather, it is about the ways in which cult film and television inspires handicrafters in their crafting, and it focuses specifically on the ways in which handicrafters who consider themselves to be fans of specific cult texts use their handicrafting to produce fan art. The book thus explores the fans' handicrafting projects in a range of fandoms. In this sense, it is an account of a participatory culture as defined by Henry Jenkins (1992), and organized around the ways in which fans remediate and transform the text through their handicrafting. In focusing specifically on the activities of those fans who are also handicrafters, it is thus about relationships between fans and also to a lesser extent between fans and the culture industries. Fan production has been well covered within fan studies to date. At least since Henry Jenkins's spearheading work on textual poaching and studies of its practice within specific fan communities such as Camille Bacon-Smith's research into *Star Trek* fan fiction writing (1992), fan production has been widely recognized and studied, but with the exception perhaps of costuming and cosplay, handicrafting in its own right has received little attention. The aim of this book is to present an in-depth look at this fan handicrafting and to give an account of handicrafting as a form of fan production and a producerly fan activity.

To this end, it presents a survey of fan handicrafting, an account of the ways in which fans incorporate their fan interests into their handicrafting, construct fan identities and forge fan communities within online handicrafting forums, and remediate popular culture texts through their knitting, crochet, spinning, and dyeing. The first two chapters set out the background, contexts, and parameters of the research. Chapter 1 locates fan handicrafting within interdisciplinary theoretical contexts, drawing on textile studies on the one hand and fan studies on the other. Fan handicrafting is framed in terms of participatory culture within which fans can be seen as playing with the text, extending it, reworking it to suit their own desires and interests, and building communities around their fan production. Underlying this, fan handicrafting is also related to the knitting revival and the ways in which handicrafting has been incorporated into feminist, DIY, and artistic practices, as well as the ways in which it is embedded in the social sphere. Chapter 2 then sets out the research design for the empirical study of fan handicrafting that forms the findings of this book. I set out the ways in which data was captured, with a focus on the Ravelry handicrafting community. The chapter also presents a description of the fan groups on Ravelry and a snapshot of quantitative data into order to provide a demographic breakdown of the fan handicrafting community.

The chapters that follow are based upon the major areas revealed by the qualitative data collected during the project. Firstly, Chapter 3 explores the ways in which fan handicrafters construct and present their fan identities within the Ravelry community. It analyzes the way in which fans perform their fandom through their personal profiles and postings, and also through identity role-play during which they stitch themselves and their projects into the storyworld. It also discusses the different ways fan handicrafting is gendered, on the one hand as a form of feminine domesticity and on the other as a fannish femininity which foregrounds the sexuality and appeal of characters in popular culture. Then, a breakdown of fan handicrafting production is presented in Chapter 4, looking at how fan interests are incorporated into projects made by the handicrafter. This analysis is organized around forms of material production as mimetic, reproducing handcrafted items seen on screen or incorporating logos and iconic imagery into projects, and which use the storyworld as inspiration, incorporating aspects of characters, objects, and events into stitchwork, color, and other aspects of the fabric. Extending the discussion of the ways in which fan handicrafting can be viewed as transformative work, Chapter 5 follows on from this by setting out the ways in which fan handicrafting and fan fiction intersect. It analyzes fictionalized pattern books, genre novels with accompanying patterns, and the ways in which knitting culture is incorporated into fan fiction. Lastly, Chapter 6 interrogates the concept of fan cultural capital in relation to fan handicrafting, extending this into a discussion of social, symbolic, and economic capital in terms of celebrity fan handicrafters and the micro-economy of fan handicrafting, alongside this considering the ways fan handicrafters resist and negotiate the culture industry's ownership of texts.

1
FANDOM, TEXTILES, GENDER

As the examples given in the Introduction suggest, characters, costumes, props, settings, and other elements of film, TV, and novel series, as well as quotes, logos, and other identifiable images, can all be reproduced in knitted or crocheted fabric. This includes, but is in no way limited to, costume elements and props or set dressing made using the fiber arts. Handicrafters who self-identify as fans and incorporate their fan interests into their projects are on the alert for anything that can inspire them in their crafting when watching the films and television series or reading the novels and comics that they love. For example, when *True Blood* fans are watching the episode "Shake and Fingerpop" (2009), they enjoy the anticipation and excitement (if not arousal) of the vampire Eric Northman giving Lafayette Reynolds his blood in order to cure the infected gunshot wound Lafayette received when escaping captivity in Eric's bar Fangtasia (vampire blood has healing power when drunk by humans). However, the fan handicrafters are also interested in an incidental element of the scene, one that has very little to do with the events in the narrative or the plot, an element that many viewers may well overlook. Their attention is drawn to the granny square blanket Lafayette is huddling under in his fever. This blanket does have signifying meaning—as a "comfort blanket" it reinforces the fact that Lafayette is ill and suffering after his ordeal in the dungeon at Fangtasia. But after watching the episode, these fans do not go online (only) to discuss the affective moments and how this makes them feel toward Lafayette (a favorite character of many *True Blood* fans whom they might themselves want to comfort) or the excitement and arousal they feel when Eric (another hugely popular and sexually appealing character for these viewers) offers Lafayette his blood (the erotic nature of the vampire itself being a strong appeal for female viewers especially). They (also) talk with other handicrafters about how they might make a copy of the blanket for themselves.

These fans thus form a distinct fan community that draws on texts as inspiration in their handicrafting, thus integrating the text into their everyday lives as an activity taking place alongside their viewing of the program and resulting in a material object. Handicrafting related to fandom in this way can thus be considered fan production. These fan handicrafters reproduce costumes and props, but they also draw inspiration from the characters and narratives in the fan text in producing a very wide range of fan art using yarn, needles, and hooks. How can this form of fan production—fiber fan art, if you will— be understood within the contexts of fan culture and in relation to the textile arts? While there are overlaps with costuming and cosplay which also involve handicrafting practices and the production or use of textiles, fan handicrafting deserves to be considered in its own right, not least because it illustrates the way in which fans draw on popular culture texts and show their love of films, television, and fictional characters and storyworlds in their practice of common pastimes which slot into everyday life and are traditionally considered a part of feminine domesticity. It is also quite distinct in some ways from more specialized and dedicated spaces of fan production, the fan forums and archives in which fan fictions and fan videos are circulated, for example. While there are fans who showcase their fan handicrafting in their blogs and podcasts, and there are groups on social media (such as the "I Made a Thing Multifandom, Multicraft Festival" on DreamWidth[1]), there is no major archive for fan handicrafting in its own right.

In addition, knitting and crochet are accepted as "normal" hobbies and widely practiced for relaxation or to relieve tension, for filling in spare or boring moments in the day, for practical purposes such as making one's own knitwear or baby clothing for children and grandchildren, for making gifts for family members and loved ones, and even for charity or acts of craftivism (yarn bombing either to create street art or political protest). In the majority of circumstances, fan handicrafting can be framed within this everyday practice of the fiber arts, as opposed to a specialized area of fan culture (although, of course, it is that too). Fan handicrafting cannot therefore be seen as straightforwardly related to fan culture. It is also embedded in social and domestic contexts, as well as the creative, artistic, feminist, and political practices of the textile arts. Furthermore, it is discussed, shared, and practiced (by and large) not within fan communities, but within online handicrafting communities. It cannot then be seen solely or specifically in the context of fan studies.

How then can fan handicrafting be framed theoretically? The objectives of this chapter are to contextualize the empirical study of fan handicrafting presented in this book with respect to key theoretical approaches and research not only in the area of fan studies, but also within textile studies. This necessitates an interdisciplinary approach to the work which, additionally, demands consideration of fan handicrafting in the context of gender studies and material culture. This chapter therefore draws together in its discussion of contexts and approaches questions surrounding how we can interpret the material artifacts produced by fans on the one hand and how we might understand them in relation to the practices of handicrafting and the fiber arts on the other. Since the primary focus here is a form of fan production, however, it is a necessary task to first untangle some of the complex interplays between popular culture and handicrafting within fan culture. In this respect, it is useful to briefly consider other forms of fan production and how they stand with respect to handicrafting, before going on to consider how fan handicrafting relates to textiles and material culture. This enables negotiation of the various theoretical approaches to fan production specifically and fan culture theory in general, before weaving in the relevant approaches of textile theory and material culture.

Fan production and participatory culture

It is already well established in the work of Henry Jenkins, Matt Hills, and others that fans make their own contributions to popular culture texts. They remediate narratives by writing stories (fan fiction), making films (fan films) and music videos (fanvids[2]), making costumes, dressing up and role-playing (cosplay) and building props (sometimes for cosplay, other times for fan films or for display in their own right), painting, drawing, and digitally manipulating images (fan art), and writing critiques of the text or debating interpretations and responses to it. As Jenkins (2007: 358) puts it, these audience members take "a more active role than others in shaping media flows and creating new values." In this respect, fans are an interpretive community, and they undertake imaginative play with the text, rereading it, extending it, and reworking it to suit their own desires and interests, all while building communities around the fan object and/or various forms of fan production they undertake. In this way, fandom is both participatory and performative. In terms of fan culture being participatory, fans do not only behave as consumers of popular culture texts but also participate in communities organized around the texts, making their own contributions to the storyworld and thus becoming producers of those texts.

The concept of "prosumption" (Toffler 1980) can be applied to these additions or adaptations to a text. As Christina Olin-Scheller (2011: 159) points out, "Fans are actors in a media landscape where the production of culture and 'user generated content' are interchangeable terms and [...] people are vital participants as 'prosumers.'" For example, Eckart Voigts-Virchow (2012; 34) discusses the "rich and varied Austenite fan-fiction universe" that has been produced by Jane Austen fans in the "affinity spaces" of "participatory culture" in the context of "prosumption." Fans not only create, publish, and consume their own fan works, "thus expanding the borders of the source text" (Olin-Scheller 2011: 159), but, as Voigts-Virchow (2012: 39) sees it, the acts of fans that turn cultural (in this case, literary) texts into "components of lived world experience" are performative. The use of Alvin Toffler's term "prosumers" indicates the fans' dual roles as consumers who also produce and circulate media in online communities and social networks.

Not all fan activities fit neatly into Toffler's prosumer model of course (fans are still often inveterate consumers of merchandise and collectibles produced by the culture industries), but taking handicrafting as an example of prosumption illustrates the significance of fans undertaking producerly activities using fiber, yarn, needles, and hooks, and the skills they have acquired as knitters, crocheters, weavers, spinners, and dyers. Although fans who produce as well as consume have also been referred to by other sometimes more convenient terms, "prosumer" is a particularly apt one in the context of discussing fan handicrafting practices since Toffler did not coin the word specifically with regard to fan's producing their own texts but in terms of the changes from the pre-industrial age to the post-industrial in human history. In Toffler's terms, prosumers in the Third Wave[3] cook their own food from scratch, repair, maintain, and decorate their own homes and household equipment, and—most relevant for this account—make their own clothes and their own entertainment. For example, a right of passage for many of the *Doctor Who* fan handicrafters is to make their own scarf, an example of which made by Andrea (female, Germany) is shown in Figure 1.1.

Figure 1.1 The *Doctor Who* scarf © Andrea Dengler. (Acknowledgment Doctor Who—™ & © BBC.)

Accounts of fan cultures have already established the importance of understanding producerly activities undertaken by fans—see Karen Hellekson and Kristina Busse's (2006 and 2014) collections on fan fiction, for example. Fans write and consume their own stories and make their own films in order to entertain themselves and for the entertainment of their fellow fans; in the context of the textile arts, they also make their own costumes, props, and merchandise. Fan handicrafters thus fit Toffler's model of the prosumer, as handicrafters they are already making their own clothing and furnishing their homes—knitting and crocheting garments, accessories, and home decorations, sometimes weaving their own fabric and in some instances spinning and dyeing their own yarn.

In the context of discourses around the production–consumption model of late capitalism, one of the comments that sock knitters report on the Ravelry forums of getting from non-handicrafters is that machine-made, mass-produced socks can be bought cheaply from high street shops and why would someone bother to make their own. Such comments reflect Toffler's Second Wave where industrialization and marketization have devalued people's own work. In Toffler's model, in the First Wave of human history, socks and hose were made by hand, as was the collection and spinning of fiber, and the weaving and fulling of cloth: "self-production" was the norm. In the Second Wave, the spinning jenny, cotton gin, and the power loom moved the production of socks and hosiery out of the home and into the factory; in *Women's Work*, Elizabeth Wayland Barber (1994) sets out the effect of these inventions of the Industrial Revolution on women's lives and the production of textiles. Representative of Toffler's Third Wave (the post-industrial), hobbyist sock knitters value personal pleasure, superior quality, and individuality, but also, as Barber suggests, the social nexus of the home, the family, the community—and the latter can certainly be extended into fan communities of individuals sharing the same tastes even though they might be widely dispersed geographically.

Fan handicrafters, like fans in general, also share their handicrafting and make their own entertainment around it (undertaking communal craft-alongs, taking part in crafting events, participating in swaps, as well as many activities that can be observed in dedicated fan communities—group viewings of the television series, sharing news and information, discussing episodes, etc.). At the same time as they are creating fan art through their crafting, these active participants are also, to varying degrees, defining themselves by their fan interests and performing their fandom within the fan handicrafting community and in their wider social spheres. Their projects form the material objects around which this activity is structured, and approaches to material culture are thus a key context for this research.

The material culture of fandom

While the fan practices mentioned earlier often involve media content creation—fan fiction, fan music videos and films, or digital art—fans also produce material artifacts. These forms of fan production can include the making of props, costumes, and other paraphernalia linked to the fan object. Some *Doctor Who* or *Star Wars* fans make their own Dalek or R2D2, for example, and fans of a very wide range of popular culture texts make costumes so they can dress as favorite characters at fan conventions and cosplay events. Steampunks "mod" technological devices with wood and brass cases—phones, laptop and desktop computers, television, vehicles—to look as if they were made using the technology of the Victorian era or create jewelry and other accessories out of old analogue watch parts. This kind of fan production can be considered a part of maker culture (itself illustrative of Toffler's Third Wave prosumption) specifically organized around a fan object. Material fan production can range from badges, t-shirts, bags, and other accessories incorporating logos, quotes, images, and other identifiable elements of the fan object, to toys, models, and other objects depicting characters, scenes, or events from the text, to accurate reproductions of costumes, props, or other items from the sets or art design. Knitted scarves or hats from *Doctor Who* or *Firefly* and crocheted stuffed *My Little Pony* fall into this category of material fan production. In this respect, it is important to contextualize fan handicrafting as part of the material culture of fandom.

As Matt Hills has already discussed (2014), material fandom is a somewhat neglected area of fan studies. But as Benjamin Woo (2014: 1.3) points out: "Things are the sine qua non of fandom, that without which it remains only potentiality and not a realized capability." Material culture is thus integral to fandom, and while this includes licensed and official merchandise and spin-offs, including action figures, models, toys, games, comics and novels, as well as DVD or Blu-ray releases of films and programs, it also includes many examples of prosumption activities, not least handicrafting. Bob Rehak (2014: 1.4) notes that:

> The "things" of fandom are more prominent than ever, offering a window into our present while revisiting the past with a freshly object-oriented historicist eye. Exploring these relationships has too often been discouraged within fan studies that privilege textual over tactile engagement.

He goes on to suggest that "the changed role of objects in fandom, new modes of both fan and professional industry, the display and record constituted by the objects of fandom hiding in plain sight" are factors that should be borne in mind. There has been a tendency in the development of fan studies, however, to see material culture as separate (and also often subordinate) to textual culture.

Jenkins and Hills both note that the norms and assumptions of fandom stand against the large bulk of work in the field of fan studies which has highlighted and explored the transformative works of (female) fandom in great depth. In recent years, Hills (2014) and Rehak (2014) have sought to explore the practices of (male) fandom that have been largely ignored by this body of work. In particular, Hills (2010, para 1) has called for a reappraisal of fan creators who "apply their skills base to materialising SF's narrative worlds." It is thus only recently that attention has been turned (back) onto the material culture of fandom with any depth of scrutiny. In Rehak's (2014) definition, the material practices of fandom include objects created through craft, commodity, collection, and curation. It is really only the first of these that is of concern here (the remaining three are organized more specifically around the accepted practices of production and consumption of products from the culture industries, rather than prosumption). One of the issues raised by this intervention in fan studies is a largely gendered assumption of material fan production as masculine. Clearly, the largely female community of fan handicrafting works against this assumption, though Hills (2014) does note my earlier work on fan handicrafting. It is therefore pertinent to reconsider some general points about material culture, and especially gendered approaches to crafts.

Material culture, while often applied in the fields of archaeology, anthropology, and museum conservation, relates to all objects with physical form or presence made or altered by human beings. It can be usefully applied to various forms of fan production (and not only mimetic crafting such as that described by Hills). Sandra M. Falero (2008), for example, discusses the fanzine (fan-made publications dedicated to the fan object) as a self-published, often handmade, form of material production (and women have long been producing fanzines). The study of material culture focuses on the material in an endeavor to "explore and understand the invisible systems of meaning that humans share" (Sheumaker and Wadja 2008: xii). Within fan culture, then, there is a material culture that creates meaning for the fans involved in that community. While much of this may take the form of clothing, costumes, accessories, house decorations, reproduction props, toys, action figures, and other merchandise that display the object of fan interest, the material culture of fandom also encompasses the fanzines which were—and in some cases still are[4]—material objects in the physical world. The fan art, fiction, articles, letters (or LOC— letters of comment), and news that occupied the pages of fanzines are now largely found on the online sites that have replaced the print 'zine, but it remains the case that the textual is contingent on the material. This is the case too with fan handicrafting, in which the textual is often encoded in the material object. And since material objects can, in many instances, be a form of material-semiotic production as well as an overt physical display of the fan's love for the particular text at the center of their fandom, it is clear that "forms of embodied and technical craftsmanship" and "fan labour" (Hills 2010: para 4) are important (and as Hills points out, somewhat neglected) areas of study. This draws attention to the very particular circumstances of fan handicrafting and how we might understand it. In this respect, what can fan handicrafting tell us about fan culture and also about handicrafting culture?

As Jules David Prown (1982) posited, the subject matter of study, material, can provide understanding of culture. The relationships between objects and people are the key to this understanding. A fan wearing a mass-produced *Doctor Who* or *Star Wars* t-shirt can tell us much about both the desire *for* a popular culture text and the commodification *of* culture by the culture industries. The *Star Wars* fan wearing a *Star Wars* Celebration t-shirt is proclaiming not just that they self-identify as a fan, but that they have been to the fan convention (or want to suggest they have), that they are part of the participatory fan community. A hand-knitted *Doctor Who* scarf or a fan-made crochet lightsaber on the other hand is also imbued with potential meanings that, like the fanzine, can tell us about the personal thoughts, desires, and imaginative play with the text of the fan who made them. If instead of a Celebration t-shirt the fan is wearing the hand-knitted jumper shown in Figure 1.2 with a colorwork yoke depicting the TARDIS, the Doctor and Rose, a parade of Daleks, and "EXTERMINATE" around the neck, what does this say?

Figure 1.2 Paper Daleks jumper © Rebecca Beam. (Acknowledgment Doctor Who—™ & © BBC.)

The wearer, Rebecca (female, 20s, USA), is declaring herself as not only a fan, and above that a fan of the David Tennant Doctor, but also a knitter, and a particularly skillful one at that with a flair for adapting and incorporating her own designs into her projects (the jumper is based on the popular Paper Dolls pattern by Kate Davis, a knitwear designer who adapts traditional Scottish knitting techniques for contemporary knitters). The fan identity is thus refracted and imbued with deeper meaning through many other levels of handicrafting practice: traditional Fair Isle, contemporary design, popular culture, individual taste, star appeal, knitting skills, the talents of a respected designer, and the artistic interpretation of the knitter commingle. Furthermore, Rebecca's Ravelry project page notes also extend this analysis of the material object into details of the knitter's fannish interest—"I'm basically in love with [the original Paper Dolls pattern] because the corrugated ribbing reminds me of Ten's Suit"—and her level of experience as a knitter—"I have never made a sweater before, nor done Fair Isle." This indicates that affective fan responses can carry more weight in choosing to undertake the project than skill and experience as a knitter. She recognizes this when she adds, "I'm planning to somehow change the chart to do a Ten, TARDIS, and Daleks marching around the top. Sometimes I think I have gone mad." But the fact that Paper Daleks is a completed—and much admired (there are over eighty comments on the project filled with excessive praise and it has been marked a favorite by 1,543 Ravellers)—project shows that lack of experience do not stand in the way of expressions of fan passion.

The attention that such examples of fan handicrafting draw within the community is thus part of the fan culture as much as the material object itself. As Ian Woodward (2007: 133) sets out, material objects assist in the formation and performance of self and social identities. Studies of youth subcultures also suggest that material objects establish a collective identity (Woodward 2007: 133) and this can also be true of fan cultures. This is evident in the way in which certain objects have come to signify membership of a fan community—a pair of goggles worn as an accessory or some gear embellished jewelry can indicate that the wearer is a steampunk fan (Cherry and Mellins 2011) or dark Victorianesque clothing, tinted glasses, and fangs might suggest the wearer is a vampire fan on their way to a vampire group meeting (Mellins 2013). Clothing can thus be important in establishing a collective fan identity, though unlike vampire or steampunk fans many fans do not dress in ways that make them stand out as having a subcultural identity. However, handicrafters—by wearing, using, or displaying their own work—are already declaring their identity as a handicrafter.

This comes into especially sharp focus within fan handicrafting, providing new understandings of popular culture and the fans' attitudes toward it. The knitted or crocheted material object links its maker to two identifiable communities at one and the same time: they are a handicrafter and a fan. And beyond this, where the handcrafted object is neither a copy of an iconic design nor displays an identifiable logo or image, the project nonetheless continues to publicly declare the identity of the maker as a handicrafter and at the same time is a private or concealed marker of fannish interest. It is worth stressing that such public–private separations of fan community membership and identity can be true also of mimetic fan handicrafting. Fan knitters frequently create patterns (which they share within the community) for items worn or used by characters in their favorite films and TV programs. The *Twilight* films, being set in a cold climate, offer many opportunities for such mimetic knitting, and popular patterns on Ravelry include Bella's mittens, baseball scarf, and La Push hat, and Alice's arm warmers (several different patterns existing for each). By making these patterns, the *Twilight* fan knitters can construct and express their fan identity for themselves and for the fan community (the fan herself is aware of the significance and such items will be recognized by other fans), though being commonplace items of clothing without logos or branding they may well pass unnoticed as indicators of fan identity by non-fans. For some, though not all by any means, this may be useful in not overtly drawing attention to their status as a fan, and this might be especially significant where the fandom is one that has been subjected to ridicule (as with *Twilight*). What it does illustrate is that the kind of mimetic crafting discussed by Hills (2014) is wider than the making of important, significant, or iconic objects from the storyworld. Fan handicrafters also make anything visible in a scene that they take a fancy to (such as a common-or-garden patchwork crochet blanket as seen in *True Blood*). In exploring this further, I do not wish to use gender to draw a dividing line between the work of male prop builders and that of female fan handicrafters, not least since there are many men who knit and crochet. Nevertheless, gender is an obvious factor in handicrafting, and the focus on it in this research serves to problematize binary divisions often inherent in fan studies around the textual/transformative/female and material/affirmational/male debate.[5]

In approaching this problematic, theories of material culture are useful in terms of understanding gendered crafting practices. Michael S. Kimmel (1997: 2) argues that gender is an interactive, negotiated, and contested process that active subjects embody, apply, and inscribe through material life. Material objects can be themselves gendered, or reveal gendered bias through their use value. Studies of fan production do show some evidence of gendered practice, for example, through dominant forms of fan fiction (slash fiction in particular) and vidding being predominantly female, and male fans tending to dominate areas of fan film production and prop making. Traditional handicrafts too encode assumptions about gender, working with textiles historically being women's work (Barber 1994) and thus connoting femininity. If we therefore position fan handicrafting as a feminine fan activity, the question of how can this be equated with ideas circulating in fan studies around the differences and intersections between affirmational and transformational fandom (Scott 2013) arises. In this binary, affirmational fandom reproduces the source material and thus reaffirms authorial status including the program's showrunner and writers or the filmmakers' power and control over their work, while transformational fandom remediates the source material to reflect the fans' desires and interests, the original material is reworked and rewritten with meanings and affect altered. Since the former gives precedence to the official status and canon of the text and the latter represents the democratization of taste and non-canonical additions to the text, the affirmational is very often sanctioned by the culture industries and the transformational more often seen as illegitimate.

This is not a straightforward binary distinction, however; as Hills (2014: 2.17) notes of mimetic fan production, there are "oscillatory distinctions that vary at different levels of analysis and appreciation." Furthermore, this also recalls the fluidity that Hills (2013) stresses in his reappraisal of the three categories of productivity set out in John Fiske's model of fan productivity (1992). Hills argues that "digital fandom's affordances and activities indicate a fluidity of semiotic, enunciative, and textual productivity" (2013: 130). Moreover, he also raises the conceptual problem of material production suggested by Abercrombie and Longhurst's (1998) separation of fans, cultists, and enthusiasts where "material production" is the defining trait of enthusiasts and "textual productivity" is generated by fans (Hills 2013: 134). As Hills (2014: 1.1) points out in his account of mimetic fan art, "the separation of material and textual production is itself far leakier" than the critics, including Abercrombie and Longhurst, allow. He suggests that:

> Rather than arguing that such material culture and fan creativity deserves an alternative concept altogether (Abercrombie and Longhurst 1998), it may again make more sense to theorize these "networked re-enactments" [...] as a type of strongly mimetic textual productivity drawing on particular craft skills. Such mimetic textual productivity may also include practices of cosplay and action figure customisation, whereas forms of fan fiction are more likely to be transformative in terms of reworking the source text rather than directly emulating it.

In this respect, fan handicrafting provides examples of textual productivity that draws on the craft skills associated with the fiber arts. Handcrafted objects might be used in cosplay or other form of role-play, and certainly stuffed toys can easily be viewed as customized action figures. The range of fan handicrafting projects discussed earlier and in the Introduction illustrates that material fandom can encompass mimetic production (Jayne's hat, the Doctor's scarf, Lafayette's blanket) and do-it-yourself (DIY) merchandise (crochet toys substituting for action figures, colorwork jumpers substituting for branded t-shirts), but fans craft projects that also play with the text—remediating it, transforming it, and telling stories in its own right, even where those projects might not seem connected to the text at a casual glance. As Hills (2014: 2.17) goes on to elaborate in respect of mimetic productivity:

> It appears to be affirmational from a distance, but transformational details are evident when viewed closely. It seems authentic by virtue of noncommerciality, but it indicates inauthentic brand extending and so-called grassroots marketing when considered from a commercial perspective. It centers on material culture and haptic presence but indicates the value of a framing immateriality, namely the cult world [...]. More than simply a part of fans' material culture, mimetic fandom thus occupies an interspace between materiality and what might be termed soul, building and branding, imitation and individuation. In addition to pervasively in-between positions, however, mimetic fandom also performs a desired bridging of text and reality.

My intent in exploring the material culture of fan handicrafting is very much to analyze the ways in which this form of fan production similarly transcends such binaries. Fan handicrafting is both mimetic and non-mimetic, it moves between affirmational and transformational works, and it is material and yet also textual. Further, in light of the material objects made and the way they are incorporated into the fans' everyday lives, they also function as a bridge from text to lived experience.

Hills's account is also useful in respect of how fan productivity might be theorized in respect of social media (where user-generated content, tweets, micro blogging, and animated gifs can all work as textual productivity, albeit not in the forms that fan studies have often been concerned with). Indeed this opens up the ways in which fan handicrafting might be approached, namely in terms of analyzing not only the material objects themselves, but the fans who produce them and their interactions within the community (this is the basis of the approach taken in terms of the empirical research design for this study as discussed further in Chapter 2). How fan handicrafters' photograph, present and contextualize their projects in the discursive environs of the fan community is not insignificant. The material objects themselves are only one part of the narrative presented to the community. In addition, many material objects produced by the fan handicrafters play with the text and transform it. And while the material objects of fan handicrafting do not necessarily transform the text by retelling stories directly, they nevertheless make contributions to transformative narratives within the discursive contexts in which they are presented. Indeed, as the case studies in the chapters that follow reveal, fan handicraft projects are worked into fan fiction, as is the practice of knitting itself: fan fiction and role-play take place around the display of fan handicrafting projects within the community, projects are made in conjunction with the viewing or reading of fan texts, and projects come to stand in for the passion that the fan feels for a desired character. The material objects of fan handicrafting can thus intersect with narratives in many ways, as well as tell stories in their own right.

It is pertinent at this point to ask exactly how material objects operate as transformative works. This is usefully illustrated by a discussion of how we might understand forms of fan production in which handicrafts play a part (such as cosplay). Discussions of the performative and transformational elements of cosplay shed useful light on how fan handicrafting can be understood, but other approaches from performative and dress subcultures are also useful.

Intersections of cosplay and crafting

Costuming (making or acquiring a copy of a costume worn by a character in a popular culture text) is the closest form of fan production to the handicrafting explored in this book, though often only insofar as it involves a set of crafting practices that overlap with knitting and other fiber or textile arts during the making of the costume. It is important to note that while fan handicrafting and costume making both encompass crafting in terms of its practice as a prosumer activity, and indeed the textile and fiber arts are central to costuming, many forms of crafting beyond knitting, crochet, and dressmaking can be involved, including millinery, metal and leatherwork (for armor or belts, for example), and corsetry, as well as other elements involved in appearance such as make-up and wigs. It is clear from the survey of groups in the Ravelry forum that knitters and crocheters often practice other forms of crafting outwith the main Ravelry crafts among their set of hobbies or prosumer activities. Fiber artists do not only knit and crochet, they often work in the textile arts (and beyond with other materials). Discussion on Ravelry often spills over into areas such as dressmaking, quilting, embroidery and needlepoint, beading, and jewelry making. Fan handicrafters also frequently discuss a much wider range of crafting activities, and this often involves making costumes from fan texts. Moreover, props are often integral to costumes for cosplay (costuming combined with role-play) and other related activities such as live action role-play (LARPing) and re-enactment (ren faires and living history events), and these also require working with different materials and tools. Whereas the clothing parts of a costume might involve needlework and textile arts, prop making is more closely associated with leatherwork, woodwork, metalwork, model making, and so forth. This illustrates that the subject of this research, handicrafting, thus represents only one subset of crafting techniques practiced by fans when making costumes or among their pastimes generally. This in itself, though, raises issues concerning perceptions of gender and the questionable gendering of crafts.

Crafts themselves often fall into sets of gendered practices or assumptions. Working with textiles and fiber is often stereotyped as "feminine handicrafting," whereas "technical crafts" (Kokko 2012) are seen as masculine. The latter include metalwork and woodwork. Barbara Brownie (2015: 145) argues that while costuming and "dressing up" have traditionally been viewed as feminine pursuits, when male fans cosplay they reframe these activities in ways that make the wearing of costumes conform to expressions of masculine ideals:

> If costume can be justified as a functional object, particularly in that it is associated with the very masculine act of combat, it can be distanced from feminine acts of vanity, and childish acts of play.

Such reframings are not only based upon the emphasis on "gear" (Brownie 2015: 147) as opposed to "costume" (as suggested in the quote in terms of armor and weaponry), but upon the depiction in the Spider-Man comic (and thus acceptability) of Peter Parker sewing his own costume. This serves to illustrate the ways in which traditional conceptions of gendered crafting can break down when exploring costuming. It also indicates that further acknowledgment of gender is imperative when engaging with fandom as "object-oriented" (Rehak 2014). When costuming, female fans often cross these perceived boundaries, working in technical crafts as costumes require it as well as textiles. For example, one fan handicrafter and Femme!Doctor cosplayer (anon) has made her own remote-controlled K-9 to accompany her Fourth Doctor cosplay, as well as knitting several versions of the *Doctor Who* scarves as part of her costume (see also Cherry 2013). This also illustrates the point that within costuming choices negotiations of gender are apparent. Unlike Brownie's male superhero cosplayers who seek to mimetically reproduce the muscular body of the superhero in their costumes, some female cosplayers work to transform gender through what is often called "crossplay." Some of the fan handicrafters who crossplay are involved in creating Femme!Doctor costumes where one of the Doctor's costumes is transformed into a female version (and indeed in crossplay the character will also be gender transformed). Costuming thus represents a useful way of exploring some of the issues around gender and handicrafting in greater depth, and it can also be an important consideration in understanding the wider practices of fan handicrafting discussed in this book.

It is useful to discuss cosplay in a little more detail here, not least in order to illustrate the ways in which clothing and costume—and dressmaking is an example of the prosumption involved in both—play an important role in fandom as both a process of material production and also through the performance of fandom. Theoretical approaches to understanding cosplay are therefore useful in engaging with some of the contexts in which fan handicrafting might be understood in terms of the wider fan culture. Cosplay (a portmanteau word deriving from the contraction of costume play) became popular through Japanese fan culture (though costuming was prevalent at fan conventions before this) and is now widely practiced by fans across the whole spectrum of fandom. It is worth considering that cosplay is a specific form of costuming, involving as it does elements of role-play and performance, though it is obviously not completely distinct from costuming. Costuming and cosplay go hand in hand of course, and are often discussed in conjunction as a single form of producerly activity, but—since the handicrafting of concern in this study, knitting and crochet are only a very small part, if any, of cosplay—it is worth teasing out some of the differences. As Nicolle Lamerichs (2014b) observes, cosplay is similar to costume design in the domain of professional theater makers. Handicrafting, on the other hand, is for the most part situated within the realm of everyday clothing and street fashion. Costumes for cosplay are typically—though not always[6]—copied from characters in cult media; they are thus strongly mimetic. Handicrafting has a role in this (costumes for the Fourth, Fifth, and Seventh Doctors from *Doctor Who* might well include the scarf, a cricket jumper, and the question mark Fair Isle sleeveless jumper respectively, for example), but it is significant that the greater number of mimetic handicrafting projects observed in this study are not (or not only) intended for cosplay, but rather for everyday wear.

What is notable here is that mimetic fan handicrafting projects, whether intended for cosplay or not, can be worn or used in ways that echo the performative aspects of cosplay. Some handicrafting projects are incorporated into cosplay performances and competitions at conventions, but in a similar way to the "'hallway' costumes that are generally worn without professional or competitive intent" (Lamerichs 2014b: 113), fan handicrafters simply wear or carry their projects to fan conventions and some even craft in public at such events. The Fourth Doctor cosplayer mentioned earlier has worked on her copy of the burgundy version of the *Doctor Who* scarf at a convention (while wearing her Fifth Doctor costume), and two other fans interviewed for this study have won a great deal of admiration at conventions—one at a *Sherlock* convention when wearing her knitted scarf based on the wallpaper in Sherlock's Baker Street flat in the BBC series and the other at *My Little Pony* conventions for her crochet Ponies. Cosplay outfits and performances "are a physical manifestation of their immersion into the fictional realms of television, games and movies, among others" (Lamerichs 2014b: 113), but these other examples of handicrafting on display at conventions (and this includes the Stitch 'n' Babble knitting group at the Nine Worlds fan convention in London) also suggest that this can be true of items worn in conjunction with ordinary clothing too. In fact, such items also perform the fan identity beyond the confines of the fan community, extending into everyday life.

The circumstances of wearing a mimetic item of clothing in everyday life is of course very different from cosplay, but the meanings and emotions involved (in both the making and the wearing) can be similar. One interviewee (anon) refers to wearing her handmade mimetic costume items as "everyday cosplay in my head." Turney (2009) does not engage directly with fan experiences in her account of knitting culture, but she does raise some interesting points with respect to the Starsky cardigan. The cardigan, she says, is "a sign not only of identification, but of transformation and role-play" (2009: 39). In Turney's analysis, the Starsky cardigan patterns make overt connections to the text:

> Directly referring to the TV show and characters, the patterns illustrate the "commodifcation" of the body, i.e. make the cardigan and transform your man into "Starsky."

The wearer, then, will "emulate the character's persona" simply by wearing the jacket. The important point here is that the wearing of the Starsky cardigan is not in the context of cosplay, but in terms of everyday life. Furthermore, Turney's reading of it is that it encapsulates the desire women have for the character. Although Turney locates the cardigan within the heteronormative relationship of a woman making the cardigan for her husband or partner, this can be extended to the fans' desires to be or be with the characters they love. This desire, alongside the adoption of the persona in wearing a character's clothing, illustrates that mimetic fan production and the making and wearing of a costume for oneself can take place outside of cosplay. While the dedicated spaces of the convention reify the adoption of the character's persona (as Lamerichs proposes), this is not the only situation in which we might observe such role-play operating.

Moreover, wearing clothing inspired by the costumes of characters from popular culture texts might also be considered in relation to style or taste cultures. Just as in Turney's account where the character of Starsky is embodied through the wearing of the cardigan, a subcultural (or in this case, fan) identity can be communicated through style and dress practices (which may themselves carry a performative aspect). The most obvious example here might be in terms of performing a geek identity (as with the geek chic trend in recent years), but some fan communities adopt much more clearly identifiable alternative style cultures. Vampire and steampunk fandoms, for example, are closely allied to Victorian, Edwardian, and Gothic styles. Although fan communities rarely adopt dress practices to the extent that vampire or steampunk fans do, Maria Mellins's (2013) observations in respect of mixing clothing styles, creativity, and performativity in everyday life are more widely relevant. Analysis of vampire fan clothing reveals the "eclecticism and general bricolage of subcultural aesthetics" (Mellins 2013: 54), mixing vampire clothing (velvet and lace garments, corsets, full-length skirts, Victorianesque or platform boots) with office wear, conventional casual clothing, and cycling gear, as work, time, or family and other social functions dictate (Mellins 2013: 51–52). This bricolage illustrates the tactics that people use in their everyday lives to build themselves worlds and identities out of readily available mass-produced goods (de Certeau 1980).

In terms of fashion, people mix and match clothing from different labels, wear them in ways other than intended, and customize them (de Certeau 1980: 322–323). Mellins's vampire fans do not wear costumes copied wholesale from popular culture—it is not cosplay. Rather, they adapt their clothing to include particular items, a sense of style or an aesthetic look; one fan, for example, cuts and dyes her hair to resemble that of Keifer Sutherland's character in *The Lost Boys* (Mellins 2013: 57). Fan handicrafters often make fannish objects to wear in everyday life, incorporating—in similar examples of bricolage—Bella's mittens (*Twilight*), Rose's scarf (*Doctor Who*), or Claire's cowl (*Outlander*) into everyday wear with ordinary items of clothing such as jeans and t-shirts. Although this style bricolage is very unlike cosplay as practiced at fan conventions, such performances of fandom can be "visible and overt" (Bennett and Booth 2015), as are the popular culture-themed weddings that Jessica Elizabeth Johnston (2015) describes and the fannish tattoos that Bethan Jones (2015) discusses. These examples too operate outside of specialized fan events or arenas. Fans are "incorporating a [fan] aesthetic into their wider fashion style" and garments from a wide range of fan texts "are then transformed into a wider sense of self and incorporated into their own [fan] identity" (Mellins 2013: 57–58).

While the wearing of mimetic accessories cannot be wholly conflated with the examples of cosplay discussed by Lamerichs (2011 and 2014b), similar observations can be made in terms of identity, embodiment, and emotional affect. The affective processes of cosplay as described by Lamerichs (2011) can indeed be applied to the fan handicrafters' non-cosplay mimetic crafting. Firstly, the crafting of a fannish project often involves the choice of character that matters to the handicrafter, just as it does for the cosplayer, though this may be focused down into a single object rather than a whole costume and changed appearance. Hermione Granger's striped sweater from *Harry Potter and the Order of the Phoenix* (2007) or Amy Pond's scarf from the "Vincent and the Doctor" episode of *Doctor Who* can come to embody the active female character that the wearer identifies with. Secondly, the creation of a single element of a costume involves study of the costume in the same way as cosplay does—handicrafters seek to identify the exact stitches and lace pattern as well as the type and weight of yarn in Amy's scarf.

Though study of the character's personality for the performance aspects of cosplay is not essential for crafting projects for everyday wear, nonetheless the character's persona is very much incorporated into the crafting. This serves to solidify the fan's relationship with the character just as acting out the character's persona in cosplay does. Thirdly, cosplay and fan handicrafting also share similar practices in respect of displaying the fan's work in fan communities and online sites. It is, as Lamerichs (2014a: 12) terms it, transmedial—that is, an "activity that is constructed at different online and offline sites." The project is discussed online (perhaps the community helps the crafter to identify a suitable pattern that can be adapted or what stitch resembles the original or to track down the right shade of yarn), the crafting itself takes place in the fan's home or other places where they regularly knit during their daily routine, but during this time they might give updates to the online community or ask for further help. The finished garment will be photographed (perhaps involving a role-play scenario with the crafter posing as the character in a suitable setting) and then uploaded to the Ravelry project page, personal blog, and any fan groups they belong to. Finally, the garment will be worn in everyday life and/or at fan events.

Determining patterns for mimetic projects is, as with dressmaking patterns for cosplay, one of the most common social undertakings in the Ravelry fan groups—fans discuss and share their interpretations of a design and how to reproduce it; I have previously discussed (Cherry 2013) an example of a stitch pattern for a jumper worn by Amy in the *Doctor Who* episode "Dinosaurs on a Spaceship" (BBC, 2012). Referring to the third stage in Lamerichs's model, the revelation of the finished object to the group, greater differences emerge between cosplay and clothing for everyday wear. This can be—as Lamerichs stresses for her cosplayers—both a positive and a negative experience. Cosplayers are undoubtedly under greater pressure wearing their costume at a convention (as Lamerichs describes) than are the fan handicrafters posting a picture of their finished object on Ravelry. The fans on Ravelry do not have to post a photo of themselves wearing the item, though some do as shown in Figure 1.3 in which Stephanie dresses as the Tom Baker Doctor at a fan convention; these photos are displayed on her scarf project page and in the Dr. Who Scarf Support Group. They are thus not subject to the same embodied scrutiny as the cosplayer might be. Such differences between cosplay and mimetic crafting carry over into the final stage in Lamerichs's affective process, the afterlife of the costume. The cosplay costume becomes fan memorabilia imbued with nostalgic meanings (not just of the character but the past performance). For a fan handicrafter, the project might continue to be worn in everyday life, and thus to provide an ongoing affective connection with the character and to the crafter's achievement in making the project themselves. Regardless of these differences, however, this does reveal key points about such crafting—its recognizability, how it transforms the text, how the wearing of the item in everyday life is affective. Fan handicrafting does not just have a relationship to the text, but to the affective processes that surrounds it both within the social fan group and on the personal level.

Figure 1.3 Stephanie's *Doctor Who* scarf cosplay © Stephanie J. de la Torre. (Acknowledgment Doctor Who—™ & © BBC.)

Since mimetic projects are often discussed in handicrafting circles and worn in everyday life, locating fan handicrafting with respect to established fan culture is also crucial. The fact that fan groups have flourished on the Ravelry handicrafting forum contextualizes fan handicrafting with respect to handicrafting culture generally. This is not to say that forms of fan production involving textiles and handicrafting do not take place within established fan communities. Fan crafting groups on LiveJournal, for example, predate Ravelry and "knitting" is used as a tag on the transformative fanworks site Archive of Our Own. However, it is not insignificant that the growth in fan handicrafting occurs at around the same time as fandom becomes accessible through social media and Ravelry is established as part of the renaissance of handicrafting that occurred in the first decade of the twenty-first century. In order to engage with what is happening in respect of fan handicrafting being located primarily within handicrafting culture, it is important to frame it in the context of the knitting revival.

Conjunctions of fandom and knitting culture

In *The Close-Knit Circle*, Kerry Wills (2007: 29) cites consumer surveys undertaken in 2004 and 2005 showing that women aged between 25 and 34 were at the forefront of the crafting renaissance, and that the knitting and crochet undertaken by women in this age cohort increased by 150 percent between 2002 and 2004. In fact, knitting and crochet activities increased in all age groups. Although these data relate to the American context, similar patterns can be extrapolated elsewhere. Ravelry's user statistics show high levels of activity in Canada, Australia, the UK, and other Anglophone countries, across Europe, in Japan, India, and Pacific-Asian countries, and in South Africa.[7] When describing this as the knitting revival as Wills does, it is not that handicrafting had died out completely—indeed that is not the case as evidenced by the vogue for crochet granny square fashion and later punk mohair jumpers in the 1970s—but that it had declined significantly in the era of mass production. However, knitting was revitalized and made trendy in the early 2000s around the Stitch 'n Bitch phenomenon.

Debbie Stoller's books—*Stitch 'n Bitch: The Knitter's Handbook* (2003) and *Stitch 'n Bitch Nation* (2005), as well as *Stitch 'n Bitch Crochet: The Happy Hooker* (2006)—and the growing network of social knitting groups defined the resurgence of interest in handicrafts in terms of feminist and political activism; Beth Ann Pentney (2008) credits Stoller's publications with the rise of feminist knitting. Stoller's position within third-wave feminism (as co-founder and editor of the third-wave feminist 'zine *Bust*) and the associated reclamation of elements of a more traditional femininity saw feminine handicrafts take on a trendy and even radical appeal in terms of reclaiming women's domestic work. Thus, in the years of the knitting revival, the very act of taking up knitting needles or crochet hook took on feminist connotations; handicrafters added a campaigning dimension to their craft and helped change the profile of what had traditionally been regarded as rather old-fashioned feminine handicrafts. Through Stitch 'n Bitch, knitters participated in knit in public events, yarn bombing their local environment, and guerrilla knitting—very different from traditional handicrafting and a mode which fan handicrafting can comfortably be associated with. Furthermore, the revival and its link to prosumption is also linked with the DIY culture, which David Gauntlett (2011: 64–66) also connects to the "making and sharing" facilitated by online social media. This has subsequently also contributed to the continuing appeal of DIY culture as part of a sustainability agenda and of the make-do-and mend attitude that has re-emerged during the financial crisis and the loss of confidence in capitalism (Wills 2007: 33).

Given the continued, if not increasing, popularity of crafting in the decade since the knitting revival, it is perhaps only to be expected that fans who also practice handicrafting would bring the two areas of their lives together. As the Stitch 'n Bitch groups illustrate, knitters gravitate toward those with shared interests, taking part in groups and communal activities. This might logically be applied not just to knitting itself, but also to knitters with other tastes in common—including fan interests. Miller's Vampire Knits group (discussed in the Introduction) encouraged lively fannish discussion resulting in the fans designing patterns inspired by the *Twilight* books and films, many of which were published in the book. Extrapolating from this example, it is possible to identify connections between fandom and knitting culture, or between making and connecting in Gauntlett's terms.

Firstly, it is a communal activity, just as fan culture is—and the social web[8] has provided an environment in which online interactions have flourished. It is also important to note in this respect that through the Stitch 'n Bitch groups, knit-ins, and other knit groups, handicrafting has become a social activity. Handicrafters have embraced crafting together in groups, socializing over their crafting and participating in communal projects (such as the making of blanket squares either for charities or as "random acts of kindness," or contributing to crochet coral reefs which are then displayed in museums and exhibitions to highlight ecological issues). Of course, this has long been the case as evidenced by stitch and bitch groups dating back to the Second World War (Wills 2007: 23), but the increase in social crafting facilitated by the social web is noteworthy. In that the social web has also allowed the growth of fan culture and shared fannish interests, it is therefore logical that fan handicrafting is a part of this.

This leads to a second point: classifying fan handicrafting as art and specifically a form of fan art. Kirsty Robertson's (2011) discussion of the connections between crafts and the art world is pertinent to this. She links the revival of crafting practice to conditions created by "the tentative opening of the art world to craft," alongside "a resurgence in knitting and crafting," and "activism involving knitting" that are in turn connected to "a shifting economy that has eviscerated the textile industry in North America and Europe" (Robertson 2011: 199). Fans, who may well already be engaged in this revival on many levels, have similarly wasted no time in carrying crafts over to the fan art cultures they already inhabit and this, in turn, has opened up fan handicrafting to many handicrafters. Case studies in this research illustrate the ways in which fans work their fandom into their fiber art, and sometimes even incorporate handicrafting into their fan fiction. Thirdly, the growth of interest in the fiber arts can be understood in the context of third-wave feminist practice (Pentney 2008). Although Pentney rightly points out that not all knitting can or should be regarded as feminist, the practice of handicrafting as art or for personal pleasure needs to be understood in relation to "the complexities of being both critics and consumers of popular culture, as well as critics and participants in gendered spaces and subjectivities" (Pentney 2008: para 23). While it is unrealistic to assume that fan handicrafting is unproblematically feminist, the expression of fandom and fan status within a handicrafting community (as opposed to a fan community) should be recognized as gendered fan practice reflexively organized around the activities and pleasures women take from popular culture.

This is important in considering handicrafting as a feminine form of fan productivity. Although many of the fan handicrafters would not identify themselves as feminist, they are taking pleasure in engaging with forms of popular culture in a gendered space, and this is significant in its own right. It is pertinent in this respect that the circulation, discussion, and sharing of fan handicrafting takes place largely within the female-dominated spaces of the online handicrafting community, rather than within the established (and possibly masculine) online fan communities that several of the fans (though by no means all) in this study avoid. Women's fandom has been frequently "demoted" in the fan hierarchy in this way, especially with respect to women's interests and their intense emotional responses. (*Twilight* is a case in point, evidenced by negative press reactions to the female audiences' excitement over Edward and Jacob, but male *Doctor Who* fans can also be ambivalent toward what they see as the excessively emotional female fans of David Tennant.) Despite the opening up of female fan culture in general, as studies of fan fiction demonstrate, women's tastes and activities are still relegated to a subordinate status in some instances. In many respects, it is unsurprising that female fans congregate in gendered spaces. As Busse (2013: 74–75) points out in discussing geek hierarchies:

> [F]ans replicate negative outsider notions of what constitutes fannishness, often using similar feminizing and infantilizing concepts. Accusations of being too attached, too obsessed, too invested get thrown around readily, and all too often such affect is criticized for being too girly or like a teen.

Female fan behaviors (and the very acts of being a fan) are still relegated in status and there is a lack of serious attention in the mainstream media or recognition by the culture industries. As Jenkins (2013: xvi) notes, while the "fanboy" is now given a central role in news sites such as io9, mainstream media coverage of Comic-Con, and central parts in TV series and films such as *The Big Bang Theory* (2007–) and *Kick-Ass* (2010), and that the fanboy is even authenticated by this, a strong gender bias still exists. Although these texts "address us as 'fans', [...] alternative forms of fan identities in popular culture" are still lacking (Jenkins 2013: xvi). In one respect, this places fan handicrafting—as a gendered activity—on a level with fan fiction and vidding, feminine forms of fan production that have not been widely authenticated by the mainstream media or culture industries (at least not to the same extent that male fan production and activities have). It is male-centric fan traditions that form the norm (at least in the fan/culture industry dynamic), and the widely held assumption of fans being overwhelming male still often predominates (Jenkins 2013: xvii). Though female fan culture is increasingly recognized, many female fans still tend to gather together into spaces and communities that they create and define according to their own needs and desires.

Knitting itself is similarly subordinated; according to Stoller (2003: 9), knitting is belittled as a traditionally women-centered activity, and while this attitude has changed somewhat since the knitting revival, it still recurs. It is telling, then, that when fan handicrafters congregate it is in the female-dominated social spaces of the handicrafting community. This goes some way to explaining why fan handicrafters have a higher profile in the handicrafting community than in fandom (and this may include female fan communities). In this respect, it can be argued that fan handicrafters form a community in their own right, related to and sharing members with, but also separate from, other areas of fan culture. Though this is not evidence of feminist practice, it nonetheless indicates a gendered position that the fans themselves have negotiated.

If this means that the fan handicrafters are "invisible" to fan culture and are not reflected in accounts of (male) collectors and prop builders, or (female) fan fiction writers and vidders, does this mean fan handicrafting is being deflected in a similar manner to that which Courtney Bailey (2000) suggests is the case with feminist art? In respect of the tensions that are raised by the association of particular fan practices with gender, the fan spaces provided within the Ravelry community could be seen as a refuge from the competitiveness of male fan communities and the recognition given to male fan production by the culture industry. However, another reason presents itself, and this is related back to the ways in which the social web has opened up both fandom and the handicrafting community. As fan culture has become accessible to any and all viewers, the line between casual viewers and intense fans has blurred. Francesca Coppa (2007) suggests that as fandom opens up there is a risk that it is remarginalizing the very female groups that once represented fan culture. Groups of female fans, such as those discussed by Camille Bacon-Smith in *Enterprising Women* (1992), now represent a very small segment of the fan audience and Coppa is concerned that they are increasingly seen as a minority voice in a "mixed gender fannish culture" (2007: para 2). This may be, as Coppa argues, a form of remarginalization, but it could also be seen as representing a new politicization (where fan handicrafting has strong links to the gendered politics of the knitting renaissance, for instance).

In this respect, it is significant that fan knitting is not necessarily organized around specific fan events and fan cultural practices. As set out in the discussion earlier in relation to costuming, fan handicrafting is predominantly embedded in the everyday. Knitting in this respect is not necessarily a straightforward fan activity, it shares its space with a traditional pastime, taking place inside and outside the home, as a hobby undertaken simply for pleasure, as craftivism, and as prosumption—the production of wearable clothing or useful domestic items, for example. As such, it brings casual followers of popular culture texts into close contact with more intensely fannish activities, and allows them to easily communicate with fans who are active in participatory fan culture through their shared knowledge, vocabulary, and interest in knitting and other crafts (while simultaneously, and rather ironically, continuing to exclude themselves from fan culture). The fan groups in the Ravelry forum provide entry points into fan culture for viewers with fannish interests in particular texts. This works to blur the boundaries of fan culture in increasingly fluid and complex ways and contributes to the mainstreaming of fannish activities. Regardless of the fact that this is taking place in a largely gendered community, it is significant that it represents opportunities for fan handicrafters to share their intense passions and renegotiate the politicized status of feminine handicrafts.

These negotiations—material versus textual, affirmational versus transformational, crafts versus arts, fiber art versus fan art—inform the analysis of fan handicrafting which follows in the main body of this book. But they also set up degrees of fannishness while also potentially introducing semantic and theoretical problems around the use of the term "fan" itself. As the account of fan handicrafting in this book illustrates, it is not always possible to differentiate clearly between different modes of fandom (even assuming they do exist—I would argue that fan handicrafting illustrates that fans and fandom are much more fluid and hybrid than this). Before proceeding to discuss relevant contexts and approaches to researching fan handicrafting, it is useful to interrogate what it means to self-identify as a fan, especially in the context of a handicrafting community and how the handicrafters position themselves with respect to fan culture.

Identifying the fan in the fan handicrafter

It seems natural to call these handicrafters fans. Indeed, this is generally what they consider themselves to be and how they refer to themselves unprompted. To apply the label "fan" in this (or any) research, though, begs the question of what do we mean when we call someone, or someone calls themself, a fan. This is important because the term "fan" itself is problematical. In general use, the word "fan"—when used as a label applied to someone who has an overriding interest or affective investment in a text or object—can cover very different sets of experiences. It can indicate support of a particular sporting team, a taste for a certain type of music or musician, or the adoration of a film star (Sandvoss 2005). All of these can involve passion, desire, and other expression of intense love of the fan object. However, over and above what might be classed as excessive consumption (going to every match, buying DVD box sets or music downloads, acquiring various forms of merchandise, never missing an episode of a TV series), fandom—particularly as it has been explored in fan studies—can also include participation in a fan community and probably also various forms of production such as fan fiction writing or fan filmmaking. It is these areas that have been widely explored in fan studies, often focusing on specific fan communities and how they transform specific texts, and discussions of fandom have often emphasized the producerly activities of fans in these communities.

It is worth reiterating that "fan" can have different meanings and applications in such studies depending upon usage. Jenkins, discussing his own points of difference with respect to use of the term "fan" by Fiske (especially in light of his own experiences of fandom), demarcates along the lines of "individualized and social accounts of fandom" (2013: xiv). Underlying this are different experiences of fandom and fan group affiliations, with Fiske writing from a position of a fan as someone who likes a particular text and Jenkins defining a fan as someone who has membership in a participatory fan culture. As Jenkins (2013: xiv) states: "the word 'fan', in popular usage, is slippery and expansive enough to include a broad range of different kinds of relationships to media, from the highly individualistic to the highly social." The meaning of fan in "popular usage" is an important consideration, since the fans in this study are not always, or indeed often, using the term in the sense Jenkins means. Jenkins (2010: para 6) argues that the Internet has "made visible a set of cultural practices and logics […], expanding their cultural influence by broadening and diversifying participation." This, he points out, is "fandom without the stigma." Fan handicrafting, while it may incorporate aspects of intensely fannish production (cosplay, for example), also broadens and diversifies participation within fandom. Kristin Busse (2006) argues that the fannish behaviors encouraged when casual viewers engage with transmedia texts in the context of the social web should not be wholly conflated with fandom per se. She proposes instead the notion of "a continuum that acknowledges the more intense emotional and actual engagements of many TV viewers today without erasing the strong community structures which have developed through media fandom" (2006: para 3). This does not, however, address the fan handicrafting scenario that represents a mixed fannish community.

The fan knitters on Ravelry represent many "trajectories" (to employ Busse's term) of fannish activity. Some are individualized fans (coming into the community as handicrafters with no prior involvement in socialized fandom), while others are social fans having come from fan crafting communities on LiveJournal or having been involved in participatory fandom. Shared involvement in handicrafting brings these trajectories of fandom together into one community. And once fans become involved in the fan groups on Ravelry, they are all already transitioning into a specific social group of fan handicrafters. The broad range of groups in the Ravelry forum also means that fans can cross and share fan interests freely, and come together in joint activities that transcend narrow fan interests. The fan handicrafting community thus works to create a sociable space for fans and others with fannish interests. This creates a support network for knitters and crocheters new to fandom and can be an intensely pleasurable shared experience for all the fan handicrafters. It is also interesting to note that some aspects of handicrafting as expressed within the

Ravelry community are themselves fannish in nature (at least in the casual use of the term "fan"). Ravelry members in general tend to describe themselves as fans of yarn brands or indie dyers, even those groups for commercial brands are flagged as being for fans of the brands in group descriptions. Furthermore, the Ravelry members who have marked a project as a favorite are listed as the fans of the project on the project page. The notion here is not only that some handicrafters are demonstrating fannish behaviors toward consumer products, but also that fiber artists can have fans in their own right.

Putting fan handicrafting on the map

The negotiations of fan identities and activities discussed in this chapter suggest that fandom has become much more fluid, not to say widespread, in the age of the social web when we are all fans now. Handicrafting as a form of fan production broadens and diversifies participation within fandom, particularly since it is accessible—and more importantly welcoming—to anyone who crafts (and crafting is a regular, commonplace, and widely acceptable hobby). Many handicrafters are also active in fan culture, but this is not to say that all handicrafters might be comfortable or interested in belonging or participating in fan culture more widely. A handicrafting community such as Ravelry permits fannish behaviors and activities outwith the conventional arenas of fandom. In several key respects, the discussion here illustrates the ways in which fan handicrafting is located on the boundaries, firstly, between the textile arts on the one hand and fan culture on the other and, secondly, between affirmational and transformative fandom. It is with this in mind that the empirical research and overview of the fan handicrafting community discussed in Chapter 2 is approached.

2

THE FAN HANDICRAFTING EXPERIENCE

A number of research questions arise from the contexts of fan handicrafting discussed in Chapter 1. Firstly, what kinds of fan art do handicrafters make? Secondly, how does this art incorporate the text in transformational and affirmational ways? And thirdly, how do fans of popular culture texts (especially since this includes all audience members on various trajectories of fannish interest) construct and communicate fan identities in non-fan online communities? The design and the initial findings of the research as set out in this chapter define the fan handicrafting community and provide a snapshot of the groups in which fan handicrafting exists.

Researching material culture and projected interactivity

Research into fan art can be approached, broadly, from two perspectives. From one angle, the study of the artifacts that fans produce and analyzing the fan art itself can provide us with information about how fans read, interpret, and use the text. From the second, the study of the fans who produce this material can reveal not only how they position themselves in relation to the text and to the fan culture itself (not least in terms of identity) but also the social interactions within the group. The affective experiences this encompasses can be in relation to both the fan art they produce (reflective of responses to the text) and the fan community they create. The inclusion of the latter means that analyzing the group interactions and discussions is as important as analyzing the fan art itself. Exploring the ways in which fans communicate and interact can contribute to a deeper understanding of fan activities (although it is certainly not the only approach that can be used).

This approach is similar to the one that Amber Davisson and Paul Booth (2007) have explored in their discussion of approaches to empirical research in fan fiction studies. Drawing on a model of projected interactivity, their focus is on the way fans interact with characters in the text. The combination of analysis of fan fiction (they are specifically interested in fan fiction, though it is also possible to apply their approach to other categories of fan art) and interviews with fan fiction writers permits exploration of the fan community (and possibly the wider audience segment). In order to better understand media fandom, studies of fan production should also take into account the fan identities that are present in the community producing these fan texts. Davisson and Booth suggest that in order to reveal the complicated identity play occurring in online fan cultures, "one needs to conceive of the three identities that are present in the activities [of fans]—the fan, the character, the community" (2007: 41). Fan fiction gives the writer control over these identities through their play with the character's traits, actions, and environment in their own writing. In this way, the fan brings the projected identity expressed in the characters in their fan fiction close to their own identity as well as the aspects of characters privileged by the communities they belong to. Exploring the ways in which fans communicate and interact with characters through the analysis of fan fiction, in combination with textual analysis and empirical studies of the community, contributes to a deeper understanding of fan activities in general and the particular fan community specifically.

Analysis of fan discourse alongside fan production, and in conjunction with interviews with individual fans, can enable exploration of the complex negotiations of text and identification that take place across multiple platforms, these including fan art as well as the primary text and other adaptations based on them. As a body of "archontic literature" (Derecho 2006: 63), which consciously positions itself in relation to variations of the text, fan fiction "allows, or even invites, writers to enter it, select specific items they find useful, making new artefacts using those found objects, and deposit the newly made work back into the source text's archive" (Derecho 2006: 65). (Again, Derecho is specifically concerned with fan fiction, but other forms of fan production—and certainly fans are actively encouraged to create texts through their fan handicrafting that expand the archive—can be considered as part of the archontic literature associated with any fan text.) In terms of projected interactivity, such archontic writing takes characters created elsewhere and places them in new situations or gives them new experiences, and may even rework storyworlds to suit the intentions of the fan fiction writer.

Fan fiction can mirror narrative features of the original text or create entirely new narrative scenarios or worlds, and while the roster of characters usually remains relatively stable, they may be substantially rewritten in order to explore different options while remaining recognizable. Derecho (2006: 72) argues that archontic writing, since it is produced by female fans who are traditionally disempowered, is able to subvert dominant ideologies. Davisson and Booth's model of projected interactivity offers a potentially productive means of analyzing the ways in which archontic literature enables fans to subvert (or at least play with) the meanings and subtexts of mainstream culture. Davisson and Booth base their model on James Gee's account of the relationship between characters in a video game and the player of the game, which he calls "projective identity" (Gee 2003). While identification with film characters might not be expected to resemble the interaction with virtual characters by video gamers, the ways in which fan fiction writers develop intense relationships with characters—and indeed interact with them in writing fan fiction—have clear parallels. As Davisson and Booth (2007: 36) state: "fans develop a relationship to the characters about which they write. This activity is an articulation of both the desires of the fans and the fan's perception of the character's desires." This consideration of projected interactivity highlights the communication and agency taking place within conjunctions of the text, the fan community, and the fan art they produce.

In terms of selecting the research methodologies that might provide deeper understanding of fan handicrafting in a similar way to Davisson and Booth's model of projected interactivity, the focus should not be restricted to the material objects alone, but to the people who create them and the ways they interact with each other. Studying the material culture of fan handicrafting—the knitwear, accessories, toys and home furnishings, and so forth, as discussed in the Introduction—permits, via analysis of the textual and semiotic qualities of the objects, the identification of values, ideas, attitudes, and assumptions of the people who create these artifacts. As James Carrott and Brian Johnson (2013: 174) discuss in relation to steampunk prop building and costuming (just one example of a fandom discussed in this book), handicrafting is "[n]ot just material culture, but ideas as well." Since the fan handicrafting community is a lively and productive one, involving much discussion (and sometimes contentious debates) about the popular culture texts that lie at the heart of fan handicrafting in addition to the material production, it is possible to identify and explore ideas (and ideologies) as they emerge via the discourses expressed in the fan handicrafting communities, specifically the fan groups on the Ravelry forum. Analysis of the discursive data, alongside the study of the material culture produced, permits identification of the fan handicrafters' responses to contemporary culture. As Carrott and Johnson (2013: 174) suggest, it enables us to see "what's going on in our culture right now, and how [fandom] fits into it." The study of material objects and ideas is thus conjoined, but more importantly it provides understanding of the way in which fans respond to texts, specifically in the context of this community via their material production and what this reveals about their responses to popular culture and its role in their lives. The empirical methods employed (participant-observation combined with focused interviews), together with the material-semiotic analysis of the material objects, enable a triangulation of data that is of value in qualitative research. In this way, representative data and patterns, as well as contradictions and complexities, can be identified.

The Ravelry community

The handicrafting site Ravelry provides an ideal base for studying the conjunctions of fan culture, textile arts, and material production as set out in Chapter 1, and in identifying practices and discourses relevant to the questions raised therein. Before giving an account of fan handicrafting on Ravelry, it is worth pointing out that other knitting and handicrafting communities exist, but these tend to have a narrower focus and are thus limited in terms of what they can offer fans. For example, The Knitter's Review forum[1] is connected with a weekly online magazine and also predominantly focused on crafting-related topics with a small off-topic area covering films, family, politics, and personal topics. Searches reveal only limited discussion on knitting Jayne's hat, a query about crocheting a Tenth Doctor figure, and a small number of posters in search of *Harry Potter* jumper patterns, but there was no discussion of any depth. The Knitting Paradise forum[2] had rather more discussion of Jayne hats, *Doctor Who* scarves, and *Harry Potter* patterns, but these were predominantly knitted as requests by *Doctor Who* fans in the family and there was no fannish discussion around them.

In preference to these sites, Ravelry was selected as the base for the research because of the links between members' profiles, their projects and the patterns they create or work from, and their posts in the Ravelry forums, together with links to members' personal blogs and podcasts, other social media profiles, and sometimes e-commerce sites, thus providing connections to the wider Internet community. It should be noted that the profile pages of the members provide automatic links to blog updates; these are flagged to other members on the user's friends list and to any groups they have joined on the forum. This interconnectedness allows fans to easily project their fan identity (if they so desire). It is also worth stressing the aforementioned features of Ravelry mean that it is regarded as a central hub of many handicrafters' online activities. It is quite common, for example, to see active users mention that they prefer using Ravelry to Facebook or Twitter for their social networking. Moreover, posts in the Ravelry forums frequently mention and link to off-Ravelry sites that the group members might find interesting, serving as a gateway to the wider social web. Ravelry thus proves invaluable in pointing to significant examples outside of the community as well as within.

In terms of the empirical research design, Ravelry was also selected since the site facilitated and enabled close observation and in-depth data collection. Discussion in the forum groups is trackable in threads on specific topics and, since it is archived and searchable, can be traced forwards and backwards in time; postings by individual members can also be tracked across groups. Out of all the possible handicrafting communities, Ravelry therefore had the most easily locatable and accessible groups of fans, offering the potential for the breadth and depth of data collection required by the research project. It was therefore chosen as the primary site for data collection in the initial stages of the project in order to construct a profile of fan handicrafting and the activities of the fan handicrafters. It thus provided a base for the recruitment of participants for interviews and the identification of case studies, each selected as representative of the various forms of fan handicrafting discussed in this book. In designing the research in this way, the majority of the data collection has been carried out within Ravelry.

Ravelry describes itself as "a place for knitters, crocheters, designers, spinners, weavers and dyers to keep track of their yarn, tools, project and pattern information, and look to others for ideas and inspirations."[3] It is the largest and arguably the most active online site both for information in the named crafts (it was primarily set up in order to provide a database of patterns and yarns) and also for discussion of knitting and other crafts, including the production of yarn used in these pastimes (this can be commercially manufactured yarn, but also includes home dyeing and spinning). The site was formed in 2007 and grew quickly in size and recognition. By November 2010, over a million members had become registered users and in the same month it won the .net Magazine Awards 2010 Community Site of the Year (beating both Twitter and Facebook).

The site consists of a database providing searchable information on yarns, yarn companies and stores, books and magazines, and patterns; an e-commerce marketplace where members can sell their own patterns or advertise goods that they sell on other online market sites such as Etsy and buy Ravelry-branded t-shirts, bags, badges, mugs, and glassware; a social network with member profiles (these allow for the recording of stashed yarn and project progress in the Reveller's notebook section, and the notebook entries are in turn linked to the relevant pattern and yarn entries in the main database, as well as friending and personal messaging); and a forum where members can join groups reflecting their own specific interests and take part in discussion or chat with like-minded members on those topics. Through the forums, Ravelry works as a close-knit social space for anyone with an interest in handicrafts. A significant reason why Ravelry proved attractive to fans is that any member can create a group in the forum and all members have the opportunity to join a very wide range of discussion groups that reflect their crafting and wider interests, thus defining their own social experiences within the site.

In terms of identifying the forms and practices of fan handicrafting, it is the projects and forums that have been the particular focus for data collection in this research. As outlined in the Introduction, the member projects and the pattern database were invaluable sources in identifying examples of fan handicrafting. But while the patterns and personal projects reflect the member's fan interests, it is in the groups that fan handicrafting communities emerge. While many groups are dedicated to local knitting groups and yarn stores, commercial yarn brands, indie dyers, sock yarn clubs, specific pattern books or designers, techniques and styles, learning to knit, and so forth, there are almost 19,000 groups in total dedicated to everything from family and homecare (e.g., cooking) to jobs and workplace to the media and arts, as well as groups for those who identify by religion, sexuality, subcultural affiliations (goth, tattooed), age (over 50), and so on. Popular culture is reflected in many groups: there are 44 film groups, 53 for television, 40 on comics and graphic novels, 39 on popular novels and novelists, 18 for science fiction, and 21 for the horror genre. Specific programs and performers with fan followings are well represented, from soap operas to pop music performers. There are a total of 61 groups chatting about various aspects of *Harry Potter* alone. Discussion of popular culture—including the kinds of cult media that seem to encourage fan production—is thus widespread.

Quantitative findings

Given the widespread discussion of popular culture and presence of cult media fandom on the Ravelry forums, it is useful at this point to contextualize the study with some quantitative data. For instance, how large is the fan handicrafting community and how significant is it within the wider community of Ravelry? The number of fans in a general population is invariably difficult to judge, although memberships in particular fan groups or organizations may be available. This is an important consideration, especially in the light of the discussion in Chapter 1 of Jenkins and Busse's points about fannish behaviors—and therefore individuals seeing themselves as fans even though they may not be active members of a participatory fandom and/or not fitting into any of the models of fan culture discussed in the literature (and certainly it must be acknowledged that an isolated individual can be a fan too). This is an important consideration for this account of fan handicrafting since one of my aims is to explore the activities and affective investments of different types of fans, especially those who fall into the less fannish categories in Busse's trajectories of fannish behavior. The question to be addressed here is how do we understand fan handicrafting in a milieu where we are all fans now, especially where the material culture of handicrafting includes examples of popular culture-inspired projects made for fun, for gifts, for one's children, or as a one-off and thus not imbued with fan status or affective investment. Not everyone who makes a fannish item is necessarily a fan (or at least would define themselves as a fan) and this means that it is difficult to ascertain the size of the fan handicrafting community. It is nonetheless worth exploring the interest in fan handicrafting on Ravelry.

The membership of Ravelry reached 5 million in January 2015 (having risen from just over 623,800 members at the start of the study in 2010), although it is difficult to accurately extrapolate from this to the percentage of members who consider themselves as fans and/or participate in fan activities. Nor is it possible to determine the numbers of fans who handicraft, despite observations of handicrafting on various fan sites. Members of the latter may not talk about their crafting on those sites; fan handicrafters may not be members of Ravelry, or even if they are, they may not be active forum participants or even join fan groups. Ravelry's own data indicates that 0.1 percent of members are active at any one time (5,465 out of 5,008,903 on February 4, 2015) and 20 percent are active over a one-week period (1,018,092 during the week ending February 4, 2015). This suggests that the vast majority of members either log on to Ravelry only occasionally or use its database facilities only when needed (looking for a pattern for their next project or when they encounter an issue with their crafting or a pattern that they need help with, for example). It is therefore logical to conclude that only a minority of members use the social networking features of Ravelry, the forum groups primarily, on a regular basis. Nonetheless, these figures do suggest that there is a substantial pool of people from which those who might potentially be active in fan groups are drawn (over 1,000,000).

Further, those members who do participate regularly are often frequent users of and contributors to the site. Forming a social group, frequent users often recognize and acknowledge each other and friendships develop; long conversations or debates can occur across several days or weeks. Every posting in the forums is also accompanied by the number of posts a user has made, both in the specific discussion thread and in total. The total number of posts of the most prolific members can reach the tens of thousands; however, these might range across any number of different subject areas and topics including crafting ones, lifestyle, and small talk as well as other interests including fan tastes. Within this, it is possible to provide an estimate of active participants and how widespread membership of fan interest groups on the Ravelry forum is. Anyone can form a group in the Ravelry forums on any subject; they are not limited to handicrafting related topics. This means that as outlined earlier many fan groups exist, and Ravellers with fannish interests can quickly find groups to suit their tastes, and where they do not already exist can easily form one of their own. Not all the groups are equal, however, some having limited appeal or few members, but others are large and extremely active. It is useful here to consider the range, scope, and size of the fan groups active on Ravelry.

Table 2.1 *Membership of Ravelry fan groups*

Group	Fandom	Membership
Harry Potter Lovers	Harry Potter	10,026
Who Knits?	Doctor Who	8,323
Big Damn Knitters	Firefly	6,349
Lord of the Rings	Tolkien	3,863
221b	Sherlock Holmes	3,415
Studio Ghibli	Anime films from Studio Ghibli	3,288
Ankh-Morpork Knitter's Guild	Terry Pratchett novels	3,149
Outlander Fans	Outlander	3,107
Downton Abbey	Downton Abbey	2,860
Twilight Saga Fans	Twilight	2,834
As You Wish	The Princess Bride	2,500
The Big Bang Gang	The Big Bang Theory	2,289
A Song of Ice and Fire/Game of Thrones	A Song of Ice and Fire/Game of Thrones	2,130
Buffy Knitters	Buffy the Vampire Slayer	2,061
Bones Fans*	Bones	1,970
True Blood	True Blood	1,906
NCIS Knitters	NCIS	1,822
Ravel Trek	Star Trek	1,806
Lost Knitters*	Lost	1,788
Welcome to Storybrooke	Once Upon a Time and Grimm	1,597
Supernatural	Supernatural	1,437
Castle	Castle	1,316
Mad Men Knitting	Mad Men	1,217
Knitting Dead	The Walking Dead	1,206
Knitting The Galaxy	Star Wars	1,090
Jane Austen Book Group	Jane Austen	917
Miss Marple's Mavens	Miss Marple fiction and adaptations	851
The Hunger Games Series Fan Group*	The Hunger Games	799
CSI Knitters*	CSI	699
Craft Bronies	My Little Pony	600
MSTie Ravelers*	Mystery Science Theatre 3000	381
Xfiles	The X-Files	338
Codex Dresden*	Jim Butcher novels	318

Group	Fandom	Membership
Warehouse 13*	Warehouse 13	312
American Horror Story	American Horror Story	297
Twin Peaks Addicts*	Twin Peaks	199
The Lemon Lymons*	The West Wing	192
Sleepy Hollow Fans	Sleepy Hollow	189
Orange is the New Black*	Orange is the New Black	176
Marvel*	Marvel comics	157
Dark Shadows knitting & crochet	Dark Shadows	156
The Eldritch Lovecraftian Book Group	H. P. Lovecraft	101
Marvel's Agents of S.H.I.E.L.D.*	Agents of S.H.I.E.L.D.	90
Hannibal*	Hannibal TV series	73
Xena Warrior Princess*	Xena Warrior Princess	49

Note: Groups recorded in this table are the largest and most active for each specific fandom; most of the fandoms have several other less active or smaller groups associated with them, some have many. Snapshot taken on February 4, 2015.

* indicates low activity levels.

As Table 2.1 shows, there are a number of large fan groups representing a wide range of cult film and television, and a number of mainstream series with active fan followings. In addition to these, there are also a number of additional groups that offer generic fan interests or signal themselves as nerds, fans, or geeks in general. Nerdy Knitters has 5,306 members, Sci-Fi Craft has 433, Horror Knits with 1,168, Steamy Stitches 2,630 (for fans of the steampunk genre), and Gamer Geeks 1,694, for example. There are specific game groups such as World of Warcrafters with 2,213 members. There are also groups for new media such as *Welcome to Night Vale* (2012–); Welcome to Knit Vale has 393 members. It should be noted that fannish discussion does take place in other non-fan Ravelry groups too. For example, the Lazy, Stupid and Godless group frequently contains threads on fannish topics, often in a way that suggests the members are avid consumers of popular culture texts, but also showing evidence of more intensely fannish activities such as discussing fan fiction and the site Archive of Our Own, thus illustrating the range of Busse's trajectories of fannish behaviors and how activities associated with fan culture are now widespread.

There are, however, interesting differences that must be highlighted between fan groups representing cult media and those dedicated to more mainstream television genres. The spread of genre interests across the Ravelry fan groups in Table 2.1 suggests that horror, science fiction, and fantasy series (genres that tend to dominate within cult media) predominate, at least in terms of larger memberships and more active discussion. Mainstream genres are, however, also well represented in the groups: crime series such as *Bones* (2005–), *NCIS* (2003–), and *CSI* (2000–2015), "must see TV" series including *Mad Men* (2007–2015), *The West Wing* (1999–2006), and *Orange is the New Black* (2013–), and historical dramas such as *Downton Abbey* (2010–). In addition to the cult genres and mainstream dramas in Table 2.1, there are also a varied range of fan groups for cult comedies, soap operas, reality TV shows, music, sport, and celebrities. However, these are not on the whole associated with notable amounts or instances of fan production, handicrafting or otherwise. It is by no means absolute, then, but the general trend is that cult genres are associated with the most active and producerly groups. In terms of the kind of transmedia storytelling, role-playing, and transformative works, as well as fan discourses that circulate around fan production and the fan objects themselves, programs, films, and novels most closely associated with cult genres are the more productive in terms of this research. It is not insignificant that these also tend to be the texts that predominate in fan culture generally; fans on Ravelry simply replicate the wider patterns of cult media fandom.

A decision was made early on in the design of the project that these fandoms would therefore be the focus of the study. This is not to downplay fans of mainstream television or other categories, many of the findings in the study apply to fans of these texts too, and there is often overlap in a fan's interest across both cult and mainstream texts. It is also interesting that the members of scientific and mathematical interest groups also identify themselves as nerds, illustrating the different approaches to and meanings of terminology that fans, geeks, and nerds use to define themselves and their interests. This indicates that it is more appropriate to consider nerd-/geek-/fandoms as a spectrum (science and science fiction interests often being linked as they are in *The Big Bang Theory* which has an active fan group on Ravelry). Indeed, handicrafters often identify fluidly across the spectrum and Nerd Wars includes a science and mathematics team as well as teams focused on art, mythology, and Shakespeare. This raises an interesting question, by implication the final set of teams here might not commonly be deemed fannish or nerdy interests, but their inclusion most definitely indicates that examples of high culture can attract the equivalent of fan followings. This clearly reflects the questions Roberta Pearson (2007) raises around the exclusion of high culture fandom (she includes Shakespeare, classical music, and Sherlock Holmes in this) from cultural studies. Where the term "fan" is used in this account it should therefore be assumed that this is inclusive of other categories on this spectrum, including "aficionados" of high culture. None of these groups have been recorded in Table 2.1 for reasons of clarity, but there is no reason to suppose that findings cannot also be extrapolated across these groups. Though the study mainly focuses on fan handicrafting in relation to cult media, other examples related to mainstream and high culture texts are highlighted where relevant.

Before looking at a demographic breakdown of fan handicrafters on Ravelry, it is also worth taking a moment to consider the patterns of fannish interests within media fandoms, since these are by no means homogenous. Table 2.1 records only the largest and/or most active group representing each fandom; in fact, many of these texts have several groups linked to it (since anyone can set up a group on the Ravelry forum, more than one fan might start a group unaware of the existence of others or because an existing group is not to their taste). And for each of these fandoms there are also often several other smaller groups focused on specific aspects of the text (e.g., on a single actor from a TV series, a group just for people knitting the *Doctor Who* scarf) or for a group in a particular demographic range (such as teen fans or fans in a specific geographical location).

To give a more detailed breakdown in a single fandom, there are forty-six groups dedicated to vampires in fiction and popular culture. These groups differ in both size—with memberships ranging from several thousand to less than ten—and levels of activity—with postings varying anywhere between 145 posts over a day (this was around the transmission of the season 3 finale of *True Blood* in a specific episode thread in the True Blood group) to less than ten posts a week in the discussion as a whole in less active groups. The largest of these groups are the ones dedicated to vampire texts in general: Blood and Yarn (with 860 members), Crocheters Darkly Dreaming (959), Horror Knits (1,068), Vampires Purrrl (225), and Paranormal Romance Novel Fans (187). In terms of activity levels, groups focused on specific examples of current vampire fiction and media are the most active at any one time; unsurprisingly, current texts generate the most interest. When this data was collected, there were twenty-four *Twilight* groups, six for *True Blood,* and two for *Vampire Diaries* (2009–), with one group each for *Being Human* (2008–2013), *Sanctuary* (2007–2011), and *Supernatural* (2005–), all of which featured recurring vampire characters or monsters. Various other groups exist for other recent novels or television series, as well as older cult series and films. Geographical or national groups also exist for contemporary series; for example, the existence of the True Blood UK group reflects the fact that British fans can fall out of the spatiotemporal rhythms of the US-based discussion due to the different national broadcast dates and scheduling patterns (Hills 2002: 139).

Just as in fan culture generally, distinct communities form around specific tastes such as favorite characters, desired relationships, and actors. Breaking down the *Twilight* groups further, there is a main group (Twilight Saga Fans with 3,603 members), a group of *Twilight* fan fiction readers and writers (Unicorns Unlimited which has 538 members), groups for specific characters or actors (♥Edward

Cullen♥ has 282 members—in comparison, groups for the characters Bella, Carlisle, and Jacob have under ten members each, making it clear where the interest lies among these fans), a group for Teenage Twilighters with ninety-one members and another for Twilight Kids with thirty-three members (discussion on the main Twilight boards tends to contain material only suitable for adults), and a group for the not-fans (Sparkles Aren't Our Thing which has 121 members). Other groups are for discussion of specific films or books in the *Twilight* series (Breaking Dawn Lovers, for instance, with sixty-one members), for crossover interest (Bella v Harry, for example, which has 116 members), or for quirky and light-hearted groups such as The Twilight Chocaholics (thirty members). Fans are thus quite fragmented across many smaller groups, but many of them belong to several with multiple group memberships being the norm. A selection of smaller or more specialized groups were also observed in the study, confirming that further patterns of discussion or fan productivity had not been missed.

This breakdown demonstrates that fan interests among handicrafters are spread across current and ongoing examples of popular culture, with lesser interest in niche examples of cult media. There is a pattern here in that the majority of the larger and most active groups are for current television programs or films. Many popular TV shows have groups formed to discuss them, with membership numbers in two or three figures, rarely more than low hundreds, and they often become inactive once the series has ended. This represents the kind of mainstream fannish interest that Busse discusses and the series that are the topic of these groups are to a certain extent ephemeral. Groups show patterns of higher activity when new episodes or repeats are in the current TV schedules with conversely low activity when they are off the air. As series end, interest wanes and group activity ceases. For example, a group for the series *Boardwalk Empire* (2010–2014) has changed its name to "Delete," posting in its header description "Delete. No activity, show is done."[4] It could well be concluded from the attitude that underlies such as request that the community in this group is closer in behaviors to a mainstream audience (one that talks enthusiastically about a series only as long as it is being broadcast—a "water cooler" series) than a participatory fan audience (which continues to discuss and add to the narrative even long after a program has ended—a key aspect of a series becoming a cult text). And certainly this group, while posting about each episode, does not exhibit any affective investments in the series through handicrafting projects or other examples of fan art. What this may be taken as suggesting in general is that the predominant trajectory of fannish behavior on Ravelry resembles dedicated viewers of a current series, as opposed to cult (or nostalgic) fandom keeping a well-loved text alive—that they are not by and large the kinds of cult fans keeping the fandom alive as *Doctor Who* fans did between the 1980s and 2005, for example.

However, there are also strong indications of cult fan audiences active on Ravelry as evidenced by the groups for *Firefly*, *Buffy,* and *The Princess Bride*, as well as the aforementioned *Doctor Who* (and group memberships include fans of the classic series and Big Finish audioplays, as well as of the current series). Groups for many of the non-current series that are the subject of cult media fandoms have much higher levels of fan productivity keeping the group active than do those groups for current mainstream series, though there may be relatively low levels of activity or slower pacing in terms of numbers and frequency of posts. Fans also migrate across groups, representing interests shifting to a similar or related series as one ends and another begins. For example, the *True Blood* group has fallen to very low levels of activity since the series ended (at the time of collecting the data in Table 2.1, there had been no posting for four months and the most recent discussion was mostly about what to watch instead and what other series cast members were appearing in, common preoccupations among fans bereft when their favorite series ends). What actually happened here was that many of the *True Blood* fans were also fans of *The Walking Dead* and migrated as a community to The Knitting Dead group.

The group Unicorns Unlimited is also interesting with the focus of the group evolving from *Twilight* fan fiction to "a fun home for the slightly insane and snarky" (though it still maintains lists of fan fiction recommendations). This indicates that fans "participation within fandom often extends beyond an interest in any single text to encompass many others within the same genre" (Jenkins 2012: 37). Further evidence of this can be found in the migratory patterns of membership in the Ravelry fan groups. These fans show interest in texts across widely different genres too. One of the Shakespeare fans on the Nerd Wars team has also played on the *Mystery Science Theatre 3000* team, for example. Pearson (2007: 102) refers to this in terms of a "fannish disposition," the evidence for which would be "many whose multiple fandoms range widely across fields of cultural production and up and down cultural hierarchies." There is indeed much evidence for this in the fan handicrafting community. The fans also develop strong social bonds of friendship that transcend one specific fan interest, often introducing each other to different fandoms. Moreover, this may be strengthened further by the shared handicrafting practices that they undertake, crafting being a particularly social activity as explored in Chapter 1. It may even be that fans can feel isolated in their everyday lives—at least in terms of their affective investments in the fan object—and thus friendships developed in fan handicrafting communities become all the more significant to them.

The active groups for older series that have already ended or been canceled are also revealing. These include *Firefly* and *Buffy the Vampire Slayer*, both Joss Whedon series, suggesting an interest, in this instance at least, in a cult auteur in addition to the series itself. Big Damn Knitters, for example, has a thread entitled "The Man They Call Joss ..." where he is a focus of discussion. The sustained interest in *Firefly* also relates to the fact it was canceled after only one series and that many of its fans feel it ended too soon. The cult status that this generates also continues to attract new fans through word of mouth and continuing

Internet coverage (one member posting, "I didn't get on board until 2013, so ..."). Big Damn Knitters continues to highlight the members' Jayne hats, a cult object around which the fan handicrafters can organize themselves, new merchandise and the *Firefly* online role-playing game,[5] their cosplays and convention meet-ups, and participation in fan handicrafting events (Tour de Fleece being one). *Harry Potter* also continues to attract a lively and ongoing fan community and in this instance it appears to be related to the transmedia worldbuilding that the book and film series sustains. This includes the Pottermore website,[6] which retells and adds to the books and provides an interactive experience for the fans, alongside books of *Harry Potter*-themed knitting patterns and events on Ravelry such as the Harry Potter Knitting and Crochet House Cup, which also involves role-play. As one poster on Harry Potter Lovers says in reference to the proposed film version of *Fantastic Beasts and Where to Find Them* (Rowling 2001), "we can go back to the world that we all wish was real." It is these extensions to the text as well as the transmedia storytelling on Pottermore (of which Firefly Online is another example) that support a cult fan community.

In summary, it is not possible to conclude for certain from this data exactly how many handicrafters consider themselves to be fans, but the snapshot presented here suggests that there is a significant community of fan handicrafters with an interest in cult media or with fannish interests in mainstream texts. The largest active fandoms on Ravelry are the Harry Potter Lovers group and the Who Knits? group for *Doctor Who* fans. The membership numbers of these groups suggest that there are at least 10,000 handicrafters on Ravelry who consider themselves to be fans, though this is likely to be an underestimate since not all handicrafters with fannish interests on Ravelry will be either a *Doctor Who* fan or a *Harry Potter* fan. The number is doubtless larger than this, but given that many members join several fan-related groups, a cumulative or total number might grossly overestimate the numbers (and those with more than one fannish interest will not be interested in every fan text). It is hard in any case to estimate fan populations, but it is certainly in the thousands and possible low ten thousands of Ravelry members. To provide some external context, in comparison to the Who Knits? group with over 8,000 members, the *Doctor Who* fan forum Gallifrey Base[7] had just over 80,000 members at the time the above figures were recorded on January 30, 2015. The *Doctor Who* audience regularly has 7–8 million viewers in the UK (Cherry 2013) with another 2–3 million in the United States, suggesting that the participatory fan audience segment is still quite a small percentage of the overall audience (many of whom might class themselves as fans but not be active in forums such as Gallifrey Base). It would be unwise, then, to conclude that the total size of the fan audience for *Doctor Who* is in the region of 80,000, and the *Doctor Who* fan knitters are thus highly unlikely to comprise anything approaching 10 percent of the fan audience. However, some other important considerations emerge.

In the forefront of these is the gender balance of different fan communities. Female fans are known to form their own communities around fanfic, cosplay, or other forms of fan art on social media such as LiveJournal or Tumblr. One *Doctor Who* handicrafter says that she "tend[s] to stay away from those forums, I stick to what I find on LJ. I'm only on like every Torchwood related group on LJ!" (LJ referring to Live Journal and "those forums" being established *Doctor Who* fan communities such as Gallifrey Base that tend to be more male-dominated). In terms of the ratio of the established *Doctor Who* fan community to *Doctor Who* fan handicrafters, little overlap between these two fan communities is indicated in the research data. One *Doctor Who* fan handicrafter said that she did not read Gallifrey Base because she found such fan sites to be too aggressive and argumentative for her liking, describing them as "terrifying, slavering, rabid beasties and they scare me." Another said that she "frequented Gallifrey Base for a while. It was a whooole [sic] different world." Three or four fans did make comments on Ravelry about threads on Gallifrey Base of special interest, including sharing pictures of David Tennant, the attitudes regarding copyright and trademark infringement of the BBC toward fan copies of scarves and knitted toys based on *Doctor Who* characters, and meet-ups at conventions. Another (a male) had been active in organized *Doctor Who* fandom in the UK, having been a member of the Doctor Who Appreciation Society and attending *Doctor Who* fan conventions independently of his handicrafting interests. Fans such as these are, however, in the minority, most never having been involved with such organized fandom or joining fan communities online or off for particular programs. This should not, though, be taken to suggest that the fannish behaviors expressed on Ravelry are less intense than those on display in other areas of fandom. On the contrary, it suggests yet another online space that a largely female fan-base has colonized in order to establish its own arena for fan production.

Profile of fan handicrafters, and a note about gender and demographics

Overall, then, it can be estimated that there might be upwards of 50,000 Ravelry members who consider themselves to be fans and/or join fan groups on the Ravelry forums because they are highly engaged with a particular series. These fan handicrafters are widely spread in terms of age, nationality, geographical location, occupation, and educational attainment. The profile generally (and unsurprisingly) reflects the demographic spread on Ravelry as a whole. The age range is largely clustered in the 20–59 age groups, with around 20 percent each in the 20–29, 40–49, and 50–59 ranges and slightly more, 26 percent, in the 30–39 range; 12 percent are aged above 60 and 3 percent under 20. Americans predominate, reflecting usage of the Internet as a whole, but other Anglophone nations are well represented (the UK, Canada, Australia, and New Zealand), and substantial numbers come from Europe, including eastern European countries. There is significant Ravelry membership in India, Japan, South Africa, Egypt, and Central and South American countries, but few members from these countries are active in the fan groups observed during this research (language might certainly be one factor to explain this).

The overwhelming majority of fan handicrafters are women, over 99 percent. This reflects the membership of Ravelry as a whole (the web analytics site alexa. com gives the gender split of Ravelry members at around 98 percent female to 2 percent male) and thereby of handicrafters generally, reflecting the stereotype of the knitter being female (though the above figures on the age spread belies the idea that knitters are elderly women). It must also be noted that non-cis and non-straight women are well represented in the fan groups, with several members making their trans and queer—including straight queer—identities, as well as sexualities, clear (this does suggest that the fan groups, like Ravelry generally,[8] are welcoming of handicrafters identifying as LGBTI).

In terms of the gendering of handicrafting, knitting and crochet are often classed as feminine pursuits. Fandom, likewise, is also gendered feminine in many respects, at least when considering the practices of fan culture which most resemble those of fan handicrafting—namely, fan fiction and other transformative works, with the sexual appeal and sexuality of male stars often privileged. However, as discussed in Chapter 1, this is not to say that the gendering of fandom or handicrafting is straightforward or unproblematical. The main finding from the quantitative data is, however, that the large majority of fan handicrafters, reflecting the split in the handicrafting community in general, are female. But within this it is important to highlight that categories of sex and gender, as with ethnicity and race, ability and sexuality, are nevertheless well represented on Ravelry. It is not always easy, however, to establish the exact demographic splits in such categories. Take gender, for example.

The Men Who Knit website (menwhoknit.com) has 5,080 registered users. On Ravelry, the Men Who Knit group has 3,183 members, Men Who Crochet has 759 members, Spinning Men has 180, and Gay Men Stitch, Too! has 1,524. Of further note, there are just under 150 Ravelry groups for male knitters or which specifically encourage male knitters to join, the majority local or national groups allowing male knitters to be in contact with others in their locality or geographical region (data collected on March 18, 2015). It is hard to give a definitive figure or even to estimate a total figure, given overlaps in the group membership, but taking an approximate figure of just over 5,000 (also reflecting the Men Who Knit membership), the percentage of total Ravelry members who are men is around 0.1 percent. This is a small percentage, but it remains true to say that male handicrafters do have a presence (there are male pattern designers, indie dyers, and manufacturers of tools, as well as those who pursue handicrafts as hobbies) and it is important to consider them as contributors to the culture of handicrafting. It is therefore also important to remember that although the vast majority of participants in the research are female, and that this does reflect the demographic spread of Ravelry in general, men do knit and crochet. Though there may be very few men in the fan groups and events observed during this research, I have selected a small sample to interview and some of their work is featured in the chapters that follow.[9]

Research design and recruitment

For reasons of manageability, a decision was made to focus specifically on a sample of representative groups and activities. Similar patterns of discourses and crafting activities were observed across groups so the findings can be more widely applied. Groups with the largest and most active communities were chosen as the focus of the study because this offered the opportunity to observe the widest possible range of discourses and activities for analysis. While all groups offered opportunities for researching responses to the text, some had much lower participation in crafting activities and fan projects related to the text (the *Bones*, *Boardwalk Empire*, and *American Horror Story* groups, for example). These groups, with discussion tending toward "water cooler" type of chat, were not included in the selection for participant-observation or case studies. Since the focus of the research is on handicrafting and textile-based fan art, as well as the communities producing these, those groups involved in higher levels of fan productivity were selected for close observation and analysis. These include groups for fans of *Doctor Who*, *Sherlock* (2010–), *Harry Potter*, and *The Walking Dead* (2010–).

Firefly, *Doctor Who*, and *True Blood* provided in-depth case studies of mimetic crafting and prop or costume reproductions. *Doctor Who* and vampire handicrafting were selected as examples for pilot studies at the beginning of the research design process (see Cherry 2011 and 2013) and these have been developed during the ongoing research to provide further in-depth case studies. Nerd Wars was chosen for participant-observation as it offered the opportunity for data collection across a very wide range of fan interests, enabling correlation of findings to other areas of fan interest. The Harry Potter Knitting and Crochet House Cup was selected for participant-observation since it presented a case study involving elements of role-play and performance. Steampunk groups were also selected because they offered the opportunity to observe the wider engagement with fiber- and non-fiber-based textile arts through costuming, cosplay, and everyday dress practices.

The account that follows draws on observations of the discussion groups noted earlier, online interviews with a selected sample of fans, with interviews being conducted by email and personal messages on Ravelry. In order to capture focused data, participants were asked questions tailored to their projects, fan activities they take part in or handicrafting practices, as well as a standard questionnaire. The selection of interviewees included indie designers and dyers, bloggers and podcasters, as well as a range of fan handicrafters from the different groups in which the participant-observation was carried out. Participants were selected for interview on the basis of, firstly, creating projects or patterns representative of various classes or examples of fan art, and, secondly, as being active participants in groups and events organized around fan handicrafting. Case studies were selected to illustrate particular aspects of the activities and production being undertaken by the fan handicrafters. Participants were approached using the personal messaging system on Ravelry, via the snowball technique—participants suggesting others or passing on the request, and via other fan sites including the fan fiction sites An Archive of Our Own and fanfiction.net, handicrafting blogs and podcasts. In total, thirty-six fans were interviewed (90 percent being female). Where discursive data was identified from group discussion, quoted participants were asked for permission and anonymity has been given. The names given in the data analysis and case studies are always those that the participant preferred (either a given name, the participant's Ravelry ID, or anonymous).

The fans who craft

This profile of the fan handicrafters that are the subject of this research reveals that they are predominantly female, largely coming from Anglophone nations and Europe, spread roughly evenly across the age ranges, education, and relationship status, with a significant minority identifying as LGBTI. However, this tells us little about their fan identities, nor about the affective investments these fans make in terms of both their fan interests and their crafting practices. The next chapter sets out the ways in which the fan handicrafters construct and communicate their fan identities within the handicrafting community on Ravelry.

3
NARRATIVES OF THE SELF AND FAN IDENTITY

Identity, whether related to aspects of gender and sexuality, family, domesticity, or social situation, is frequently constructed and communicated within Ravelry (just as it is in other social networks both offline and on). More importantly, in relation to fan handicrafting are the ways in which a Raveller defines herself as a fan or as having a "fan disposition," as Roberta Pearson (2007: 102) suggests. The key point here is to consider the ways in which fans construct "narratives of the self" in a mediated world, focusing in particular on how handicrafters construct and project fan identities within an online handicrafting community. Analyzing the discourses identified members' profiles and in the chat within fan groups reveals the ways in which fan identity can be communicated. In particular, Ravellers construct and perform fan identities through their personal profile, the projects they make, the groups they are active in, and the community building—organized around the fandom—that they undertake.

Presentation of self and performative identity

As Lucy Bennett and Paul Booth (2015: 1.1) point out, "performance is an integral part of fandom and fannish experiences," and fans are "constantly negotiating their own performances, both online and off." Such performances can be overt or can hover beneath the surface: fandom is not "a particular behaviour," but includes "characteristics of being that permeate a fannish identity" (Bennett and Booth 2015: 1.3). Bennett and Booth suggest that the social web is an important factor: "In the digital space, everything fans post, create, or share could be considered a type of performance." (2015: 1.4). A "social establishment" in Erving Goffman's account in *The Presentation of Self in Everyday Life* is defined as a place in which "a particular kind of activity regularly takes place" (1959:

239). Such places can be extended to include online communities, as Rebecca Bley (2009: 44–46) sets out with respect to LiveJournal's hyperlinks to profiles, personal messaging for one-to-one conversations, groups on specific themes or topics for one-to-many interactions, threaded postings which emulate conversations, and management of friends into distinct groupings. Ravelry presents a very similar social establishment (though it does not have quite the flexibility as LiveJournal for presenting different identities to different groups or sets of friends through filtering). Bearing this in mind, Ravellers make use of their personal profile, photographs on their project pages (and the projects themselves), and their user avatars displayed on forum posts (referred to as a Ravatar in this community).

In terms of signposting identity, it is the personal profile, incorporating a username (also known as the "Rav ID" or sometimes "Rav Handle") and a Ravatar, that can be used to most obviously perform an identity. Many members of Ravelry choose usernames that reflect their real name or a nickname, indicate a family relationship, or give an indication of regional identity or profession. Many others choose usernames to indicate their crafting skills. Some do choose a name that reflects their tastes or likes, but overall usernames linked to fan interests remain a very small minority. This really tells us nothing beyond the nature of the umbrella community and its focus on crafting practices and the textile arts. It is to be expected that in fan communities many more members choose names reflecting character or storyworld preferences; this is the case in the steampunk community, for example, where members adopt a steampunk name (or *nom-de-steam*) and sometimes constructed personas (Cherry and Mellins 2011). We would expect a community geared to handicrafting to have more members with usernames reflecting crafts, family, and social situation. The Ravelry username is also semipermanent (it can be changed but this is only permitted twice and is not encouraged, so occurs infrequently), and for most users it reflects their choice at the moment of joining. Joining a handicrafting community is likely to inspire the member to choose a craft, domestic or family related name (and certainly members are not necessarily thinking of fannish interests or fan handicrafting when they joined—as the quote from *Vampire Knits* in the Introduction suggests Genevieve Miller was not).

However, a small number do choose a name that suggests fan interests or passions. Names indicating a fannish disposition incorporate the terms "nerd," "geek," or "fan" somewhere in the name—for example, nerdyknitter, knittinnerdy, geeky-squeaky, GeekyGirl, GeekLady, CathleenFanGirl. Incorporated in these identifications as nerds, geeks, and fans are tastes in music, comedians, actors, film directors, games such as World of Warcraft, and comic book superheroes. Other fans choose a Ravelry name incorporating an interest in a specific text (their dominant fandom perhaps) or interest in particular characters, but again this is a relatively small number. Usernames chosen by some vampire fans, for example, include Blooferlady, vampirate, spikeknits, MinaHarker, and teamedward18. Some *Doctor Who* fans have usernames such as dr-who-fan, TARDIS-InA-Teacup, and DWImpossibleGirl. Other examples include jedisparkles, fireflykiwi, Lothlorien93, supermoonie (a reference to *Sailor Moon*), Cheetoy (for Cheetor from *Transformers*), and Kinnexa (after a character from the EE Doc Smith *Lensman* series).

A few usernames are characters from cult media such as AliceCullen (from *Twilight*), PamelaDeBeaufort (from *True Blood*), and TardisType40, these being used for specific instances of role-play. Paul Booth (2010: 154) defines such adoptions of a character as a form of "identity role-play" in which fans "act as if they were the character and 'play' with the characteristics of the character." PamelaDeBeaufort, for example, is a sockpuppet account in the Fangtasia group, the owner of this account making posts as if she were Pam to comment on group members' projects in the thread Pamela's Closet: Blood Will Spill. In the storyworld, Pam is known for her love of fashion and the color pink, and in response to a member thinking about making a particular cardigan pattern, PamelaDeBeaufort says, "I'd suggest a lovely shade of pink—or red if you're spending time with Eric." Booth (2010: 155) sees this as a form of parasocial interaction whereby the fan inhabits the character. And, of course, this offers opportunities for role-play by all the members of the group as they interact with their own version of Pam who enjoys knitting.

Other Ravelry members use the "About Me" section on their profile page to define themselves as fans of particular texts or of a genre. The moderator of the True Blood group gives "Vampire Gail" as her name on her profile. Steampunk fans in the Nerd Girl Yarns group gave each other codenames such as The Ruffled Cravat, The Clockwork Coronet, and The Strawberry Aviatrix and displayed these as their first name on their profiles. Other Ravellers incorporate snippets of dialogue or catchphrases from a favorite series as their "Fave curse word"[1] including "F'n Sookie!" (*True Blood*), "Frell" (*Farscape* 1999–2003), and "Frack" (*Battlestar Galactica*). The *True Blood* fan here goes on to declare her specific fan interests mixed in with biographical information, her status as a stay at home mum and number of children, other fan interests including sports team, and other hobbies—scrapbooking, sewing, baking, as well as being a collector of nail polish. She writes, "My weekly indulgence is *True Blood* (Team Eric!) and *The Walking Dead* (Team Daryl!)." She adds, "I'm also a *Doctor Who* fan." Thus, she indicates not only the range of cult media that she watches as a nomadic fan, but her affective investments in particular characters.

The option to link to a personal blog also permits the fan to synchronize their profile with fan-related postings on their blog. Blog updates are hyperlinked from their Ravelry profile and can also be linked from the groups they are members of. For example, a *Sherlock* fan interviewed in depth for this study, WhoGroovesOn (female, single, 20s, American, educated to degree level in computer animation), links to her Tumblr[2] page that includes her Sherlock Goldfish fan art—characters from the series drawn as fish—and her poster designs for the fan convention Necronomicon 2014. This means that her reblogs of *Sherlock*, *Doctor Who*, Benedict Cumberbatch, and other assorted fan art is also linked on her Ravelry profile. From her Tumblr, there are links to her fan fiction on Archive of Our Own and to her Society6 page where other fans can buy prints of her goldfish, as well as back to her projects on her Ravelry profile. On her Ravelry profile, she also provides links to her DeviantArt site and Twitter account. All of this constructs a complex presentation of who she is as a fan. As narratives of the self, these instances illustrate the way in which fan identity is embedded in a broad set of interests, including sport and cosmetics, and sits alongside family and crafting. The fan identity is presented as a significant component of the self as performed within the wider handicrafting community.

Furthermore, overt displays of fan identity are performed via the use of Ravatars. This is significant in terms of the performance of fandom (especially in the wider community) since other members of Ravelry will not necessarily visit the profile page, but can see the Ravatar on the fans posts when reading the forum or looking at their project pages in the database. The Ravatar can be chosen and changed easily, as often the member desires, with currently unused or older Ravatars being displayed on the profile. Thus the Ravatar can be used to reflect ongoing and current interests in a flexible way. Whereas the username is not necessarily the best place to communicate fan identity, especially where the fan interests may be varied and nomadic, the Ravatar can reflect multiple aspects of identity including fan identities, even fluid or nomadic ones.

Again, the commonest categories of Ravatar, even among members of fan groups, are photos of the member, their pet, their children, family or spouse, or favorite project or piece of handicrafting of which they are most proud. Other popular categories are archive photos, including film and TV stills that are not fannish in nature (Cary Grant knitting is a recurring one, for example), art and other found imagery, and pictures of sheep. Popular choices for Ravatars that project a fan identity are favorite characters: Eric and Spike are the two most popular characters by far in vampire fan community; David Tennant as the Doctor and pictures of the TARDIS are extremely popular among the *Doctor Who* fans; *Supernatural* fans often have pictures of Sam and Dean Winchester— both separately and together—or Dean's 1967 Chevy Impala; and Benedict Cumberbatch or Martin Freeman from the BBC series are popular Ravatars with Sherlock Holmes fans, as are photos of the street sign for Baker Street or 221b door furniture. Often the images chosen for Ravatars are of characters in sexually appealing poses, thus reflecting the tendency "fangirling"[3] among these communities (see also Cherry 2010). Ravatars such as these are sometimes used to display desire for sexually appealing characters, or the desire to become or be with the characters. One Ravatar of Eric from *True Blood* depicts him naked in bed and another proclaims, "I'll knit for a Viking any time" (text is frequently added to images used as Ravatars), another shows Spike, naked from the waist up, in an intimate scene with Buffy, and one has a close-up of Richard Armitage as Thorin in *The Hobbit* films (2012–2014) which highlights the intense, sultry gaze of the actor.

One thing that comes across strongly in all of these is that the fan identities being displayed are organized around characters that arouse desire, thus communicating the affective investment of the fan in the character and/or the actor. Funny, quirky, or jokey Ravatars are also common. For example, one *Sherlock* fan has a Ravatar depicting Sherlock and John Watson in the style of Minions from *Despicable Me* (2010), a vampire fan has a picture of Grandpa Munster looking disapproving with the text "Sparkles? Really?," and one *Supernatural* fan has a convention photo taken with Misha Collins, who plays Castiel in the series. In the last example, the actor is pulling a face and pointing at a handwritten note the fan is holding while she smiles goofily; the note reads "Castiel owes me child support." This is explained further in a thread posting where the fan (anon) writes that she craved cheeseburgers during pregnancy to the extent that her husband joked, in reference to a scene in *Supernatural* where the character eats dozens of burgers, that Castiel must be the father—inspiring the jokey convention photo. One member of Team TARDIS who breeds and shows rats as a hobby has Ravatars displaying a rat photoshopped in *Doctor Who* costumes (one in Tom Baker's costume and another in Peter Capaldi's), as well as a "Captain Ratmerica."

Ravatars are also used to display participation in fan handicrafting events, for example, Nerd Wars and the Harry Potter Knitting and Crochet House Cup. These fans indicate their fan allegiances via team membership (itself a declaration of fan identity) and display this in their Ravatar. This often involves text with team declarations or adopted team logos, but can also add thematic elements to pictures (which most often are shots of characters or iconic imagery). Members of Slytherin in the House Cup often have green-tinted Ravatars. Players on Team 221b in Nerd Wars have a silhouette of the London skyline—with the London Eye prominent as in the BBC publicity posters for *Sherlock*—superimposed on theirs. These images variously communicate playful crossovers of different texts, fluid fan interests, fan group affiliations, anti-fan status (*Twilight* is disliked by many of the vampire fans), and personal history.

An interesting observation here in terms of presentations of fan identity to the community is that other members of the social or fan groupings come to associate the Ravatar with the individual, to the extent that members sometimes joke about hearing the post read in the voice of the actor in the Ravatar or failing to recognize each other when they change their Ravatars. The Ravatar is thus an extremely significant component of the profile or persona the fan wishes to project. Members make knowing or playful, jokey remarks about the distracting appeal of the character displayed, but also about the Raveller being the character depicted in their Ravatar. A fan handicrafter might display Eric or Spike in their Ravatar because they like or even desire that character, but the character becomes a kind of alter ego for them too, and thus a form of identity role-play. This relates to the construction of narratives around the fan herself, her participation in the community, and her work.

Matt Hills's (2002: 43) discussion of projects (or reflexive narratives) of the self, in which he suggests there are links between discourses of fandom and the fan's biographical sense of self, is relevant here. As Hills (2009) points out, within digital culture "self-identity is not only presented and displayed through the embodied self." Presentations of self also work through profile images, avatars, and personal digital photographs in social networks and other spaces of digital culture. These are all available to the fans on Ravelry, via their Ravatars, the photos they use on their project pages, and in their postings in the forum groups. As the examples explored earlier illustrate, fan identities can be projected in the Ravelry profile via appropriations of the text, borrowed and transformed images, quotes, and statements of fandom, as well as affirmations of fandom by joining fan groups on the forum. The latter becomes an integral part of the personal profile since the profile page includes the logo or badge for each group that the Raveller belongs to, effectively becoming a display of iconic images from the fan objects the member affiliates to. The fan's project pages in their Ravelry notebook—linked directly from the profile—might similarly be used to display their love of the text. In addition, the experiences of the fan handicrafters as relayed to their fellow fans in the groups (including their participation in fan activities outside of Ravelry) and their accounts of personal fan histories strongly signal their fan identities and histories.

In this way, the Raveller performs their fan identity, and this is true irrespective of the trajectories of fannish behavior they fit into. According to Hills (2009: 118), social networking sites "place a new-found digital-cultural emphasis on the presentation of self." This is a highly salient point—even though Ravelry's primary function is to provide a database of fiber arts-related information, the social networking aspects are a major attraction for many of its active members (many stating that they prefer Ravelry for this than Facebook). Hills goes on to discuss the way in which consumer taste is heavily foregrounded in social media, and the self is presented through fan-consumer identities (though these are not the only factors involved). Certainly, fan identity and performativity are defining characteristics in the sociability of the fan handicrafters, even where they have little non-Ravelry experience of participatory fan culture or typical fan competencies.

For Goffman, presentation of self is a performance designed to elicit an emotional reaction in others. But this may raise challenges in relating presentations of self to the performance of fandom, especially as it relates to, or is tangential to, everyday life. Cornel Sandvoss (2005: 45) puts forward the notion that performance of fandom is related to the fan community, fandom is only performed when others acknowledge the fan identity. In this way, the fan groups on Ravelry perform an important function in performances of fan identity, but it is important to note that others can also see this fan identity whenever the fan handicrafters post in other non-fan-oriented groups or when others check out their Ravelry profile and projects. In this way, fan identity is not only performed for the fan community, but is observable within the entire Ravelry community. Because this performance of fandom exist within a much larger online community, fans' presentations of self thus spill over into the wider community and are recognizable by others outwith the fan handicrafting groups. To illustrate these points further, it is useful to look at the formation of the fan groups and activities on Ravelry. These not only reveal the enmeshing of handicrafting and fandom, but more importantly the ways in which the embodied self (the physical acts of knitting and handicrafting) and the narratives of self displayed in the virtual community coexist.

Entry points: Bringing handicrafting and fandom together

Fan identities constructed and displayed by Ravelry members frequently draw on personal experiences and life histories that include fan dispositions. Regardless of an individual's entry point into fan culture—or, indeed, regardless of whether that individual has actively participated in a fan community or not, the sense of being a fan is a lifelong one. Interview responses suggest that many of the fan handicrafters in this study have fannish interests that date back to childhood. David (male, gay, married, 30s, American, working in finance) says, "From a very young age, I was interested in the Greek myths, superheroes and the supernatural." Similarly, Samantha (female, single, 20s, UK, full-time student) says, "I am a big Dr Who fan (it's what was on TV when I was the right age and I got hooked). I was an obsessive fan of *The Matrix* in my teens." And Hannah (female, single, 20s, USA, office worker) admits, "Way back in my sordid youth I was really into *The X-Files*." Furthermore, a fan disposition does not always predict participation in fan culture. A significant number of interviewees report never having been involved in a fan community. Jess (female, married, 30s, USA, works from home as a virtual assistant while home schooling, mother) says, "I mostly keep my fandom to myself," and Carol (female, single, 50s, USA, carer for elderly relative) says, "No, I do not [take part in fandom]."

For these fans, finding the Ravelry fan groups opens up possibilities for becoming part of a fan community and—through intersections of crafting and fandom—becoming involved in fan production. JaimeLouise (female, single,

20s, USA, self-employed in arts and crafts) says, "Joining Nerd Wars opened up a whole new world to me, as I had teammates and members of other teams suggesting that I try new things." Fans like JaimeLouise thus come into contact with other fans (some with more extensive experience of fandom that they can share) and experience the sociability of a fan community. Yvonne's (female, single, 50s, USA, writer and artist, grandmother) experience of the sociability of fan groups illustrates a typical example:

> The Knitting Dead on Ravelry is my Rav "home." I'm on that forum every day chatting with friends. I participate in knit-alongs, discuss lots of shows, share my daily life, and have even met some of the forum members in real life. This is a particularly nice group. We just don't have the flare-ups that you see in many groups on Rav. It's a safe place (as safe as any online group can be) to hang out, chat, and laugh.

It is important here to also note that many of the participants are already experienced handicrafters prior to joining Ravelry and finding the fan groups. However, some fans move from participatory fandom to Ravelry specifically when they wish to undertake mimetic projects. Yvonne, for example, says, "I learned to knit so I could make a Jayne hat." Learning handicrafting for this fan came about because she was already an active fan, including in a LiveJournal fan crafting group, and her Jayne hat knitting (she has made several and proudly displays a photo of herself, her son, and her grandson all wearing Jayne hats alongside the actor Adam Baldwin on her project pages) started prior to her Ravelry membership. Mimetic fan crafting was thus the route into Ravelry (as opposed to the handicrafters who became fan producers on finding the Ravelry fan groups). One further entry point worth mentioning is that a very small number of fans join Ravelry specifically to take part in fannish events or activities, usually by invitation or encouragement of fellow fans already involved in the various Ravelry games.

While these entry points into fan handicrafting, as with the entry points into fandom generally, vary, they are illustrative of the way in which fan production is itself the focus of fan communities (just as fan fiction writing or model making is). Sociability is key here with the creation of fan groups allowing fans to share their affective investments. Fans were quick to colonize the Ravelry forum and to organize fandom-related communal activities and events. As Susan Strawn (2007: 197) has noted:

> It has been online technology [...] that has brought knitting enthusiasts together as never before. Knitting has always been an inherently social activity, and technology has accelerated the ability of knitters to interconnect, exponentially so. This acceleration of interconnectedness is a phenomenon of the social web, and this has facilitated access to fandom and fan communities.

Fan groups were formed within a few weeks of Ravelry being launched, and it is worth noting that this carried over from fan activities on other Internet sites (as opposed to being a Ravelry-specific phenomenon). However, the crafting focus of Ravelry provided an ideal, specialist location for those interested in fan-related handicrafting. Ravelry's forum permits any member to create a group on any topic and the forum groups are run as the founders, administrators, moderators, and members of those groups see fit or deem appropriate; the Ravelry staff or moderators in the main Big 6 groups do not monitor or input into any other groups (or at least only to the extent that the Ravelry terms of service apply across the whole community). It is therefore very open, allowing fan handicrafters to organize themselves into fan communities in whatever way they wish.

What is clear from this (aside from reinforcing the difference between mainstream and cult media audiences) is that fan handicrafters are very active fans and eager to bring their affective investments into handicrafting. The speed at which the fan groups arose on Ravelry is also indicative of this. One of the earliest fan groups, the Big Damn Knitters group for *Firefly* fans (the group name plays on the term "big damn heroes" from the episode "Safe"), was formed on August 7, 2007, by a member who had joined Ravelry the day before, making this one of her first actions on joining and the introductory post on the group only her second forum post. This demonstrates how Ravelry was inhabited from the very early days by fans. Other early groups formed between 11 July and 17 December were Who Knits?, Outlander Fans, NCIS Knitters, MSTie Ravelers, Buffy Knitters, Lord of the Rings, Codex Dresden, Harry Potter Lovers, and the Geekcraft Group. As the example of Yvonne moving from LiveJournal crafting groups to Ravelry makes clear, fan handicrafting did not originate with Ravelry; fans often imported their crafting discussion from other online communities.

The Harry Potter Lovers group was created out of a thread in the Needlework on the Net group (one of the main groups that all Ravellers are members of) on July 7 about the next *Harry Potter* novel and the possibilities of having a knit-along for *Harry Potter*-themed patterns. At that point in time, a knit-along was already in progress on the Harry Potter and the Book Seven KAL blog[4] (on which several Potter-themed patterns, yarns, and projects were also being discussed), the hogwarts-sock-swap-two was about to commence,[5] and the book *Charmed Knits: Projects for Fans of Harry Potter* (Hansel 2007) had just been released. During the discussion, a Harry Potter Ravelry group was suggested: "Well, if there are groups for people who happen to live in certain areas, I don't see why we can't have a Harry Potter Fan group!:D." This not only indicates the fan's affective investments, but also puts fan communities on the same level as communities linked by geography. This signals the fan community as a social one, albeit one linked only by online access. In response to this, the group was formed within three minutes. The ellipses, multiple exclamation marks, and word spelt out in capitals—"YAY! Group up and running ... go and join!!!"—communicate excitement and pleasure in forming a fan community and the anticipation of the activities that this promises.

Sociability and pleasure

It is useful here to consider accounts of the pleasures of crafting. Kerry Wills's (2007: 57) discussion of contemporary American knitters suggests that knitting (and by implication other fiber arts) offer a number of avenues for pleasure and satisfaction:

> Knitting continues to fulfil needs that are rarely acknowledged or even named, though they are acute. Knitting satisfies needs for leisure, creativity, aesthetic and sensual stimulation, meditation, and contemplation. Knitting circles and online communities gratify the knitter with the pleasure of a community that appreciates ones' talents and hard work.

There are a number of commonalities with the setting up of fan handicrafting, namely leisure, creativity, sensual pleasures, and community. Nor are these the only similarities between handicrafting and fan communities. As Rosie Patch (2007) points out, "Knitting also offers [...] comfort by providing a sense of belonging to a universal culture that goes beyond the sense of belonging to a particular time and place." Again, this has echoes in the fans' sense of belonging to a fan culture that is expressed via a fan identity or narrative of the self. As Strawn (2007: 197) also observes, "Knitters also share photos of pets, children, severe weather, food, books, and at times their personal lives." Is it any wonder then that they would share their fan interests?

This can take the form of photos of the fan in costume, at conventions, wearing fan paraphernalia (often hand-knitted), with actors, but most of all (and just like other fans all across the Internet) they share photos from the television series concerned—screen grabs, official or press images, preview shots, and sometimes images other fans have taken during location shooting (and videos of the same). Fangirling is often to the fore with photographs of favorite actors from the series, in their other work, and in their off-screen life. These are often accompanied by expressions of the intense emotions the fan feels, often eroticized. Pleasures come both from working fan interests into their handicrafting and from the communities built up with other fan handicrafters who share the same interests. For female fans who have not otherwise been involved in participatory fandom, and for some who have but did not find it a pleasurable experience, finding a community of like-minded fans with a shared passionate interest in the text and in handicrafting is a significant pleasure. The social networking or online community aspects of fan handicrafting within Ravelry are thus extremely important.

This is further illustrated by several quasi-competitive[6] events that are as important as the fan groups in terms of defining the pleasures of fan productivity for handicrafters. These events include Nerd Wars, The Harry Potter Knitting and Crochet House Cup, Star Fleet Fiber Arts Corp, Battlestar Galactica FPB, Disney Adventures, and The Shire Games. These are not unlike the Ravelry-wide game activities organized alongside major sporting events such as the Olympic Games and the Tour de France. Many fan groups organize themselves into teams for these events, so that even in the wider Ravelry community fans of various cult texts are visible. In addition, there are many smaller scale activities, including groups which run challenges such as Sock Madness, swap groups, and many and various craft-alongs, often organized by specific designers or dyers for the fans of their work. Some of these are fandom-themed. The Odd Duck Swaps of Ravelry group organizes fan-themed swaps and swaps on other associated topics of interest to nerds and geeks such as Lego, Ancient Civilisations, and Cryptozoology. During Super Sock Scare Fest in the weeks running up to Halloween horror fans knit socks from patterns written by members of the group while watching the horror films that inspired the patterns. Swaps and craft-alongs also take place, sometimes with regularity, in the fan groups.

Some fan handicrafters participate in multiple activities, sometimes frequently. Yvonne, a member of Team TARDIS in Nerd Wars, says that she likes to participate in knit-alongs, spin-alongs, crochet-alongs, and watch-alongs, and adds Nerd Wars for its "team challenges." She also joins swaps "when I have the funds." It is often in the communal events that highly pleasurably fan experiences are experienced through the sociability they provide. She goes on to say that:

Inclusion is a big part of it. Communing with people who are into my particular brand of nerdiness. I don't feel isolated in my fandom. In fact, I make friends and have loads of fun. The Knitting Dead has become a giant community. We've knit chemo hats for one member's mother, baby gear for new mothers, performed random acts of kindness for each other, and more. We also provide lots of moral support for one another. It's really astounding.

The pleasures of participation and sociability are thus key motivating factors for handicrafting and drive the interactive events that bring fans together.

The Harry Potter Lovers group was one of the earliest to create an interactive event for fans; the Harry Potter Knitting and Crochet House Cup formed in July 2008. This arose from a thread started on July 1, 2007, suggesting "a Fiber Arts Tri-Wizard Tournament OR a House Championship." The idea for a House Cup was well supported with the main reason being that many fans of *Harry Potter* identify with a particular House or characters associated with a House. *Harry Potter* handicrafters on LiveJournal had previously attempted a Triwizard needlecrafts tournament, though this had not been particularly successful.

In the case of Harry Potter Lovers, though, it may have been because they were already in a dedicated handicrafting community that allowed the House Cup to work well and grow, attracting handicrafters from across the Ravelry community. The fans discussing the idea also quickly settled on a framework based on the Hogwart's curriculum—classes in transfiguration, herbology, and potions, with Quidditch matches a popular addition. Much of the discussion was on how the curriculum—especially Quidditch—could be adapted for craft-based projects. Some of these were quite literal, for example, "knit a magical creature" for Care of Magical Creatures and "something with stars" for Astronomy. The House Cup group was set up on July 10, with volunteers acting as Headmistress, Caretaker (keeping the peace), Groundskeeper (awarding points), Heads of Houses, and Teachers for the various classes. In this way, the group and its moderators were modeled on Hogwarts and designed to resemble the experience of becoming a pupil at wizarding school, just as Harry does in the novels. This underlines the importance of role-play and affective investments to the pleasures experienced by the fans.

Almost 100 people enrolled for the first House Cup and the Headmistress allocated players to House teams. But echoing the sockpuppet accounts set up for identity role-play discussed earlier, in later terms a SortingHat account was created which allocated players to their Houses. Again, this emulates Harry's experience in the book. When the first Cup opened in September 2008 (this "Autumn term" ran for three months, designed to resemble a traditional school term), classes set personal challenges such as making a hemp or cotton washcloth for Herbology, or making a project inspired by the canonical spells Wingardium Leviosa or Lumos for Charms, with a Quidditch cooperative game alongside to recreate the sense of playing on a team. In these several ways, there is clearly a sense for players that they are entering and experiencing life in the *Harry Potter* storyworld and this offers a dimension of imaginative play and potentially role-play for the participants.

This also implies that participants in the games require a high level of *Harry Potter* knowledge. They need to be familiar with the narrative of the novels and have a sound grasp of the language and imagery not only from the novels but also of the wider transmedia storyworld, for example, the games, the films, and secondary texts such as the *Fantastic Beasts* (Rowling 2009) and *Quidditch Through the Ages* (Rowling 2001) books, and latterly the Pottermore website.[7] Players who do not possess high levels of knowledge are not necessarily disadvantaged, but with chat in the main and House groups often using terminology from the books and films, the acquisition and usage of fan competencies involving spell names and uses, historical figures and events, locations, and relationships between characters is encouraged. This facilitates entry for newer fans into the fandom, allowing them to acquire knowledge and attain insider status.

There is, moreover, an inbuilt narrative distinction between insiders and outsiders to the group (and the fandom) with the use of the term "muggles," further creating a sense of belonging. For example, players often use the phrases "In my Muggle life," "my Muggle job," or "In the Muggle realm" to differentiate their social situations or professional lives from their fandom as performed in the House Cup. And sometimes the term "muggle" is used to designate people in their everyday life who are not on Ravelry or do not practice handicrafting, as in "my Muggle family" and "my Muggle friends." One comment that "All I want to do is sit and knit ... but Muggle demands are creeping up on me after a full weekend of full on contact knitting" equates crafting with the magical world and differentiates this from the mundane (housework). The post goes on to say that the "dishes look like a full party of dwarves ate here yesterday," and this crossover of storyworlds—here into Tolkien fandom—is commonplace. This reconfirms the status of handicrafting as a pleasurable creative activity separate from mundane everyday chores. But at the same time, it aligns that handicrafting with fandom and the pleasures of imaginative play or role-play that this affords.

Many of the pleasures obtained from playing in the House Cup also relate to affective investments in the storyworld of *Harry Potter*. One aspect of this is identification, not just with major characters but also with one of the Houses. The green-tinted Ravatars of the Slytherin players reflect such emotional investment and are even referred to as "robes." Moreover, the fans tend to incorporate the characteristics of each House in their role-play. The group for the players sorted into Slytherin, The Snake Pit, is themed as a dungeon, Ravenclaw's as The Tower, Hufflepuff's dorm is in The Den, and Gryffindor on The Seventh Floor. Locations at Hogwarts are emulated, just as the classes for study and the school terms are. The personality types of each House are also role-played. Slytherins play at being resourceful and plotting to win in a common room with a bar where players are served exotic green drinks by characters (or actors) they find sexually appealing. As in all the House dorms and common rooms, role-play actions are indicated with italicized or otherwise delineated text: "*swishes around in her azure robes,*" "*///hauls her trunk in then sends it to float on up to the Elder Dorm//,*" "*-runs a cloth over the shiny dark wood of the bar counter-,*" and "*The pocket of her apron bulges with skeins of yarn and needles.*" Role-play posts can become quite long, elaborate, and include dialogue:

Sits down at a corner booth and pulls a large alpaca shawl out of her overstuffed knitting bag. A crumpled piece of parchment falls out as she shakes it out and gets ready to knit. Puts the knitting to the side and uncrumples the piece of parchment. Raises an eyebrow as she looks at a small sketch of a phoenix in flames:: "Where did you come from?"::Shrugs and figures some Gryff must have missed a trashcan with the wadded ball of parchment during one of her classes. Grins evilly thinking about applying it to whomever threw it in with her knitting with a sticking charm.

I refer to these as action and dialogue because they function to create a stage with actors. This is not quite on the same level of the adoption of a character persona in identity role-play, which Booth (2010, 154) defines as "fans insert[ing] aspects of their own personality into the character to rewrite the narrative around this fan/character amalgam", since they make no pretense of adopting an existing *Harry Potter* character persona. These fans are role-playing themselves, or at least their performative fan identity. They are, however, inserting aspects of their own personality into the storyworld. And, just as the identity role-players do, they are rewriting the narrative—with the difference that this is around a fan identity/narrative construction and thus removing the layer of canonical character. Moreover, the interactions within the role-play call out (via magic links, Ravelry's form of tagging) to friends and fellow fans, contributing to the feeling of belonging in the community and the sense of fan sociability this engenders. Not all fan groups provide a setting for such role-play, and not all players in the House Cup take part in it all the time, but this nevertheless illustrates one of the pleasures within which the fans' handicrafting is situated. Moreover, such imaginative play, whether incorporating overt role-play or not, can be part of the material production process.

Fan competencies and sharing

The role-play of the House Cup illustrates the way in which shared fan competencies are important in establishing community. Nerd Wars provides an interesting contrast to this. Information about the game was posted on fan and gaming groups across the Ravelry forum in December 2010 and January 2011. A snowball effect took place as people interested in forming a particular team posted to the fan groups they were already involved with or brought the game to the attention of their friends. The game was designed to expand on the single fandom theme of the House Cup, allowing fans of all persuasions to take part. Players were thus able to organize themselves into fandom-centered teams as they desired.

In the first Nerd Wars tournament, fourteen teams formed, including already very active fandoms of contemporary series such as *Battlestar Galactica*, *True Blood*, and *Fringe*, well-established cult media and literary fandoms such as *Doctor Who*, *Star Trek*, *Star Wars*, *Harry Potter*, *Discworld,* and *Lord of the Rings*, other cult series such as *Babylon 5*, *Firefly,* and *The Big Bang Theory*, and gamers had options to join video game or multiplayer role-play game teams.

Since the fan handicrafters taking part were spread across such a wide range of fandoms, the themes for challenges had to be broad. Unlike the House Cup which could role-play around the Hogwarts curriculum and in which all players shared the same set of fan competencies, different Nerd Wars teams might have very different sets of generic conventions, storylines, and world-building details to draw on.

Nerd Wars' challenges were therefore designed around broadly academic subjects that nerds (as distinct from fans) might be interested in: Scientific, Intellectual (which covered culture and history), and Technical (this focused the technical aspects of crafting itself), with the addition of two more overtly fannish challenges, Team Spirit and Nerd Culture (for the specific fandom of each team and more general fannish interests, respectively). Nerd Culture was based around typical nerdish characteristics, such as always "having one's nose in a book" and going to fan conventions. It also included crafting itself as a nerdy activity: one challenge was organized around crafting in public and another around yarn bombing. The depiction of crafting as a wizarding skill (as opposed to Muggle pastime) in the House Cup and the inclusion of crafts in nerd culture in Nerd Wars identify crafting itself as fannish. But however much players in Nerd Wars share crafting competencies, they might have little knowledge of the fandoms of players on other teams. This is not to say that Nerd Wars is a less cohesive fan community, but it explains why role-play is not observed so frequently. Regardless of this, being a multifan community means that players with several fan interests can demonstrate fan competencies in more than one storyworld or serially join different teams as they desire, thus performing fluid fan identities without leaving the community.

In Nerd Wars, displays of fan knowledge take the form of links that projects make to storyworlds. During the study, the vast majority of players added such team tie-ins to their challenge entries (over 97 percent) and players enjoyed the opportunity to create tie-ins. Clever and interesting tie-ins are admired by other players. One member of Team Browncoat (the *Firefly* team) linked a book cover she had crocheted to the character Shepherd Book, making a play on words. The project also had the Chinese ideogram for "book" embroidered on the cover, linking to the fact that Chinese is the predominant language used in the *Firefly* storyworld. Book was the subject of clues throughout the series that he was not who he appeared to be (a missionary). The word "book" on the cover is the character's name, but in terms of it being a cover for a book, it gives nothing away about the particular book it is covering. It thus signifies that, like Shepherd Book himself, "you should never judge a book by its cover" (he turned out to have a violent, military past). In this way, the fan displays the complex interplay of knowledge about the character and the storyworld to all the players, many of whom count *Firefly* among their set of fan interests regardless of their team affiliation. Among the several replies, one reads, "I love how many levels your project works on. Great team spirit tie-in." Players thus gain attention not only for their work but their ability to link their work to the fandom, contributing to a mutually supportive and enjoyable environment that works in a very similar way to feedback in fan fiction communities.

Identifying tie-ins also adds to the atmosphere of team sociability by offering communal activities. Teams had opportunities for choosing team-building exercises (Team Unity) to represent their fandom to the whole Nerd Wars community. In one tournament, Team TARDIS all made stuffed adipose toys, one of which is shown in Figure 3.1, which they posted in the challenge threads on the same day to recreate the "march of the adipose" in the *Doctor Who* episode "Partners in Crime." This created an impact in the challenge threads, providing moments of amusement for all players. In another team-building exercise in Tournament 9, the Tolkien team Team Precious organized a unity for all teams that wished to join in on the theme of dragons—"All Dragons, All the Time: The Epic Unity Crossover"—with players connecting their projects to dragons in their own fandom. The level of participation was high, with 33 out of the 39 teams joining in either formally or as an optional extra tie-in,[8] with high numbers of posts saying how much this was appreciated, and this again enabled sociability and different teams to feel connected.

Figure 3.1 Knitted Adipose for Team TARDIS unity project in Nerd Wars © Brigid Cherry. (Acknowledgment Doctor Who—™ & © BBC.)

As noted, many of these handicrafters express multiple and fluid fan interests and perform their varied fan competencies by taking part in multiple events. Many play in both the House Cup and Nerd Wars, submitting the same projects to a class or a challenge as fits. This is interesting in respect of how crafting projects reflect the fan's affective investments. In one tournament, Kaye (female, married Canada, indie dyer, work-at-home mother) was simultaneously a member of Team TARDIS in Nerd Wars and a Slytherin in the House Cup. For her House Cup Divination class, she submitted her skein of handspun yarn in the context of a fictional account of her practicing palm reading on one of her friends (a fellow member of Slytherin). In this role-play, she is

> sitting in the Slytherin common room reading a book on palm reading to study for her Divination class. She didn't quite believe in it, but sometimes getting information from a variety of sources could help give different perspectives on things, so she didn't want to completely rule it out.

Having set the scene, the action can begin. When her friends arrive, one of them offers her hand and asks, "Who's the man of my dreams?" In the continuation of her story, she makes reference to a DVD box set of the third season of *True Blood* with the exclusive Eric Northman cover:

> She took [anon]'s hand into her own and traced the lines on her palm curiously. While looking down, she noticed [anon]'s bag was slightly opened … and lo and behold, on top of it looked to be a muggle DVD with a picture on the cover. It was the same man that she saw in [anon]'s head when she was practicing legilimency!

This reference to legilimency demonstrates Kaye's fan competencies, legilimency being the wizarding art of navigating the layers of another person's mind and correctly interpreting the images therein. Mentioned specifically in several of the novels, *Harry Potter* fans assume this form of divination was also used on a number of other occasions when one character appears to be reading another's mind, and they incorporate this into their fan knowledge of the storyworld as a common phenomenon, which Kaye draws on here. Moreover, the *True Blood* reference acknowledges her friend as a self-confessed fan of the vampire series, or more specifically the character Eric whom she describes as "hot and sexy" and "*doesn't* sparkle" (another expression of *Twilight* anti-fandom). This is yet another instance of how female fans invest in certain characters (or actors) deemed to be sexually attractive. Here, Kaye plays on her friend's affective investments, continuing her story with an account of a teasing interaction between friends:

She lifted [anon]'s hand again and traced more lines on her palm. "The man of your dreams is tall. He's tall, and pale. He has white blonde hair and piercing blue eyes. A veritable nordic GOD," she stated. She leaned in close and whispered, "And he's a VAMPIRE!!"

Her friend is aghast and leaves in a huff, while her Slytherin housemates giggle. This reflects the way close friends might interact in real life, or more appropriately perhaps teenage girls (these, of course, are grown women but the role-play here is key to their pleasure in taking part in the House Cup) might interact at school, teasing each other, taking offense, and making up to be bosom buddies once again.

In her story, Kaye completes this friendship arc by visiting her friend in her dorm room and gifting her the skein of yarn—an appropriately Eric-themed color of dark blues and reds—that is her Divination class homework. The colors in the yarn Kaye has spun also allows this to be easily fitted into the Scientific challenge for that month in Nerd Wars on the topic of anatomy, namely that the red and blue represent the veins and arteries of the human body. This is one of the challenges that does not require knowledge of the fan object, but Kaye chooses to acknowledge *Doctor Who* for her team tie-in points by linking the colors to the red and blue bow ties that are the distinguishing feature of Matt Smith's costume in the series.

Several aspects of fandom and pleasure can be identified here: knowledge of the text, the opportunity to role-play being at Hogwarts, acknowledgment of friends within the fandom, and their incorporation into the storyworld, and the enjoyment of creating short works of fan fiction. In addition, Kaye is able to reference other fan interests, strongly emphasizing that fans are not only nomadic but also merge one fannish interest into another in crossovers. Fan identities are not performed in terms of single-minded pursuit of a singular passion (though they may of course be), but are free-ranging and varied in their allegiances. Further evidence of this is clear from the chat in the Slytherin common room where players—in another example of imaginative play—have "hotties" (sexy companions selected from among the actors the players find attractive). Hotties are effectively servants, or perhaps devoted lovers, bringing them drinks from the Dungeon bar and spoon-feeding them or giving them massages.

The majority of hotties are stars of cult texts, including David Tennant, Jason Momoa, Nathan Fillion, Viggo Mortensen, John Barrowman, Johnny Depp, Alexander Skarsgård, Felicia Day, and Gina Torres, with Severus Snape also being chosen frequently. As seen with the choice of female actors as hotties, non-straight sexualities are represented but "girl crushes" are also fairly commonplace and it is not seen as unusual for a heterosexual female player to select a female hottie. Similarly, no distinction is made for an actor or a character's actual sexuality as when Zachary Quinto or Captain Jack Harkness are claimed as hotties. This does not necessarily indicate a queer identity or sexuality, but it does represent a rejection of heteronormativity by some straight female fans to some degree. This is borne out by the fact that straight fans often ally with their LGBTI fellow fans. For example, during the Ravellenic Games played in parallel to the 2014 Winter Olympics in Sochi, many Ravellers joined protests against the controversial Russian laws on homosexuality. Perhaps most significantly, however, it illustrates the way in which this kind of fandom objectifies the male body and also sometimes female ones.

The fact that characters and actors cannot always be separated in these discourses is evident (sometimes Eric Northman is specified, sometimes Alexander Skarsgård; Captain Jack Sparrow is cited in some cases, Johnny Depp in others). The conflation of character and actor is made clear in the way they are put on display as "eye candy," as also evidenced by the "picspam" threads in other fan groups. For example, photos of David Tennant and Tennant playing the Doctor are shared around for the mutual pleasure of the group members in Who Knits?, Team TARDIS, and in the tellingly named "Gallifrey Ladies Auxiliary High Tea and Smut Society" thread in the Dr. Who-ites group. Talk of hotties takes up a significant element of the chat in The Dungeon, being a significant discourse alongside delectable yarn, cocktails, and cake. These discourses are incidental in the main to fan handicrafting, though sexually appealing characteristics are often referenced in links fans make to their projects (Eric's blue eyes, for example, for projects made from blue yarn). This reproduces female fan interests in attractive male (and sometimes female) bodies.

While these examples of imaginative play are a performance of sexual desire, others are undertaken in jokey, ironic, or light-hearted ways (this also reflects the split in the examples of Ravatars where some fans express desire for characters and others display humor). This contrasting discourse can be seen in the Rachel's Attic blogpost[9] about a skein of yarn (that the fan names "SherlockSkeiny") she has received from the indie dyer Gnome Acres. This is a navy blue and light gray variegated colorway inspired by the address (and named by the dyer) 221B. Inviting her readers to play along with the conceit that the skein is a living guest, she writes:

> I have had a guest skein in my house who wanted to see the sights of Londontown, specifically those pertaining to Mr Holmes. My only instruction was to take SherlockSkeiny to 221 Baker Street. I was glad to oblige.

The blog post then proceeds to show the tour, taking in the Baker Street tube station with its Holmes mural, the Holmes statue outside the tube station, the Sherlock Holmes Museum on Baker Street with its 221b numbered door, the Sherlock Holmes bench in Woburn Square Garden,[10] Russell Square, St Bart's Hospital, and outside the 221b flat entrance next to Speedy's Sandwich Bar & Café—the last three all used as locations in the BBC TV series.

The skein of yarn is posed on benches, held up to the camera in a selfie pose, and in one case accompanied by the actor playing the Victorian-era policeman outside the Sherlock Holmes Museum. When the yarn takes a break on the Sherlock Holmes bench in Russell Square, it is raining and the yarn is kept in its plastic bag: "it was spitting so he kept his raincoat on." These details from the blog post resemble something a tourist might post. But it is also a fan paying homage to the production of the series with a tour of locations. At St Bart's, which replaced the Reichenbach Falls in the *Sherlock* adaptation, the skein and blogger "pay our respects." The expressions of intense passion that fans feel visiting locations are transferred to the yarn: "SherlockSkeiny was overcome with excitement and needed to sit down." On the GnomeAcres Ravelry group, where Rachel links to her blog post, she also says: "Sherlocky skein keeps reminding me that I can't knit with him yet as he hasn't been to see Scotland Yard."

This anthropomorphization of yarn is not commonplace, but it does illustrate the ways in which handicrafters can construct discourses around fan-themed yarn in terms of their affective fan experiences. Color, softness, and squeezability are often remarked upon, yarn is viewed as "pettable": it can be stroked, cuddled, and fondled, with a common turn of phrase being that a skein of yarn is "squooshy." Comments frequently include things like "My inner geek/nerd squeals happily over all the different inspired yarns"—the reference to "squeals" here playing on the fangirl practice of squee. In the context of fan-themed yarn, the qualities of the character can be transferred to the yarn. The fan may never "possess" the desired character or storyworld (outside of their imaginative play), but they can have the skein of yarn that bears the name. In her GnomeAcres group on Ravelry, the dyer similarly refers to her Sherlock yarn as "he": "Here's some Sherlock eye candy for you.;0) Just finished his photo shoot. I'm glad you likey!" She also responds to Rachel's blog post, saying her yarn had been "Sherlocked," a reference to the term used for becoming a fan of the series (taken from text on a computer screen in "A Scandal in Belgravia"). This then provides an encouraging environment for light-heartedly treating the yarn as a living person, and moreover as a substitute (fetish object if you will) for the transference of the desires the fan has for the character. I do not intend to suggest that there is any psychological perversity to this—and nothing in the fans' postings suggest that is anything beyond a knowing and often joking nod to their fan obsessions. Rather, it serves to illustrate the ways in which fiber arts can be seen as transformative and contribute to projected interactivity.

These accounts of sociability, productivity, and role-play surrounding fan handicrafting illustrate the pleasures inherent in the affective investments the fans are expressing, but further analysis is required in order to explore the way identity relates to crafting. Clearly, affective investments carry over into fan handicrafting projects, but—conversely—what roles do handcrafted objects play in everyday life and narratives of the self? In order to engage further with questions relating to identity and pleasure, a case study of *True Blood* afghan blankets is illuminating and reveals many of the inherent links and contradictions surrounding narratives of the self and identity.

Vampire fandom, threat, and domesticity

The first point to stress here is the linkage between handicrafting and domesticity (not only in terms of crafts being carried out within the home, but that next to clothing and accessories many of the resulting completed projects are material objects used and displayed in the home). Many fan-themed patterns are available in the Ravelry database for household items including teapot and cafetiere cosies in Hobbit hole and Dalek designs—the latter titled "Caffeinate!," a range of *Star Wars* character cup cosies, and all manner of character, prop, and logo designs on dishcloths and washcloths for the kitchen and bathroom. The TARDIS is replicated on blankets, various cosies and cushions, and hot water bottle and tissue box covers. In all these examples, however, it is iconographic elements of the fan text, including logos as well as identifiable objects, which are incorporated in various ways onto random household items. More interesting from the point of view of recreating the settings and locations of the storyworld in the fan's own home are mimetic projects that reproduce items depicted on screen, most usually from the domestic space belonging to favorite characters. Many choose to reproduce objects that provide some meaning or function for the character.

As with the majority of popular culture texts, many examples of cult media depict domestic environments in which handcrafted objects are displayed and used. As a case in point, the afghan blanket in particular has become an iconographic signifier of homeliness, security, and comfort, being seen in many American TV series. These afghan blankets are homeware items, found in the domestic spaces of the living room and bedroom, and they facilitate the incorporation of fan handicrafting into home décor. Although these might be props in homely settings, they are not always depicted in homely scenarios and this provides an interesting case study in femininity, domesticity, and fan pleasures. The key example in this respect is the way in which the domestic setting of human characters pushes against, sometimes in a contradictory manner, the threat and sexual appeal of vampires in the TV series *True Blood*. The domestic setting of *True Blood* (a Southern Gothic text depicting small-town rural life) offers several possibilities for mimetic crafting for the home, of which Lafayette's blanket discussed at the start of Chapter 1 is but one. Several different blankets, both crocheted and knitted, as well as other items such as Gran's knitted picture frame, have all drawn the attention of fan handicrafters. This raises some points in relation to how fan crafting intersects with the construction of domestic and feminine identities in everyday life.

For the fans who adopt similar homely styles in home décor especially, this is a significant narrative element of the series that offers strong appeals and points of identification. The homespun look of Sookie's house, characters such as Gran—who is recognized as a fellow handicrafter with her baskets of yarn and tools—and the many blankets all reflect the interests of this group of fan handicrafters. They recognize the work and love that would go into these items. They connect with the series not only because they are vampire or *True Blood* fans, they also have a connection in terms of their knitting and crochet hobbies, their tastes in home décor, and their domestic situations. This is not to say that all the *True Blood* fan handicrafters are drawn to the homespun style depicted in the series, or that the tastes of the handicrafters might not run counter to this style (some just want to display their fan interest or join in for the fun of a crochet-along). But it does draw attention to the fact that fandom and handicrafting can be integrated components of a fan handicrafter's domesticity and that their fandom is not divided off from the domestic.

The most important finding here is that props seen on-screen are recognized by the fans as useful domestic items which can be appropriated for use within their own homes, but which nonetheless also bring the narrative and the characters of the storyworld into the personal and domestic space of the fan (a reverse of the fans writing themselves into the *Harry Potter* storyworld in the House Cup). Pictures of finished items are displayed on project pages in a domestic setting. This relates to the gender politics of handicrafting and fandom. As Sandvoss (2005, 16–18) argues, fandom per se is not necessarily gendered, but specific fan interests, activities, and communities are often marked out as feminine or masculine. Vampire fandom, of which *True Blood* is a facet, is a culture that has always attracted a significant female demographic. The vampire has always held great appeal for female viewers (see Williamson 2005; Mellins 2013), and readerships for *Twilight* and other paranormal romances are largely female (Clarke 2010: 3). With the handicrafting community being predominantly female (and the membership of the Vampire Knits group on Ravelry is over 99 percent female), it is little wonder that fan handicrafting, in part, is focused on domesticity (some of these fans are very unlike the ones adopting a Gothic style in Mellins's account).

The *True Blood* blankets can thus be part of the do-it-yourself (DIY) or maker culture, as well as signifying the fan identity of the maker. And since these blankets represent a traditional form of crafting—the crochet patchwork square dates back to the mid-1800s (Weldon and Company 1974: 165–167)—they can be located within the trend for shabby chic[11] and what has been termed "New Domesticity" (Matchar 2013). This trend is strongly linked to traditional femininity with soft colors and floral sprigs predominating, and also with the traditional domesticity of the war-time homemaker with her make-do-and-mend ethos drawing on traditional feminine skill sets. It is of course important to recognize that this is a consumer trend and is to all intents and purposes inauthentic; it is a heavily commodified faux-antique, "retro" fashion trend. Nevertheless, it has been linked with the knitting renaissance. This should not necessarily be interpreted as a wholesale embrace of traditional domesticity and rejection of feminism, however. For Beth Ann Pentney (2008), the act of taking up needles has feminist connotations, and certainly it may have sociopolitical meaning in terms of prosumption, contributing to the make-do-and-mend attitude that has re-emerged during the financial crisis and the loss of confidence in capitalism. And for some women, for instance those who choose homemaker roles, the DIY crafting aspects of shabby chic might well be appealing.

An example of this is seen in a version of the Water Lily Blanket from Arlene's house seen in the *True Blood* episode "I'm Alive and On Fire" (2011). A narrative of the self is clearly expressed in terms of Melanie's crafting both on Ravelry and off. The post about the blanket on her personal blog Cosy Living[12] (which itself has the look of shabby chic and a focus on traditional housewifery, emphasizing home cooking, handmade tea cosies, and retro styling for the home) suggests anything but the dangers experienced by the characters in *True Blood* or offered by vampires in general. Melanie's water lily blanket is largely removed from the scenario in which Arlene and her children are huddling, scared, under the blanket. The Cosy Living post reproduces the screen grabs just to show the blanket as a beautiful and desirable object without engaging with the plot or emotional contexts of the narrative. There does not seem to be a contradiction for Melanie in this. While she is not a member of any of the *True Blood* or vampire fan groups on Ravelry, she is a declared fan of *True Blood* as well as *The Walking Dead* and *Lark Rise to Candleford* (2008–2011). More tellingly, she is a member of several vintage and retro crafting groups on Ravelry and active in the Thriftiness group that advocates the homemade and make-do-and-mend attitude. This eclectic narrative of the self is interesting in that it shows free flow between her individualized fandom and her domestic role. A blanket seen on a vampire television series is not out of place in a lifestyle modeled on New Domesticity; in fact, this is facilitated by the way the small community and the home are significant in *True Blood*.

There are a number of issues raised by this presentation of self in the context of shabby chic and New Domesticity. The fact that Melanie does-it-herself, making home furnishings and baking from scratch, places her firmly in the category of prosumer, rather than the consumer of commodified shabby chic as a fashion trend, but this is not an unproblematical position. As Karen Halnon points out (2009: 510), shabby chic can involve refurbished old objects found in junk shops, charity shops, and flea markets, but with respect to the costs of refurbishment, shabby chic is expensive (she calls it "not-so-shabby chic"). It is important to remember that handicrafting is not necessarily an inexpensive pastime, and crocheted or knitted garments, accessories, or home décor items are not always (or indeed often) a cheaper alternative to mass-produced versions. Fan handicrafting projects thus represent an example of the entanglement of fandom and consumerism (Hills 2002: 133) when considering the yarn purchases required.

Another important consideration in this respect is that in creating a shabby chic aesthetic crafting can be classed, as well as gendered.[13] Shabby chic style represents middle-class taste and affluence; Melanie's blanket represents her own labor, but it is displayed in the middle-class home. In a discussion of lifestyle television makeover shows, Julie Doyle and Imri Karl (2012, 93) argue that shabby chic is positioned as a middle-class style in opposition to lower-class cheap and trashy "Essex girl" bling. Shabby chic contributes to respectability, "one of the most ubiquitous signifiers of class" and, as "a property of middle-class individuals," an aspirational standard (Skeggs 1974: 1–3). Shabby chic, in other words, serves to other a cheap and tasteless working-class sensibility. This echoes Turney's (2009: 58–59) discussion of the knitted twin-set as a "classic" and therefore a sign of wealth and status.

It can thus be argued that respectable styles such as shabby chic represent the security afforded by a middle-class lifestyle. However, considering the mimetic production of *True Blood* blankets in the context of New Domesticity exposes contradictions vis-à-vis the storyworld and readings of the text. The fan-made *True Blood* blanket discussed here is presented in the context of a domesticity that is classed in opposition to that depicted on-screen. As a Southern Gothic text, *True Blood* depicts a rural community the members of whom, while not necessarily impoverished, are not particularly affluent. The heroine Sookie Stackhouse comes from an established family, but the family home is down-at-heel. Arlene's house is rented. Like many of the other inhabitants of Bon Temps, Sookie and Arlene are not in the demographic that might be labeled "poor white trash" (though the series contains other representations of this group with the Rattrays who try to drain Bill in the first episode and the were-panthers of series 3), but they both work as waitresses and lack disposable income (Sookie is often short of money in the novels). Their blankets are not displays of ostentatious consumption or deliberate aesthetic choices in fashion, but family hand-me-downs representative of their rural family roots.

This difference in domestic context between Arlene's blanket and Melanie's mimetic fan project is an example of the way in which she elides meaning, in this instance at least, seeing a material object she would like to incorporate into her home décor rather than a family under threat. In the series generally, knitted and crochet blankets are often props in scenes where the characters are under attack. Arlene and her children huddle under their blanket when she is being haunted by a supernatural entity, Lafayette under his after he has been imprisoned, chained like a slave, and shot by vampires. Moreover, Lafayette is black and gay, his clothing, environment, and mannerisms code him as camp—the very antithesis of New Domesticity.

Figure 3.2 Version of the Lafayette afghan from *True Blood* © Jennifer Hill.
(Acknowledgment True Blood—™ & © Home Box Office Inc.)

The Lafayette blanket projects such as one made by Jennifer shown in Figure 3.2 are certainly more integrated into affective investments and responses to the text, providing an emotional connection with a well-loved character. Lafayette, who is extremely popular with the fans, is colorful and flamboyant and his home reflects this, allowing the fans to incorporate bright colors into their own home décor (and wardrobes)—again, ostensibly at odds with the Gothic style of vampire fandom. On-screen, the blanket is depicted as one element in an excessively decorated, camp space with clashing bright colors, candles, and lights reflecting from sequinned surfaces. These blanket colors are much less feminine. Whereas Arlene's blanket is in pastel shades of blue, white, and pink (traditional feminine colors) and evokes the floral with a flower pattern called Waterlily, Lafayette's is a traditional geometric granny square in black and primary shades. It is not only brighter, it reflects his over-the-top personality.

In fact, after making her Lafayette blanket, one anonymous interviewee says, "I wish I had used the same colours in more garish hues. I think it was the following series that showed Lafayette's afghan in daylight and it was very brightly toned." She expresses emotional attachments to her afghan which parallel those around the plot and the character. The blanket connects directly to Lafayette: "I was in love from the moment I saw it wrapped around him on my telly. And right now it is wrapped around me!!!" and "It makes me smile, and being wrapped up in it is the closest thing to a hug you can get." It is worth noting that the sexual aspect of the scene in which Eric heals Lafayette with a vampiric exchange of fluids—giving his blood to Lafayette to drink—is of no little significance here. This fan goes so far as to say: "Lafayette would also be nice to marry, I reckon, I LOVE his humour. And he's very caring." Not only does this indicate likings for particular characters (or the actors who play them—an extremely important factor in fan passions for characters), it also spills over into expressions of desire for them, even as here where the character's sexuality would seem to exclude such a relationship with the heterosexual female fan.

Just as some of discussion in the Slytherin group does, this challenges heteronormativity. Furthermore, such imaginative play is not limited by the definitions of the character within the series and in this respect at least draws attention to the ways in which mimetic crafting can be transformative. As Jenkins (1992) has argued, drawing on theories of gendered reading, female fan production is often constructed around the emotional dimensions and relationships of the characters, and the narratives constructed around the fans handicrafting projects occupy similar positions as fanfic (especially slash fiction) in this respect. Such expressions are clearly playful and knowing, transforming the canonical characters while foregrounding their attractiveness and emotionality. There is a strong emphasis on the characteristics the fans associate with an idealized masculinity or what they look for in an ideal partner (including humor).

The fans' comments around their reproductions of Lafayette's and Arlene's blankets are thus encoded in terms of oppositional femininities. The trajectories of fandom and forms of fan production discussed here are tied into complex negotiations of gender, sexuality, class, and race. The discourses used in the Lafayette's blanket craft-along thread, this being a far more popular pattern and talked about more than Arlene's, are also indicative of an oppositional attitude toward domesticity and femininity. The thread is titled "Lafayette's moth-eaten afghans," thus subverting the semiotic meanings of shabby chic by making an ironic reference to an object of fear among fiber artists—the clothes moth. Of more significance, the participants make much of the fact that crocheters use hooks to manipulate the yarn and work stitches, and thus sometimes refer to themselves ironically as "hookers." They align themselves with Lafayette's use of the term to refer to his female friends. The introduction to the thread reads: "Or as Lafayette would say.. 'Get yer crochet on hookahs!'" and one poster comments "I'll be rockin' these when I want to channel my inner hookah!" in reference to a Lafayette-style granny square cushion with accompanying fry cook badge and black nail polish she receives in a *True Blood*-themed swap.

It could be argued that the appropriation of the term "hooker" is itself a negotiation of, and possibly a rejection of, the notion of handicrafting as indicative of domestic femininity. It echoes the kind of reappropriation of language that has been seen in the SlutWalk protest marches, for example. Certainly it is a refusal by this segment of handicrafters of traditional domesticated femininity. Certainly not all crocheters would be comfortable using the term, but for those that do, it is a knowing ironic terminology that sets them up in opposition to traditional domesticity. Furthermore, at least within the *True Blood* handicrafting community, it aligns these fans not with the romantic ideal (Sookie and her heteronormative relationships, albeit with a vampire and a werewolf) or with models of maternal domesticity (Arlene, albeit she has been in a series of failed marriages), but with gay masculinity and a sexuality that confronts rather than embraces heteronormativity. This is much closer to feminist acts of craftivism (Robertson 2011) than it is to Emmanuelle Dirix's (2014) description of crafting linked to New Domesticity as "the dark side" of the knitting revival.

From fan identity to material culture

As explored in this chapter, the ways in which handicrafters construct narratives of the self and fan identities are varied. Identities may not be presented or performed in a straightforward way, but come together through conjunctions of personal profiles and images of various kinds that become attached to the profile (including, but by no means limited to, projects that the handicrafter has made). These are further elaborated via the social interactions and online discourses that are expressed in forum discussions with others. And, in fact, multiple identities might be presented as, for example, when fan identities are performed alongside family and social situations. In fact, fan identities cannot be entirely separated out from other aspects of identity, not least those that are associated with handicrafting as a feminine form of craft. The domestic and the personal are often to the fore in presentations of fan identity, with aspects of gender and sexuality dominant, although expressions of class identity and personal tastes in fashion or subcultural affiliation are also prevalent. Together with the reframings of femininity that take place, the constructions of fan identity and the performance of fandom discussed herein provide the context for the further analysis of the material culture of fan handicrafting in the following chapters.

4
HANDICRAFTING AS FAN ART

Having looked at the ways in which handicrafters construct fan identities through their online profiles and craft-related fan activities, it is now relevant to turn attention to the work they produce and how different kinds of projects relate to and invoke the storyworlds the fans are invested in. This chapter analyzes the ways in which fan-themed crafting forms a dialogue with the text and functions as transformative work. In order to explore these transformations and remediations of the text, it is necessary to consider handicrafting as a form of fan art. With respect to this, the examples of fan handicrafting discussed in this chapter are inspired by texts and the responses that the fans have to those texts.

Positioning handicrafting as art and as fan art

As Joanne Turney (2009) establishes, there are significant "arts and crafts" debates around the status of the fiber arts such as knitting and crochet. In this context, it is important to consider how fan production in general and fan handicrafting specifically relate to these categories. Gary O. Larson (1997: 13) argues that the arts are not something that exist "out there" in a world alien to many ordinary people, but are an essential part of their lives. Arguing for adopting a perspective of the arts as vernacular culture, he draws on folklorist William Wilson to point out that art is all around us, it is "in the things we make with our words (songs, stories, rhymes, proverbs), with our hands (quilts, knitting, raw-hide braiding, pie crust designs, dinner table arrangements, garden layouts)." This has obvious links to fan art as a vernacular culture. Fans make their own artworks, whether drawn or digitally manipulated, written, videoed and edited, or knitted and crocheted. Fan artists do not make art (or at least not usually) for the exhibition, gallery, or museum spaces (the usual places one might expect to find art). But its creation often resembles artistic practices (painting, drawing, fiction writing, poetry) and the end product often functions as art (for display in the fan's home, or for publication in fanzines or online, for showing to other fans). Joli Jensen (2002: 149), drawing on Larson's point, suggests that this is "repositioning the arts as everyday activity." Fan art is appropriated (rather than original) art, but fans who are involved in making such cultural borrowings play with the material in many creative ways as part of their everyday activities. It is thus transformative rather than derivative (Schwabach 2011, 67).

It is important also to acknowledge that art extends into many areas of crafting practice. Jensen (2002: 196) counsels against the traditional, elitist position in which "the arts must never be confused with the media or with hobbies," an approach that results in the dismissal of "such mundane activities as knitting, leather tooling and bass fishing." She contends that these practices have "salutary power." The implication here is that fan art (as a kind of vernacular art) has personal and social benefits. Moreover, yarn and fiber are already a medium for contemporary artists (Padovani and Whittaker, 2010). Mark Newport's hand-knitted suits are an interesting example, illustrating the context of handicrafting inspired by popular culture. His suits (which cover the entire body, encompassing feet, hands, head, and face much like a "gimp" suit) are designed to construct hero personas, sometimes of his own invention, and sometimes based on his childhood heroes and comic book superheroes. The latter include Batman, Spider-Man, Superman, Iron Man, Captain America, and Mister Fantastic from the Fantastic Four. Although the suits are wearable (with the exception of the Mister Fantastic suit which is elongated to convey the superhero's power of being able to stretch his limbs to abnormal length), they are exhibited in gallery spaces and in photographic reproductions empty and saggy as if lifeless.

These suits cannot be classified as fan art necessarily, though they do draw on the nostalgic feelings of the artist for his childhood. They are "childhood memories of the ultimate man—the Dad every boy wants, the man every boy wants to grow up to be" (Newport 2010: 46). Newport goes on to say that he also intends them to be a statement on gender, they "combine their heroic, protective, ultra masculine, yet vulnerable [superhero] personae with the protective gestures of my mother—hand-knit acrylic sweaters meant to keep me safe from New England winters." However, it is not difficult to see connections with fan art, specifically costuming, and how this also conveys discourses of gender. As Bainbridge and Norris (2009: 7) argue, cosplay can be described as a "ritual of identification" which aligns the cosplayer with their fictional hero or heroine through procedural play—just as Newport's suits do. He says that the superhero suits "become the uniforms I can wear to protect my family from the threats (bullies, murderers, terrorists, pedophiles, and fanatical messianic characters) we are told surround us" (Newport, 2010, 46). Critiques of the discourses surrounding gender, patriarchy, and the role of the father figure in the family are inherent in this. In exhibiting his suits hanging limply on hangers, Newport states on his website that he is "challenging the standard muscular form of the hero and offering the space for someone to imagine themselves wearing the costume, becoming the hero."[1]

By contrast, Barbara Brownie's male cosplayers create suits with padding to transform their bodies into the muscular body of the superhero. Superhero cosplay "requires participants to aspire to an unattainable physique" and for bodies which do not meet the ideal "costumes are designed to enhance the physical characteristics associated with masculinity" (Brownie 2015: 149). She adds:

Such padded costumes enable the wearer to not only dress like a superhero, but also to extend his physical presence. With chest padding, a cosplayer may occupy equivalent physical space to his favourite hero, thereby more accurately replicating the experience of being that hypermasculine character.

Newport's costumes are similarly designed to "reflect the physical qualities we attribute to the hero." But whereas the cosplayers fill out their costumes with padding, Newport allows his to expose the contradictions, stating on his website that: "The proportions of Batman 3 are based on those of a very muscular action figure, scaled up to my six foot tall height, resulting in a costume that is too large for me and that drapes and sags even more than the others." While there are differences from cosplay in artistic statement and intent here, there are nonetheless commonalities that relate to identity, persona, and play.

As the example of Newport's hand-knit art illustrates, the fiber arts can be eclectic, nostalgic, and kitsch (Newington 2010: 26). Knitting "now appears in unexpected guises with intentions and meanings that stray far outside the realm of the domestic and utilitarian" (Hemmings 2010: 9). These quotes are taken from accounts of vintage heritage knitting and knitted art respectively, but they can equally be applied to fan art. This chapter now considers some of the eclectic and unexpected guises knitting and other crafts take on as they are co-opted as media for the production of fan art.

A taxonomy of fan handicrafting

The working of fan interests into handicrafting falls broadly into three types: mimetic, in which objects seen on screen or described in the text are copied; emblematic, the work uses or incorporates logos, character likenesses, iconic objects, or elements of the text; and interpretive, the work is inspired by the text, but does not overtly reproduce identifiable elements. The intent here is not to present a taxonomy for categorizing individual examples of fan handicrafting, that is something that could too easily become reductive or proscriptive, and in any case examples do not always fall clearly into single neat categories. Rather, my aim is to explore ways of understanding the approaches fan handicrafters take in expressing their love for the text, and drawing attention to the ways in which such fan art is complex and interconnected (e.g., in respect of transformative work and identity role-play). In this way, it is intended to engage as much with the cultural, historical, and gendered contexts of fan production, as with handicrafting practices and the meanings of material objects.

Mimetic handicrafting is the form most obviously connected to Matt Hills's (2010: 2014) discussion of mimetic crafting. Hills is concerned with prop builders, but there are equivalents in the handicrafting community that recreate knitted and crocheted costumes and set designs (including the Jayne hats, *Doctor Who* scarves, Mollie Weasley's cardigan, Starsky's cardigan, and *True Blood* blankets discussed previously). Emblematic fan handicrafting is also in part mimetic, though the aim is to incorporate recognizable images related to the text into other projects. This includes extratextual material such as logos, as well as images of characters and iconic objects, and quotes from the text. Another form of emblematic crafting is to use color palettes or patterns to signify the text, as when fans make striped socks in the *Doctor Who* scarf colors. Images can be reproduced either as two-dimensional pictures—for example, portraits of characters in colorwork or illusion knitting—or as three-dimensional sculptural figures—such as crocheted amigurumi. Many examples of emblematic handicrafting offer overt and easily recognized connections to the text and the fandom, thus signaling the fan status of the crafter.

Interpretive patterns and projects are distinct from both mimetic and emblematic examples in that they have a much looser connection to the text. The status of the work as fan production may not be as easily identifiable either to casual viewers or even to other fans at first glance. This form is therefore a much more personal activity on the part of the fan, and in most cases is not designed to signal fan identity but functions much more as a transformative work—inspired by but playing with the text. Nevertheless, the work holds great meaning to the fan, and moreover it allows the fan to secretly carry or wear signifiers of their fandom in everyday life without offering an obvious sign that they are fannish in any way. This is not to say that such fans are necessarily ashamed of being, or being labeled, a fan. It may be that they work or live in situations where the wearing of fannish clothing is not an option (in a workplace or formal situation, for example). Alternatively, the fan may just find the pattern appealing, the connection with the fan text simply being an additional appeal or what led them to select that pattern in the first instance.

This taxonomy or categorization of the ways fans integrate the text into their handicrafting raises interesting points around the nature of fan production as it has been discussed in terms of the transformational/affirmational binary of fandom. This also has relevance to considerations of gendered fan practices and forms of production. Regardless of the category or categories which a fan project fits, all examples of fan handicrafting are discursive. All tell stories, whether personal and private or open to the group and public, of the artist's own status as a fan and of their love for particular texts or aspects of the text. Moreover, the projects themselves form part of a dialogue with the text in terms of material-semiotic production. The work of the fans incorporates their responses to the text and—potentially of the greatest interest—how they rework it or play with the text according to their own desires vis-à-vis the storyworld.

Furthermore, fan narratives are often created around the projects. In exhibiting their fan-themed projects in the group threads or on their own project pages, fan handicrafters often stage or photoshop their projects with or alongside other images representing the text. Interpretive fan handicrafting projects can be overtly linked to the text in this way. For example, a project by a member of Team Bite Me in Nerd Wars includes pictures of Eric Northman in the bath from a season one episode of *True Blood* and then poses her bath set (comprising a knitted washcloth with runes and crochet bath puff in light blue cotton to match both Eric's eyes and a sweater—extremely popular with the Eric fans—he wore in episodes from season three) on the edge of a similar roll top bath. Figure 4.1 shows Jess modeling her hat pattern inspired by Rose Tyler from *Doctor Who*. To evoke thematic elements of Rose's story, Jess poses against a wall on which the words "Bad Wolf" are chalked—a recreation of a story arc trope from the 2005 series of *Doctor Who*. Fans are already accomplished users of the Internet and social networking, and such remediation using screenshots, publicity stills, other artwork, and their own staged photographs echoes the remix culture also observed in vidding and the photo manipulation as seen on microblogging site Tumblr. In the following sections, examples of each category are analyzed in greater depth to illustrate these points.

Figure 4.1 Jess's Hat for Rose © Jessica and Jillian Cook. (Acknowledgment Doctor Who—™ & © BBC.)

Mimetic handicrafting

As discussed in Chapter 3, there is widespread interest in the handicrafting community for spotting examples of knitwear and other textiles in television programs and films, with some handicrafters then being inspired to reproduce a version of their own. In this, there are echoes of the way in which the fashion industry has typically been enmeshed in the merchandising of film and TV costumes or stars. Clothing and cosmetics have long been tied to Hollywood films and film stars (Stacey 1994: 182), and fashion filters down from cinema (Goulding 2015: 56). Discussion in Ravelry groups such As Seen In the Movies helps members identify a similar pattern for a design they have seen on screen or identify patterning details. Items discussed from January and February 2015 include Siobhan's sheep jumper from the *Ballykissangel* episode "River Dance" (BBC, 1997), Jack's jumper from *Into the Woods* (Disney, 2015), Katniss's shawl from *The Hunger Games: Catching Fire* (2013), Galadrial's wrap from *The Hobbit: The Battle of the Five Armies* (2014), and Sophie's hat from the *Doctor Who* episode "The Lodger" (2010). These examples do not necessarily illustrate the point that these viewers have fannish interests—the people asking for guidance often just spotted an item that drew their eye and they would like to knit. This kind of interest in costumes is very different to fan costuming and cosplay—there is no desire to dress up as the character and no role-play involved—but such projects can nonetheless embody affective responses to popular culture and bring the character or the storyworld into the everyday life of the viewer.

In terms of fan production specifically, the development of a pattern for the Jayne hat illustrates the intensity of these affective responses for fans. It is also an example of the way in which detailed knowledge of crafting—and in particular, how to deliberately make mistakes—combines with fan competencies and knowledge of the text. On her blog,[2] Keiyla describes the way in which she constructed her Jayne hat pattern. Rather than adopting an existing hat pattern and making it in the colors of Jayne's hat, she analyzes the screen images showing Jayne wearing his hat in great detail, much as the fans making props in Hills's account of mimetic fan production do. Knitting her first prototype Jayne hat was a process that she describes as "yield[ing] some interesting and entertaining insights for me, and quite a few questions." She concludes that Ma Cobb "was not an experienced knitter," basing this conclusion on the fact that the hat has uneven (or no) ribbing around the bottom edge, lacks any edging on the ear flaps—the flaps are knit in stocking stitch and therefore roll up; the hat has unfinished ends of yarn that are dangling from the flaps; and there is no decreasing to shape the top of the hat. She analyzes this in close detail:

> I suspect she simply didn't mark her rows. If she cast on, hid the tail by knitting the two together, and just knitted a bunch of ribbing, she might not have realized where she started, and instead accidentally knit say, 2 and 3/4 rows of ribbing instead of 3, especially if the piece got flipped accidentally. This would account for the extra ribbing on the sides and back that is not seen in the front. In addition, an accidentally flipped work-in-progress (easy to do in the beginning stages of a ribbed work for an inexperienced knitter …) would create a short row when the work was resumed and got knit in the opposite direction. (Go ahead, ask me how I know!) If she continued then to knit around, and still did not see where she started, she may have joined with yellow before the last round was complete, which would make the stripe slightly shorter on the incomplete side—the front.

This detailed analysis, including Keiyla's close observation of screen grabs, also goes into great detail in terms of schematic measurements (circumference of the hat, ear flap width), gauge (stitches per inch), depth of the stripes (number of rows per color), and weight of yarn (bulky or worsted held double). She uses these details in creating her pattern for the hat, but it is noteworthy that her analysis of the flaws in the hat is so that she can recreate these faults (including what happens if a knitter puts down their work and then mistakenly starts knitting in the wrong direction when they pick it up again) in her pattern in order to produce as authentic a hat as possible. Equally importantly, Keiyla also reflects on what the hat means within the text:

> All of these, ah, interpretations of a hat design lead me to conclude that this was Ma Cobb's first hat. Not only was it her first hat, but she designed it herself. I deduced this because, if she used a pattern, the pattern designer would not have incorporated the … choices … Ma Cobb made. […] Therefore, Ma Cobb designed and knit her very first hat—to mail across the galaxy to her boy Jayne.
>
> A mother's love, my friends. In addition, that Jayne immediately put on and wore the hat—as jarring as it may have been to his tough-guy image—speaks volumes about Jayne's own love for his Mama. I find their love for each other heartbreakingly sweet.

These interpretations illustrate what is potentially so important about the hat for the fans and what drives so many to knit one for themselves. This illustrates Hills's (2014, 2.17) point that while mimetic crafting is affirmational—as here with the extremely close attention to the details of the on-screen object, it also incorporates transformational responses. It may be simply because it is a quirky hat, but its significance may also be part of the affective relationship the fans have with the text, it represents the reading of familial love between a favorite and well-loved character and his mother, reflecting the fact that many handicrafters knit hats and other garments out of love for their children. As one comment on Keiyla's pattern says: "It seems a wonderful analogy for parenting, really. We do things for our kids that aren't what they wanted. We often don't do these things terribly well. We sometimes seem a bit ridiculous. But we love them, and they know it, and it turns out that was all that mattered anyway." For knitters such as these, family relationships feed into readings and interpretations of the text. Furthermore, the authentic elements of this Jayne hat pattern are signifiers of the mother–child love that is not otherwise expressed in the text.

More generally, authenticity is highly valued in mimetic production, as for Hills's prop builders, and for the cosplayers discussed in the work of Brownie and also Lamerichs. Fan handicrafters tend to employ the same distinctions; for example, the author of the *Doctor Who* scarf site Witty Little Knitter[3] examined one of the original scarves in order to identify the most accurate colors for selecting yarn. The Starsky cardigan analyzed by Turney and discussed in the Introduction raises some interesting points about authenticity in relation to handicrafting. The Sirdar pattern referenced by Turney is only an approximation of the jacket. As several potential fan knitters point out in Ravellers' discussion of the jacket, the

Sirdar pattern is knit in stocking stitch rather than the textured stitches of the original visible in publicity stills. Just over twenty projects are linked with the Sirdar pattern in the Ravelry database, but some knitters wish to make a more accurate version, and discussions take place about identifying the textured stitch used. Some categorize the cardigan as very similar to Cowichan designs, an acculturated art form that combines European and Aboriginal Canadian methods for creating textiles, and refer to a very similar jacket worn by Marilyn Munroe. Other knitters examine the stitchwork closely and identify honeycomb brioche (brioche is a style of knitting using tucked stitches—yarn overs knitted with slipped stitches from the previous row—that creates a reversible ribbed fabric) or a combination of slipped and twisted stitches. The French designer Agnès Dominique offers a pattern for a Starsky cardigan[4] using a brioche stitch, though those in favor of a twisted stitch in turn dispute the authenticity of using brioche. Others again identify a Jacquard machine knit fabric.[5]

This debate around the reproduction of a material object demonstrates the complexities of identifying the knitting techniques required for a thoroughly authentic reproduction. Similarly, there was much discussion around identifying the exact lace pattern in Amy's scarf from the "Vincent and the Doctor" and "Vampires in Venice" episodes of *Doctor Who* (2010). Here screenshot enlargements were the subject of close scrutiny, the fans working out the stitches and techniques needed to reproduce the patterning as closely as possible using compendiums of knitting stitches such as Barbara Walker's *Treasury of Knitting Patterns* (1998). The fans determined that the closest pattern was Frost Flowers, as shown in a section of a reproduction in Figure 4.2. Though it did not apply in the case of Amy's scarf, in other instances a commercial source can be identified. The relevant fashion brand's online catalogue can be used for reference material since close up pictures of the item or the ability to zoom in and magnify a section of the fabric can provide more details and visible detailing. This happened with Amy's blue and cream jumper mentioned in Chapter 1; fans were able to reference the pictures of the jumper on the Reiss website (Cherry 2013). In these instances, one or more fan—especially those who have particular knowledge or access to stitch glossaries—might then work up a swatch for further discussion. This can then be incorporated into an existing pattern, or as the basis for writing a complete pattern. The disagreements that emerge in these discussions often lead to several patterns being developed by different designers, leading to some patterns becoming more highly valued than others. But more importantly, this also illustrates some of the difficulties in reproducing knitted items—namely, the fact that textiles are fluid and the reverse side of a knitted fabric is often quite different in appearance to the right side—as is the case with Amy's scarf where the folds and movement of the fabric work against clear identification of the pattern.

Figure 4.2 Pattern detail in a reproduction of the Amy Pond scarf © Brigid Cherry. (Acknowledgment Doctor Who—™ & © BBC.)

Authenticity, then, may have to be compromised. Often knitters have to adapt existing patterns or create their own in order to reproduce items as closely as possible, evaluate several possible stitches or designs until a consensus is reached on what is the best to achieve the most authentic look, as is the case with the frost flowers stitch for the Amy scarf. As with one opinion on the

Starsky cardigan, knitwear costume items, especially those purchased from fashion and clothing chains, might well have been machine knit on commercial knitting looms. This does raise an interesting conundrum for hand knitters since it is not always possible or practical to reproduce the fineness and texture of fabric or specific stitches of mass-produced knitwear exactly. The fans well recognize that hand knitting cannot exactly mimic the fabric or stitch pattern of the mass-produced item since the yarn used in mills can be of a much finer gauge than is practical in hand knitting a jumper. Available knitting time thus becomes a crucial consideration, and knitters trade off authenticity for a reduction in the amount of knitting by working with thicker yarn.

In the case of Amy's Reiss jumper, for example, discussion focused on how it might be adapted for hand knitting and improving the design rather than achieving an authentic look. One fan comments:

> The stitch pattern in the original sweater is a lot more complicated than I originally thought from looking at the screen caps ... I don't really understand why the back panel is just smooth cloth though, while the rest of the sweater (sleeves and front) is in the stitch pattern. It feels very off! That's the beauty of making something like this instead of purchasing it. If you don't like an aspect of it, you can just change it. Once I figure out a stitch pattern for this, I'm planning to make it with the stitch pattern all-around.

The fans in this instance want to have an item with a similar look, but they value their own handiwork more highly than the authentic—not least, because the mass-produced item is seen as deficient. Projects are thus improvements on, rather than reproductions of, costumes. Like fan fiction writers, handicrafters remediate and rework the text in order to bringing it closer to their tastes and desires. It also illustrates the way fan handicrafters make use of the fashion industry as prosumers. In one sense, fan handicrafters negotiate the tensions inherent in being simultaneously inside and outside the processes of commodification as Hills proposes, but it also illustrates the ways in which cultural competencies are very relevant to this community. Alongside knowledge about the cultural text, knowledge of handicrafting techniques and artistic skills are privileged.

Material fan production such as this can therefore be seen as transformative work. This can also be seen in the way female crossplayers make female versions of male characters' costumes, thereby challenging gender roles and remediating these characters, and in the way steampunks adapt original texts in costuming and fan art projects to make it look as if it was made in the Victorian era, thereby reworking texts into an imagined past in order to reclaim the present. Considering this further, Hills's (2014: 1.1) reference to material fan production being "strongly mimetic" leads to the thought that some instances of fan production might be "weakly" mimetic. Hills's argument concerning oppositional maneuvering among fan activities is thus very pertinent to fan handicrafting. This is pertinent when considering the recreation of non-textile props in yarn (something that is extremely common in fan handicrafting), thus destabilizing the physical properties of material objects. Among the mimetic projects observed during the study that are made from yarn are bottles of Tru:Blood, Mr Pointy stakes from *Buffy the Vampire Slayer*, *Star Wars* lightsabers, the Doctor's sonic screwdrivers, or an Elven leaf brooch from *Lord of the Rings*. There are also many reproductions of costume items and even make-up elements that are not originally knitted or crocheted—a knitted version of Gimli's helmet and a crochet version of his beard from *The Hobbit*, Spock and Elf ears, or even a knitted version of Loki's silk scarf from *Marvel Avengers Assemble* (2012) for example. Handcrafted replicas of various props (and also characters in the form of amigurumi figures) are not, of course, straightforwardly mimetic. Neither of the knitted objects in Figures 4.3 and 4.4—a *Buffy the Vampire Slayer* Mr. Pointy stake and a version of *Doctor Who*'s sonic screwdriver respectively—can ever fully capture the texture and solidity of a sharpened stick of wood or an extremely detailed, illuminated metal object. The softness and texture of such "weakly mimetic" objects suggests that knitters and crocheters are negotiating a place in fan production that is in opposition to the authenticity of strongly mimetic prop building.

Figure 4.3 Knitted version of Mr Pointy stake from *Buffy the Vampire Slayer* © Brigid Cherry. (Acknowledgment Buffy the Vampire Slayer—™ & © The WB Network, United Paramount Network (UPN), Mutant Enemy Inc., and 20th Century Fox.)

Figure 4.4 Knitted version of *Doctor Who*'s sonic screwdriver © Brigid Cherry. (Acknowledgment Doctor Who—™ & © BBC.)

The example of an entirely knitted cosplay outfit further illustrates the ways in which transformations of material objects using knitted textiles can exist both in opposition to and alongside strongly mimetic production. The Wonder Woman costume made by Victoria (female, UK) that is shown in Figure 4.5 is based on the bodysuit pattern by Chris Wass,[6] but also includes the knitted boot toppers (that completely cover the footwear worn underneath), wrist bands, tiara, belt, and lasso that Victoria improvised. Knitting, in this instance, provided a way into cosplay without acquiring additional skills in other crafts. As Victoria explains, "I can't really sew, and all my friends were planning their costumes for a big event." Having previously made smaller knitted cosplay projects such as a *Futurama* brain slug and an Alien egg, she says:

> I really liked [the Wonder Woman pattern] but it took me a couple of months to decide to give the pattern a go. During this time I did a lot of research into Wonder Woman's look and costumes over the years and it was really interesting. [...] I wanted to get a look that was very recognizable as Wonder Woman but there wasn't one particular version I was aiming for.

Victoria "wasn't happy with any of the accessories that were available as they didn't match the aesthetic" and so she devised her own versions, "I'd never designed anything before so it really challenging to get it all to work." The boots were a particular problem to knit, and she added buttons to hide an obvious seam, but says that this embellishment is "one of my favourite aspects of the costume." The combination of an existing pattern with accessories that she selects from various versions of the costume and her own artistic interpretations thus allows the fan to express artistic creativity.

Figure 4.5 Knitted Wonder Woman cosplay © www.alasdairwatsonphotography.com. (Acknowledgment—™ & © DC Comics, Inc.)

Certainly, fan handicrafting—with the exception of handcrafted clothing or homeware—does not often fit neatly under the definition of "strongly mimetic." Mimetic crafting of scarves, hats, and blankets only accounts for one category and a very small proportion of material objects produced by the fan handicrafting community. The end products of fan handicrafting more often arise from and relate to the handicrafters' love for the text and the imaginative play they undertake around it rather than accurately reproducing material objects from the text. Fan handicrafts thus move back and forth between affirmational and transformational work, and many of the projects of fan handicrafting blur these boundaries. Authenticity has less value in these instances than the enjoyment of crafting and using (wearing or displaying) the items. In another crucial difference with the mimetic fan production Hills describes, perfect copies are not held up as the ideal by fan handicrafters. As Howard Risatti (2007: 184) argues, the qualities of hand-made-ness mean that craft objects hold a unique relationship to the body. Each object is unique through the qualities of the chosen yarn and, more importantly, the stitchwork of the maker. When fan handicrafters make a sonic screwdriver, golden snitch, or Star Trek communicator pin, it will always be obvious that the item is handcrafted, the knit or crochet stitches and the texture of the fabric always being visible, and some compromises might have to be made in terms of detail and shape.

Although individual handicrafters vary as to degrees of perfectionism, flaws in handcrafted objects are not necessarily avoided or reworked. Rather they are seen as something that reflects the individual's style and skill level, resulting in a piece of art made with their own hands, and their levels of skill. Flaws or differences from a written pattern—and in this case from the prop that is being recreated—can be seen as serendipitously beneficial or aesthetically pleasing (something that is ironically mimicked in the Jayne hat pattern discussed earlier). Artistic re-interpretations are also used to impart individuality in such projects—as Melanie says of her *True Blood* blanket: "I used a slightly darker blue for the blanket, with a khaki green color for the leaves, and about the same shade of pink for the pink flowers, and the exact shade of white for the white flowers." The pattern for Buffy's Mr Pointy leaves it up to each knitter where they will add the increases and decreases that emulate the knots and grain of a wooden stake, thus each project has a degree of uniqueness—and none will reproduce the exact shape and form of prop used in the series exactly, even as fiber art.

In fact, within the fan handicrafting community, individuality and customization are often privileged, sometimes to reflect personal tastes, sometimes to accommodate economic or availability issues, and sometimes—of no little significance—to reflect a range of fan interests. The latter can be seen as equivalent to crossover fanfic that merges different narrative worlds or takes a character from one world and places them in the universe of another text. An important consideration here is that handicrafting is, in and of itself, not a slavish adherence to the pattern. As Maura Kelly outlines (2008), handicrafters make many choices that individualize each project, choices regarding color, make and type of yarn (component fibers), adapting the pattern for individual size and body shape, accommodating differences in tension and gauge caused by the crafter's own technique, tools, or yarn choice. No two items made from the same pattern are likely to be identical. For her Cogwheel shawl (part of the Clockwork Collection of steampunk shawls designed by Remily Knits[7]) shown in Figure 4.6, Nassira (female, USA) adds a third color for alternate horizontal stripes and a bead to the center of each circular lace cog.

Handicrafters, then, are very accommodating of individual differences and do not hold authenticity up to intense scrutiny. Already used to substituting whatever yarn they can into a pattern depending on personal preferences, budget, or allergies, they are more open to adaptation and thus not slavish to the original. The *Doctor Who* scarf knitters, for example, are very aware that they would never be able to replicate the colors in the Tom Baker scarf exactly, nor would they be able to reproduce the knitting style of the original knitter. Furthermore, the *Doctor Who* scarf went through several versions during the Tom Baker years, none of which is definitive nor can be analyzed exactly (which the fans recognize). Even where a fan decides to acquire the yarn specified on Witty Little Knitter's site, yarn companies frequently change their catalogue discontinuing some colors and replacing them with different shades. In many instances, an accurate or near-exact reproduction of the scarf would be impractical—the sheer

Figure 4.6 Detail of customization in Nassira's Cogwheel shawl © Nassira Nicola.

length of the original making it unwearable for the many knitter's significantly shorter in height than Tom Baker. On "The Official 'I'm Finished'" thread in the Ravelry Doctor Who Scarf Support Group, one member posts:

> After a month and three days of hard work, I finally completed my season 12. It was my first knitting project and I'm quite pleased with the results, even if I made some mistakes here and there. My scarf is made for everyday wear, not cosplaying so I used smaller needles and ended up with a scarf around 3 feet shorter than the original, I didn't block it though, so I suppose it will stretch a lot in time.

Some of the members also make deliberate changes, using the scarf template but personalizing the color choices to reflect individual tastes. One fan used the gang colors from the PlayStation game Saints Row: two shades of purple and apricot. While another took "artistic license with the colors," using pink, teal, purple, burgundy, and cream to knit her version of the scarf to the template for season 12.5. She defends this saying, "but my TARDIS is the wrong color as well" in reference to a photo of herself beside a red telephone box while wearing the scarf. Inauthenticity does not mean projects are not awarded kudos or status in this group. This scarf has seventeen love clicks on her post, in comparison to fifteen for one in more accurate colors posted immediately before hers (love clicks range from eight to twenty-four in this thread). Nor is the knitting competitive in terms of either perfection or speed. The amount of time spent making the scarf varies considerably, one knitter taking three years of intermittently working on her scarf, another completing hers in a month of intense knitting. Knitters also mention the mistakes or perceived flaws in their own work without concern or shame, and this is often passed over by others who offer praise or encouragement.

As this analysis suggests, mimetic crafting can be quite fluid, incorporating transformational details or embodying affective responses to the text. In terms of being signifiers of fan status, mimetic productions are not always overtly so, or might incorporate multiple fandoms. Moreover, handicrafting skills are foregrounded both in the discussion of projects and the material objects these fans produce.

Emblematic handicrafting

Like mimetic crafting which involves the identification of stitchwork and possible pattern writing skills or confidence to adapt patterns, emblematic projects involve a range of handicrafting techniques in order to create words and pictures out of yarn, some requiring relatively advanced skills. Such techniques—stranded knitting, Fair Isle or intarsia, and three-dimensional crochet—are often necessary in producing emblematic fan art. Many examples of emblematic fan handicrafting are similar to other forms of fan art such as portraits of characters as displayed on DeviantArt, Tumblr, and other online fan art sites. Portraits can be created in colorwork and illusion knits, for example. The equivalents of model making are to be found in crocheted figures and other three-dimensional objects. One point that has been observed in this study is that fans very often learn more advanced techniques specifically in order to produce fan art. That said, fans do not necessarily have to be advanced in terms of handicrafting or artistic skill sets.

There are examples of emblematic handicrafting that can be quickly and simply made. Simple textural images can be produced using combinations of knit and purl stitches, as in the many fan washcloth patterns. These simple items, basically squares made in solid colored cotton yarn, feature designs such as "221b," Batman, Flash, Captain America, and Green Lantern superhero logos, a Pokemon Pokeball, the triforce logo from the Zelda games, and a range of *Doctor Who* images including the "DW" police box logo, the TARDIS, the seal of Rassilon, a Dalek, K-9, and catchphrases—"don't blink," "jelly baby," and "bad wolf." Some fans have knitted up multiples of such squares and sewn them into fan-themed blankets. However, more detailed representations do require more complex techniques.

Colorwork can range from simple two-color motifs (such as those used in traditional Fair Isle knitting, for example) to extremely complex pictures involving many shades of yarn (such as those Kaffe Fasset is renowned for in the wider knitting culture). Various emblematic patterns use different techniques, but stranded methods such as intarsia or picture knitting, Fair Isle, and double knitting (providing a reversible fabric with the image appearing in negative on the reverse side) are often used; crochet colorwork can also be carried out simply by changing yarn as required. Such work can depict detailed images relatively accurately. Several wall-hanging portrait patterns are available for characters from *Harry Potter*, *Twilight*, and *Doctor Who*. These take the form of a still or publicity shot from the film or series that is pixelated and translated into the required number of stitches (usually double crochet stitches since these are approximately square) in different colored yarn. The images are rendered in monochrome color schemes to cut down on the number of colors required—typically black and white plus three shades of gray, though one portrait of Edward from *Twilight* makes a highlight feature of his bright golden eyes. The Name of the Doctor double-knit scarf incorporates the circular Gallifreyan writing from the Doctor's crib in the episode "A Good Man Goes to War" (2011), and since this requires fine detail, it is knit in lace weight yarn.

Working with such a high number of strands, or even less strands but on a large project or with finer yarn, can be daunting. The TARDIS Afghan blanket, for example, creates a near-life-size picture of the iconic Police Box in five colors. One knitter frogged her project because "it was too much of a headache to follow nearly 400 stitch rows in a chart." Another used her participation in Team TARDIS during the 2014 Ravellenic Games as encouragement to complete hers. Finer details are not always possible, but fans find ways around this. Some fans choose to embroider smaller details onto knit or crochet fabric. Samantha (female, UK) does this with the Federation crest and motto on her *Star Trek* blanket shown in Figure 4.7; this forms the centerpiece to a patchwork blanket made up of squares in the Federation uniform colors of red, gold and blue, each with the Enterprise symbol in crochet colorwork.

Samantha's blanket is a statement of her identity as a fan of *Star Trek*, just as the TARDIS blankets are of *Doctor Who* fandom, but many fan handicrafters identify themselves as fans of multiple texts. Emblematic projects permit such handicrafters to display their mix of fan interests. The Geek-along blanket is an interesting use of fan handicrafting in the incorporation of symbols and images from a wide range of cultural texts into a highly customizable project. The individual blankets can thus reflect each crafter's sets of nerdy, fannish, and geeky interests through the squares they select from the choices on offer. The resulting blankets are not a representation of a singe text. Rather they display multiple fan interests. The Geek-along blanket is a clear example of how some fans do not focus solely or exclusively on a single text, but have wide-ranging interests that cross between several (or many) texts and even other nerdy or geeky interests (science, technology, gaming, for instance) at the same time. "Being a fan" (or a nerd or a geek, depending on how the individual defines themselves or chooses as the most appropriate term) is as significant in this respect as "being a fan of…." In this way blankets move away from the connections to domesticity and fashions such as shabby chic (as explored in Chapter 3) when, as in this case, they become, in the hands of the fans, emblematic of a fannish disposition.

Other colorwork techniques can be used; these include mosaic knitting and illusion knits. Illusion knitting, also referred to as shadow knitting, exploits the

Figure 4.7 Embroidered panel on Samantha's *Star Trek* blanket © Samantha Goodrick. (Acknowledgment Star Trek—™ & © CBS Studios Inc.)

different appearances of knit and purl stitches to create a series of ridges that appear as narrow stripes worked in alternating colors of yarn when viewed directly from the front as with the Woolly Thoughts Deathly Hallows shawl in Figure 4.8. But when viewed at an angle as in Figure 4.9, a picture is revealed, in this instance of Harry Potter. Illusion knitting can be used to create simple logos or graphics or, as here, detailed portraits. This shawl was created to mark the release of the final *Harry Potter* film, *Harry Potter and the Deathly Hallows Part 2* (2011).

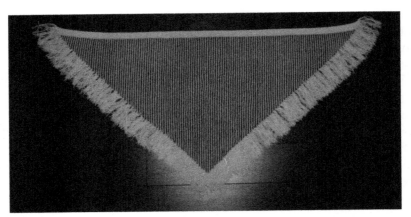

Figure 4.8 The Woolly Thoughts Deathly Hallows shawl seen straight on. Harry Potter Illusion knit shawl designed by Steve Plummer © Steve Plummer and Pat Ashforth. (Acknowledgment Harry Potter (film series) — ™ & © Warner Bros.)

Figure 4.9 Woolly Thought's Deathly Hallows shawl seen at an angle. Harry Potter Illusion knit shawl designed by Steve Plummer © Steve Plummer and Pat Ashforth. (Acknowledgment Harry Potter (film series) — ™ & © Warner Bros.)

Woolly Thoughts is interesting in relation to nerdy interests (in this case, maths)[8] as distinct from fannish ones. Steve Plummer, one half of Woolly Thoughts, developed a new charting process to facilitate the creation of complex images. His view is that illusion knitting "only allow[s] very primitive illusions that were little more than silhouettes," whereas his technique "allows different levels of shading to be incorporated into a design rather than the simple dark and light that was possible before." He has created patterns for a wide range of iconic imagery including famous people (Albert Einstein, The Beatles, Elvis), artworks (The Three Graces, The Scream, Girl with a Pearl Earring), mazes, and symbols (a green man, the Pendle witch, a first class stamp). Although Plummer does not have strong fan interests himself, he says that "I need the image to be recognisable. I need people to say, 'Wow, that's Harry Potter' [...], instead of 'A face, that's clever'." His illusion knits of Harry, Hagrid, Snape and Draco Malfoy, Edward and Bella from *Twilight*, the David Tennant Doctor and a Dalek, and Gollum from the *Lord of the Rings* films nevertheless tap into fan handicrafting activities (and of course portraits of the Beatles, Elvis, Marilyn Monroe and other iconic stars are also of fan interest). A number of fans have made the Harry Potter shawl for their House Cup entries, for example.

Portraits are important in expressing fan interests and identities, but as suggested often involve investments of time and effort in complex projects. The third form of emblematic crafting is often more accessible to many fans, being quick to make and using small amounts of yarn. "Amigurumi" are simply small figures or toys, the term originating in Japan and deriving from the Japanese word meaning crafted—*ami* (this can refer to crocheted or knitted, though crochet is more often the craft used in this case)—and the word for stuffed doll—*nuigurumi*. Following in the pattern of its Japanese aesthetic, amigurumi are often given a cute look, though realism is also valued. Kati (female, Hungary) designs and makes amigurumi based on characters from a wide range of television series including *Doctor Who*, *Game of Thrones*, *Firefly*, and *The Hunger Games*. Designed around a basic figure, it is the attention to detail in the clothing, accessories, and pets—her Columbo amigurumi shown in Figure 4.10 is accompanied by his dog—that create the character likenesses of her figures. Some are fairly easily accomplished. She says that this

> depends on how familiar I am with the character, and how complicated their costume is. For example the Doctor has a large screen time, and at least in his recent incarnations wears fairly straightforward clothing, so pretty much can be made from memory (though it's a good excuse to rewatch a good episode or two).

Figure 4.10 Kati's Columbo amigurumi with pet dog © Kati Galusz. (Acknowledgment Columbo—™ & © NBC and Universal Studios.)

As with the Jayne hat pattern, fan production is linked to the viewing pleasures and the affective experiences this provides even where the fan does not actually need to undertake additional viewings for their crafting.

As Kati emphasizes though, research is often a requirement in the design process and its execution. Of characters like her Shae and Melisandra amigurumi from *Game of Thrones* shown in Figure 4.11, she says:

A minor character in a more unique outfit will need more research. I usually just do a picture search and see what I can find. Publicity shots are nice because they are well lit and detailed, but rarely show multiple angles of a costume. Screenshots and watching episodes might help, but not always. Wide shots are not all that common, and quality might be poor as well. With a bit of luck, if it's a famous franchise, there might be exhibitions with costumes on display. Not that I have much chance to attend, but fans often share their photos— without the color filters etc used on the shows, these pics are very informative.

Figure 4.11 Amigurumi costumed as Shae and Melisandra from *Game of Thrones* ©Kati Galusz. (Acknowledgment Game of Thrones—™ & © Home Box Office Inc.)

Just as for the Amy scarf knitters, identifying details is not always straightforward, and Kati draws on multiple sources. Her comments on this also illustrate the link between crafting amigurumi figures with accurate costumes and cosplay itself. Describing cosplayers as her "secret resource," she says:

> They are of course proud of their work and love to show it off from all angles. Often, they will also share WIP pictures and layers, which help to understand how a complicated costume is actually put together—it's very useful to have somebody else do the deciphering.

This emphasizes the shared basis of much fan production and the links that can be drawn across communities, despite lines often being drawn between forms (as with affirmational and transformational communities).

A case study of WhoGrooveOn's colorwork scarf shown in Figure 4.12 also illustrates the ways in which emblematic crafting can include affective investments in fandom itself. Here the emblematic element is the wallpaper used in the set design of Sherlock's flat in the BBC series, one that is not necessarily obvious to non-fans but which fans associate with the character and in particular a much loved, iconic scene. Although the wallpaper is present throughout the series, attention is drawn to it in the episode "The Great Game" (2010). Sherlock says he is bored and shoots several times at the wall, aiming at a piece of smiley face graffiti painted on it.

Figure 4.12 Eryn "WhoGroovesOn" Mitchell's *Sherlock* wallpaper scarf. Photograph: © Michelle Mitchell. (Acknowledgment Sherlock TV Series—™ & © Hartswood Films, BBC, and Masterpiece.)

This is a popular scene with the fans and the wallpaper design, often combined in various ways with the smiley face, and the word "bored" is widely featured in fan art on DeviantArt and Tumblr. At least forty-eight fabric prints of the wallpaper design are available on print-to-order, custom fabric site Spoonflower,[9] and these are often used to make knitting tool and project bags (as well as other fabric items) sold on e-commerce sites such as Etsy. Fan-themed accessories made out of these fabrics are widely available. Of all handmade items on July 2, 2015, Etsy lists 240 items featuring the wallpaper, including shirts, hair bows, jewelry, cushions, and fabric-covered notebooks. It should be noted in general here that fan-themed fabrics and textiles are becoming increasingly widely available. Slipped Stitch Studios offers monthly limited edition knitting bags and accessories featuring fan themes. As well as fan-designed fabrics offered on Spoonflower, licensed fabrics are also available. American *Doctor Who* fans were excited when the US-based company Joann Fabric and Craft Stores carried several TARDIS and Dalek prints in March 2015.

In knitting her scarf, WhoGroovesOn follows the knitting chart provided in the knitcetera, whatever blog,[10] as do many other of the Sherlock fan projects. Charts are an important element of producing knitted colorwork fabric that is worth considering in terms of design elements. Creating charts for designs such as the Sherlock wallpaper requires degrees of image manipulation and artistic adaptation. Knitting stitches are not square, and so designs must be translated onto rectangular grids (as opposed to the more usually square graph paper). The matter of scale is also important, small images may lose detail (as with pixelating any image), but ensuring detail is not lost may mean that images become too large for a particular project (the more stitches are required, the larger the width and height of the motif will be). The wallpaper chart is offered in two scales—The Wallpaper Had It Coming (the title is a play on the line "Oh the wall had it coming" that Sherlock utters when John questions him about his behavior) is a simplified twelve-stitch by thirty-six row two-color chart and The Wallpaper Had It Coming Too a more detailed twenty-four stitches by sixty-two rows. Sixty-two knitters have created projects incorporating the chart, including bags, cowls, jumpers, scarves, hats, and phone cosies. Most projects retain the brown and ivory color scheme of the original wallpaper, but some, according to taste, are made in other colors—blue and white, yellow and blue, self-striping rainbow yarn on white, and a negative of white on black. Some fans embellish their finished items with embroidered smiley icons in yellow yarn.

Whogrooveson's scarf uses the larger and more detailed chart, and she knit it as a tube so that the fabric is doubled. In this technique, the scarf does not have a "wrong" or reverse side, thus avoiding the colorwork floats being visible. She stays with the brown and white color scheme, but adds a purple stripe and fringe to the ends to represent Sherlock's "purple shirt of sex."[11] Her project page emphasizes the work that went in to the scarf: casting on 144 stitches so that she had six repeats of the chart (three on each of front and back) and knitting six feet of fabric excluding the fringe. She says that "this was an easy to make scarf it just took a long time to do because of the complexity of the pattern and length I wanted." Further, she links the making of the scarf to her attendance at fan conventions:

I started this at 221b Con 2013 and finished it a few days before 221b Con 2014 (there were a couple months in between where it fell by the wayside but otherwise yeah it took me roughly a year to make it).

Her main project photo shows her wearing the scarf at the second convention.

In fact, it is through this scarf and wearing it at conventions that WhoGroovesOn has found her fan handicrafting and other fan art attracting attention (her participation in the data collection for this research came through the snowball technique, she being recommended to me as a person to interview by an earlier recruit). WhoGroovesOn welcomes such attention for her projects:

> Well, in the case of the wallpaper scarf, and usually any of my fandom knits, I knit to impress. The thought when I started the wallpaper scarf was "I love that pattern, oh and its super noticeable and people at 221b Con would recognize it! If I can make a pattern of it that's nice and detailed that'd really impress people at 221b." Then I ended up finding the pattern on Ravelry, and made the scarf, and people seemed to like it so much at 221b I started planning to make another one, which is the black and yellow 221honeybee scarf I'm almost done with.

However, the attention that she invites is not that of seeking the status of a fan celebrity (although she does achieve this). It is rather she wants her art and her work to be recognized, saying: "I like contributing, I like making things that impress people and much as I don't like drawing attention to myself I like making things that will draw attention." There is a sense here in which it is important for the fan artist to both be confident of her place within the fan community and also to acknowledge that it is her work that is more important, it stands between the self and the community as well as being the symbol of belonging to the community.

WhoGroovesOn's art is thus an expression of her fandom, but it is also inspired by the fandom. She adds:

> Fandom inspires me to do more because my work seems to make people happy. […] I loved it when people saw my wallpaper scarf and after months and months of working on it (and getting odd looks from people who weren't fans when I explained what the pattern was from) I walked into the convention and had people going "oh my god its the wallpaper! you made that yourself?!" There's something very satisfying about putting all that work into making it myself, and people finally seeing it, and seeing stars in their eyes over something small that I made.

This establishes the fan's place in fandom, and not only as a fan celebrity. It also represents an extremely important aspect of fan culture and that is the sense of community. WhoGroovesOn measures her work in the sense that she can give something back to the community that brings her pleasure:

> And there's so many other fan artists and crafters. I love absorbing it, and after years of absorbing it […], I finally felt good enough personally that I finally went "I can contribute too" and so I started contributing by drawing then realized

knitting was kind of rare as far as the fan works went so I decided to use my knitting skills too.

The fact that she draws very strong connections here between her art and her handicrafting is also important, deciding that her handicrafts were a way of adding to the affective experiences of other fans. Moreover, this is indicative of Jensen's (2002: 196) point that the practices of everyday art have "salutary power." The implication here is that as vernacular art, fan art—as is exemplified in WhoGrooveOn's comment—has personal and social benefits.

The reception of WhoGroovesOn's scarf illustrates the way fan art is embodied in terms of community interactions at fan conventions, but this sense of belonging can come about through the "disembodied" social web. And on Ravelry, this can be in recognition of fan-themed patterns published in the Ravelry database unrelated to group membership and community. An anonymous *Doctor Who* fan who designs washcloths says:

> I love it when people comment on my knitting designs. I post my patterns for free because I just want to share my nerd-dom. And I often "squee" when I see people post things made from my designs because a little piece of me can't believe how popular my patterns are.

Fans thus build profiles through their designing and this too can contribute to the performance of a fan identity online.

Furthermore, recognition of the creative process brings pleasures in its own right. Hanka (female, 30s, single, Czech Republic, works in IT), a *Doctor Who* fan who has made many Doctors, companions, and villains figures (adapted from Kati's basic amigurumi pattern), says that "making crochet amigurumis is my biggest joy." Going on, she adds:

> It's creative. I love to see how a bundle of fibre (and some stuffing) grows [into] a character in my hands. It's a great challenge to try to give them the features to look like the character—to find some characteristic features and details and then find out the way how to make it in fibre with crochet hook. I'm often also angry during [the] process because things aren't going as they "should" (as I've naively imagined them to be) or when I bump in some problem I have no idea how to solve. But it brings great joy when it come[s] out well or even much better than I've expected.

Despite the difficulties she mentions, one amigurumi Hanka made—the Silurian Alaya from the *Doctor Who* episode "Cold Blood" (BBC, 2010)—was widely acclaimed for its accuracy by her fellow players in Nerd Wars.

For such fans, these pleasures are "salutary experiences" centered around the crafting experience and the production of art, but they also embody the emotional connections with the storyworld and characters on the one hand and the wider sphere of the fandom on the other. Through their crafting, they can achieve a sense of emotional connection to and possession of the text. However, this does not come about only through mimetic production or incorporating identifiable imagery into their projects. It is also pervasive across many crafting projects that do not on the surface appear to have any connections to the text.

Interpretive handicrafting

Awilda's (female, married, New Zealand) series of patterns for accessories representing *Doctor Who* companions are a case in point and illustrate the expression of fan identities and affective investments in non-mimetic material fan production. She has designed patterns for an Amy scarf (similar to the one from the series discussed previously, but not identical), shawls for Donna and Rose, and a River Song cowl. The patterns do not necessarily incorporate any recognizable imagery for either the character or for *Doctor Who* generally. Rather, Awilda says:

> I have been trying to capture what defines that character for me, physically or personality-wise or both. For To The End of the Universe, or River's pattern, I wanted the pattern to reflect both sides of her personality. River is such a complex character that it's hard to capture that in one particular motif or pattern feature, so each part of the pattern reflects something I find inspirational about her. First, her story arc is amazing—the first time we meet her is the day of her death, and we basically see her life backwards as we travel with the Doctor. So her pattern had to be a cowl to represent the cyclical nature of her story—beginning and ending with the Doctor. Then, I wanted to represent both her strong badass side and her feminine side, and perhaps a bit of the crazy from her early days. So that is the patterning: the top and bottom edges are her strong side, very angular and bold; the long slipped stitches are the crazy, and their linear nature and repetitive patterning also belies some of the ruthlessness of her early days while their being skewed a bit from one edge to the other adds to her being a bit "off" at that Melody Pond stage; and the centre portion of the pattern is all curves and lace, to represent her femininity in her tough badass shell/edging.

The design process is thus driven by personality traits and/or significant moments in the character's storyline—narrative elements—as opposed to any visual imagery. They are thus interpretational patterns, but they also include key elements that identify them with the companion.

For the River Song pattern, the yarn made to complement the pattern (the series is produced in collaboration with an indie dyer) was "a nod in the colouring." Awilda goes on to describe her collaboration with the dyer further:

The colourways were a complete collaboration with Maylin. She has got a brilliant eye for colours, colour combinations and pairing colourways with fibres. When we were first conceiving the concept of a series, we talked through which companions would be used, what the concept behind each pattern would be in terms of what aspects of the personalities would be inspiring the patterns, and what kinds of projects we would be creating. Then we worked through what would both reflect that companion and work best for the yarn weight and fibre. What we came up with was a range of colourways and fibres that complement the designs and give us both yarns we really love to work with. I usually give her an idea of what colour(s) I think would work best, and the kind of effect I want to achieve. She suggests fibre content and what colours and saturation would work best with it. And together we decide what the final strategy is and whether or not we like the test run. There are some exciting things on the way with the next five patterns, including a couple of things we've never tried before! I'm really so excited about all of them and they are all my favourite.

In the case of the River Song colorway for Awilda's cowl pattern, a particular moment from the character's journey is evoked:

River's colourway was mainly inspired by a particular scene of making an entrance in the American desert, gun in hand, full of confidence and cheek. The colours of the desert, her hair, and the shadows playing around her were the inspiration for a colourway full of golds, browns, and neutrals. Maylin chose the fibre content to work with the strong-yet-feminine theme of the pattern, as well as giving a lovely drape for a lace weight cowl. And the final colour/fibre combination was something we were both proud of.

There are references here to specific events in the *Doctor Who* storyworld, but the design choices made in terms of both pattern writing and yarn dyeing evoke atmosphere and character rather than directly represent any specific objects or recognizable iconography. They are no less fan themed than mimetic or emblematic crafting, but they do not necessarily contribute to a performance of fandom (though of course they may).

Patterns and projects such as these can loosen the connection to the text. Awilda adds that "the patterns are all named after quotes or partial quotes that aren't the typical 'Hello Sweetie'-type iconic quotes…I wanted to be more subtle than that and not alienate non-*Doctor Who* fans." In one key respect then, this approach does not limit sales of Awilda's patterns to a niche group—thus potentially enhancing the success of her micro-business. But this does not mean that the work is any less fannish. In another respect, the design process described earlier suggests a transformative work, and the crafting of the project by fans, especially those using Maylin's (female, France) yarn specifically created for that pattern, while discussing it in the designer's group reinforces affective experiences and responses to the character. It is interesting in this respect that Awilda has chosen the most popular companions—Rose, Donna, Amy, and River—for the first set of patterns released, thus reflecting the discourses in the *Doctor Who* fan groups.

Other fan activities are also linked to interpretive crafting. For example, handicrafting can also be linked to the storyworld simply by taking place alongside the viewing of a program or the reading of a book. The *True Blood* fans chose a pattern which they could link to the characters in the series as they knit-along to each new series. They have selected patterns such as My Vampire Boyfriend socks, Vlad shawl, and Tiger's Eye scarf (there are weretigers in the Sookie Stackhouse novels) that they customize through the choice of yarn color or naming of the project to represent the fan's favorite vampires or other characters. The projects made during these knit-alongs demonstrate the popularity of dark blood red and other Gothic colors such as deep blue and purple, but also specific colors associated with characters—Eric's blue eyes and Quinn's violet ones, for example. Project names add meaning through links to characters (North Man), narrative development (Jessica's Tears), quotes from the series (Rug All Wet, Sookie's admonition to Eric after he has killed a werewolf in her house), and extra-textual elements (Do Bad Things, a line from the title music). This illustrates that almost any crafting can be interpretive and incorporate material-semiotic meanings.

Pattern designing in conjunction with knit-alongs can be particularly meaningful for fan communities, illustrating that handicrafting not only takes place as an additional activity during other fan events, such as the communal viewing of a series, but that fan handicrafting projects can become the focus of the group in its own right. Sherlock's Great Afghan Adventure, for example, consists of knitting blanket squares each inspired by one particular Sherlock Holmes story (resulting in a blanket as shown in Figure 4.13). The fact that the pattern was released in installments as a combined knit-along and read-along in a dedicated Ravelry group of the same name facilitated a communal and sociable experience. The patterns, each blanket square representing elements in one of the Conan Doyle stories, were released monthly across a year, itself maintaining group interest, but the knitting patterns were also strongly anchored in the text with discussion of each story that inspired the square that month.

The iconography of the pattern pages is based on sepia tones that evoke the Victorian era, and each includes a silhouette of the classic Holmes illustration with

Figure 4.13 Sherlock's Great Adventure Afghan © Susan Woodley Designs. (Acknowledgment inspired by Arthur Conan Doyle's Sherlock Holmes stories, illustrated by Sidney Paget.)

deerstalker and calabash pipe. Knitters are encouraged to read the story that inspired each month's square and three trivia questions are included in each pattern as shown in Figure 4.14 with the Charlington Hall square, with prizes awarded for those submitting answers at the end of each quarter. This not only encourages the knitters to keep up with the pattern and complete a blanket within the year, but it also links crafting with reading and the discussion of cultural texts. With the trivia questions, the crafting of the blanket takes on the feel of detective work, in keeping with the narrative and building on the affective investments in the text. The main pattern page also states, "Here is a clue for you mystery hounds who may want to get a jump start reading our first story: We begin at the beginning." Each month new clues are offered for which story is coming next. The knitters thus get to role-play the detective, albeit in some small way.

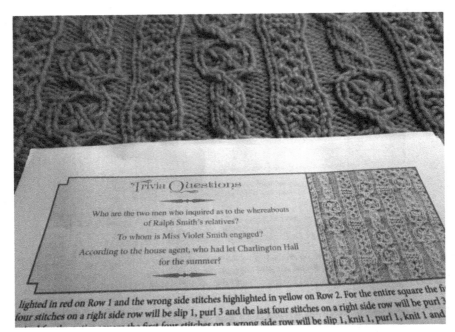

Figure 4.14 Trivia questions in the Sherlock's Great Adventure Afghan pattern © Susan Woodley Designs. (Acknowledgment inspired by Arthur Conan Doyle's Sherlock Holmes stories, illustrated by Sidney Paget.)

The handicrafters joining in the KAL are all Sherlock Holmes fans, though not only of the original works. This example thus facilitates, or at least offers opportunities for, connections between different trajectories of fannish activities: the original literary-based fandom, which Pearson (2007: 105) considers it to be the oldest established fandom in existence; an extremely active contemporary fandom producing a wealth of fan fiction and art around the lead characters/actors of the television series; and a broader community of steampunks interested in the Guy Ritchie films and the Victorian milieu of the original. This facilitates entry into the wider Sherlock Homes storyworld as fans discuss different versions and adaptations, making it a transmedial experience. Susan (female, USA), the designer and organizer of the KAL, is a lifelong Holmes fan:

Sherlock Holmes has been a part of my life since I was a young child. My first encounter was the Basil Rathbone movies which led me to purchase *The Adventures of Sherlock Holmes* at my school's book fair. The librarian assured me it was over my reading level—and at the tender age of 6 she was probably right, but when I was ready to enjoy them a few years later I had the book at hand.

It is often the case that childhood tastes for material deemed to be beyond their age grow and develop with maturity into an intense fan interest (rather than being childish interests put aside in adulthood). Hills (2002) and Pearson (2007) both describe similar experiences, as do some horror fans (Cherry 2001).

In following this trajectory, Susan has expanded her interest while retaining a sense of nostalgic love for her entry point into the storyworld:

> Since then I absorb any variation of the stories when I can, so yes I would definitely consider myself a fan. I love most of the movies and television adaptations, and enjoy various audio versions too, but nothing compares to the original stories for me—they're just great reads.

This is not therefore a straightforward nostalgia or longing for what the fan experienced in childhood. Susan's pattern is an example of how a set of lifelong affective investments feed into her designing:

> The stories are so textured with characters and plots and language that I find them great sources of inspiration for my knitting designs. Combine an insatiable desire to knit and with a craving to reread all the stories again and rediscover the great prose of Conan Doyle once more and you get Sherlock's Great Afghan Adventure.

As this comment suggests, knitting and fandom are intimately connected. Elements of the fan's inner life, not least the pleasures that the fan object brings, cannot be separated off from regular, often daily, activities. More importantly here, the interconnectedness of these elements also suggests that fandom can be an outlet for creativity and artistic talent. The fact that many fan handicrafters on Ravelry have become pattern designers is significant. They are using the experience and skills acquired as handicrafters to explore the storyworld at an artistic level, just as fan vidders, artists, and fiction writers do.

Susan's account of her Sherlock Holmes blanket illustrates one possible form this artistic expression takes:

> When I first created this mystery afghan read- and knit-along I looked to my favorite literary character Sherlock Holmes for inspiration. Reading is much more than simply devouring the words before me, Conan Doyle's stories are a great source [of] visual inspiration for my imagination and very much the beginning of my design process. Admittedly sometimes I have a preconceived idea of what I want the design to be—especially with the stories I'm more familiar with, but for the most part I let the stories and characters lead the way.

Whereas an artist using a medium of paints or pencils might choose a scene to paint or draw, Susan selects narrative elements to represent in knitted stitches and stitch patterns, sometimes in quite abstract ways, as shown in Figure 4.15 with the Winchester Road design. While a designer working in colorwork (as with the Sherlock wallpaper scarf discussed earlier) might choose to design a pictorial representation of the scene in the same way as an artist using paint, Susan works in a more conceptual way, choosing small background details or themes which capture an element of the story, sometimes one aspect of a place or an environment, or a part of the story suggested by narrative developments and characters.

This, then, is an example of imaginative play in order to design a stitch pattern using cables or twisted stitches. Susan explains how she selected narrative elements in her designing:

Figure 4.15 Winchester Road square from Sherlock's Great Adventure Afghan © Susan Woodley Designs. (Acknowledgment inspired by Arthur Conan Doyle's Sherlock Holmes stories, illustrated by Sidney Paget.)

For example on my Briony Lodge square, inspired by A Scandal in Bohemia, it struck me how much of this story played out by various fences—sometimes by the one down mews lane or other times by the one in front of Briony Lodge and those fences made me think of wrought iron work. In the curves of this "iron work" I could tell the tale of the three great loves of this story—a past misguided love, a current true love, and the enduring love our detective has for "the woman"—and the heart shaped cable design came to life. The Winchester Road square design, inspired by The Adventure of the Copper Beeches, played upon the idea of braids and the intertwining of two young women's lives for its entwined cabled elements. For Charlington Hall, the square inspired by The Adventure of the Solitary Cyclist, Miss Violet Smith's cycling trips back and forth to the train station were the springboard for the design elements that made up this square. Disc cables represent our cyclists, alternating cables build our hedges, and a staggered column of small cables creates our bicycle track.

Although the squares are representative of the story elements, they are thus also abstract designs in their own right. The links from the chosen narrative elements to the designs would not be obvious to a casual viewer, but for those knitting the squares they not only connect to the stories being read but also convey the narrative.

Literary fandom may be on a different trajectory than that of either an avid fandom associated with an ongoing series which is the subject of a wealth of transformative works (which the Sherlock fans belong to), or a maker culture intent on developing a retro-futuristic aesthetic in their material culture (as the steampunks are). But they come together and find points of contact around projects such as the Sherlock Holmes blanket. These different interests and entry points are evidenced in the variety of the blankets produced. One blanket maker decides on dark brown, ivory, gold, and blue to represent the wall in Sherlock's flat in the TV series. Brown and ivory for the wallpaper predominates in this finished blanket with accent yellow and blue squares for the smiley face graffiti and blue skull poster background. Another chooses colors inspired by the Baker Street platform on the London Tube with gray for the Sherlock Holmes mural tiles, red and blue for the London Underground station name logo, and yellow for the line on which Baker Street station is a stop (this knitter was working from a photograph of the Circle Line platform). A third pulls her colors from a publicity shot of Benedict Cumberbatch and Martin Freeman in costume posing before the door to 221b in which blues and grays predominate.

However, it is interesting that specifically Sherlock-themed color schemes taken from images of popular adaptations are in the minority overall. Many color choices and combinations reflect different criteria: practical—such as the fact that "my afghans get a lot of wear …"; artistic—wanting "to do each square in a different color" that incorporated "color gradations both vertically and horizontally" (shades of browns, orange, green, and grays); personal taste—"old fashioned colors [...] with a touch of masculine" (browns and creams); to match the décor or furnishings in the room the blanket is intended for; favorite colors; or simply using yarn from stash (i.e., whatever is to hand in sufficient quantities). Masculine color schemes are the most frequent, often chosen to evoke the general idea of Sherlock Holmes (earthy, neutral, natural colors). The resulting blanket, however, is not an item that specifically signals fan interest or tastes. Just like a Holmes story, the clues are present for those in the know but the meaning of the item itself remains hidden from casual view.

These two case studies, Awilda's *Doctor Who* companions series and Susan's Sherlock Holmes blanket squares, illustrate the ways in which interpretive projects loosen, but do not sever, connections to the text. Although the fan identity might be less obvious in interpretive projects than in the mimetic forms of crafting, some examples of crafting by fans of cult genres might in fact be overt even though they are original designs rather than reproductions of material objects in the text. In steampunk crafting, for example, the links between artistic interpretations of texts and design features of handcrafted projects can be made explicit since they are based on a generic style or aesthetic that is immediately identifiable. Steampunk also provides an interesting case in point with respect to debates about arts and crafts, and the levels of creativity involved in "modding" (making modifications to existing technology or hardware to make it look as it were made in the Victorian era). Or in the case of handicrafting, adapting patterns, seeking out historical designs, or embellishing finished projects. A search on "steampunk" in the pattern database on Ravelry reveals that many patterns draw on Victorian, Edwardian, and sometimes Georgian or 1920s/30s styles in their design approaches, design features, or other aspects of the pattern. In many instances, these have been tagged with "steampunk" in order to reach a niche group of handicrafters interested in genre. Other patterns are designed around a more specifically steampunk aesthetic, incorporating design features of cogs, clocks and clockwork, airships, steam-driven devices, and elements based on Victorian science fiction.

The Remily Knits Clockwork Collection draws on this retro-technological aesthetic of steampunk, consisting of three shawl patterns each of which is inspired by clockwork machinery—a cogwheel, a flywheel, and a mainspring. Cosplay is a highly significant and well-developed component of steampunk fandom, and this is reflected in the illustrations for the Clockwork patterns. Figure 4.16 shows the designer modeling the Flywheel shawl while dressed in Victorian style with long skirts, corseted leather waistcoat, watch-chain, and elaborate hat. The photo shoot took place at a location featuring machinery from the Industrial Revolution. Rebecca, the designer behind Remily Knits, thought "it was the perfect place." Rebecca's fannish interests, like those of many fan

Figure 4.16 Steampunk styling for the Remily Knits Flywheel shawl © Rachel Henry.

handicrafters, cover a broad spectrum, steampunk, science fiction, and science or mathematics often coinciding. She describes the way her fan interests inspire her designs: "I'm a big fan of a variety of film, books, and television. Right now I'm working on a shawl collection inspired by Oz—in fact, a dirtied-up and mechanical version of Oz that is steampunky in its own right."

As with the illusion knits designed by Steve Plummer, mathematical interests underlie the design process. Rebecca explains:

> Cogwheel is the most literal of the shawls—the notched edge resembles the gear teeth, and the smaller circular lace motif also looks like a gear [see Figure 4.6]. I tried to balance this literal interpretation of the theme for each shawl with something that was also pretty in a knitterly sense. If the design isn't balanced, it doesn't appeal to me. Flywheel and Mainspring [...] both have hints of the mechanical buried in the stitches. I have a very mathematical mind, so almost all my designs have underlying repeats and symmetries.

As this illustrates, it is often the case, given steampunk's focus on modding and adapting material objects, that steampunk handicrafters incorporate technological elements into their work with textiles.

An interesting point in relation to handicrafting is that, like some of the mimetic crafting, hard technologies involving metal clock mechanisms and steam-driven machinery are reproduced in knitted fabrics. D'gou's (male, 50s, USA) innovative top hat further illustrates the conjunction of textile art and the technologies of steampunk. It epitomizes the kind of innovation widespread during the height of the Industrial Revolution and the Victorian era in general, also bringing to mind connotations of the Victorian inventor and the patenting of innovative and eccentric objects (Halls 2014). D'gou has a large collection of sample skeins of yarn that he wanted to be able to work from "without having to make them into cakes [balls] first." His problem was that "I could use a regular swift at home, but then I would be stuck working the skeins only at home." His swift hat shown in Figure 4.17 was designed to allow him mobility, crafting with yarn that was unwound directly from the skein as he crocheted. The technical construction of the hat, using hard plastic mesh to support a wooden yarn swift and soft crocheted fabric to make the iconic Industrial Revolution-era stovepipe hat, shifts the hat itself in terms of its place in the material culture of handicrafting, locating it in Brownie's masculine cosplay recategorization of costume as "gear" (2015). It is important to point out that female crafters incorporate such elements and materials into their crafting too, the selection of a male crafter's project here is not to suggest that only men make "gear" (as opposed to clothing). One Femme!Doctor cosplayer interviewed in this study has made her own scale model K-9 and another steampunk has designed a bustle constructed with wire and fabric that has a compartment she can use to carry personal possessions in when she is cosplaying. Nonetheless, the nature of D'gou's project emphasizes innovation, particularly in the context of steampunk. Although D'gou does not consider his hat to be wholly steampunk in nature—saying, "It's not steam powered!"—it nonetheless brings to mind invention and the spirit of the industrial revolution.

D'gou's presentation of self in the wearing and use of his swift hat constructs a persona much as steampunk cosplayers do (Cherry and Mellins 2011). This persona combines elements of the Victorian inventor (the combination of fashionable accessory and piece of technology), the do-it-yourself attitude of the prosumer (crocheting his stovepipe hat rather than buying one to customize), the enthusiastic handicrafter (the hat being made so he can keep crocheting without having to wait to wind a skein of yarn), and the steampunk adventurer (his other handcrafted accessories worn in Figure 4.17 emulate the ammunition belts and bandoleers often worn by steampunk cosplayers). As interpretive fan art, projects such as D'gou's swift hat thus construct narratives. D'gou's project is based on the generic aesthetic of steampunk, as opposed to a specific film or program like Awilda's *Doctor Who* companions designs and Susan's Sherlock Holmes blanket squares. It illustrates the wide range of approaches fan handicrafters adopt in remediating the text. All of these projects represent the ways in which artistic vision and handicrafting skill combine with fan competencies in similar ways to the imaginative play also undertaken by fans writing fan fiction and producing fan art. As such, these handicrafting projects work to transform the text, not only in terms of embodying affective responses but also to create narratives in their own right.

Figure 4.17 D'gou's swift hat © Doug Philips.

Transformative works

The case studies of fan handicrafting explored in this chapter illustrate the range of ways in which handicrafters incorporate their fan interests into a hobby (and sometimes a micro-business) many of them practice regularly. For these fans, the handicrafting process and the material objects they produce (the making and the made) are part of their responses to and transformations of the text. In the context of fan culture, handicrafting is a medium for the artistic and transformative work of fans on a par with other forms of fan production. Although many fan handicrafting projects take the form of affirmative work—mimetic projects that reproduce objects from the text or which incorporate logos and other iconic imagery to produce their own collections of props, action figures, and branded clothing—much of it is also transformational, making connections with the ways in which fan fiction writers also remediate the text. Leading on from this, the next chapter therefore focuses on the ways in which fan handicrafting works in similar ways to fan fiction and in some instances is framed in deliberate conjunction with fanfic.

5
TEXT AND TEXTILES

As the discussion in Chapter 4 indicates, handcrafted items that encode the fan text are not restricted to mimetic or emblematic projects, but can also be interpretive designs that link to the narrative in terms of color, texture, and other properties of the fabric. The ways in which the characters and storyworld inspire the designer or crafter are of paramount importance here. Projects not only reflect the text but also create narratives in their own right. In other words, handicrafting projects can be one of the ways in which fans produce transformative works. Just as David Gauntlett's (2011) arguments in terms of making as connecting are important in terms of the sociability and the building of fan communities around fan handicrafting, making as storytelling is a significant act.

As Mary M. Brooks stresses (2010: 34–35), it is important to "explore making and the made." According to Brooks, the practice and experience of making is a vital factor in handicrafting and this is particularly significant for fans as the fan object is itself incorporated into acts of making. In Brooks's terms, "the artefacts are the physical evidence of an activity." Where that activity is carried out within a fan community and shared with other fans, as it is in Nerd Wars, the House Cup, and various craft-alongs, the activity encompasses not only the crafting of the project itself but also the discourses surrounding the making. These include the ways in which fans remediate the text during the making and how their affective investments in fan objects are knitted into the fabric of the work. The making and the made thus incorporate aspects of textuality, and both can be analyzed in relation to transformative work.

This connection between narrative and crafting is an important one in the context of this study. As Matthew Hale (2013) sets out in relation to steampunk maker culture, material-semiotic production is significant in terms of constructing personas and storyworlds. The concept of material-semiotic production is similarly significant in terms of fan handicrafting. Like steampunk culture, fan handicrafting is predominantly a maker culture. As with steampunk, fan handicrafting is not (or at least not only) mimetic. As Hale (2013: 7) states:

Narrative explanations for each object and entire ensembles formed a complex whole of textuality and materiality. Behind each object there were stories, and behind each story there were objects. The oral and the material were inseparable.

Similarly, with interpretive fan handicrafting, textuality and materiality are often enmeshed.

Designer Awilda's comment on her design process reflects the way in which fan handicrafters indulge in imaginative play within the storyworld:

> I am like every other fan in that I love to follow character arcs and immerse myself into the shows and movies I love. But I take more inspiration from what else could be in that world rather [than] recreating what already is. For example, what would a pair of gloves crafted in Rivendell be like? Or what other magical gear would Harry Dresden be able to create if he could enchant fabrics to do a particular job? That's the kind of thing that excites me, being able to add to that world rather than take from it, if that makes sense.

The approach to the storyworld she describes here is very similar to the extensions to the text that fan fiction writers create, the desire to "add to the world." Her comment fits the pattern of the story-oriented fans that Mary Kirby-Diaz (2013) describes in her account of fan fiction writers. These are the fans who produce transformative art, viewing the text as "raw resources to shape to their liking" (Kirby-Diaz 2013: 39). Awilda imagines "what else could be in that world" and although her transformative art is in the form of knitted fabric, this is not so very different in nature from fan fiction writers who "play with plotlines, relationships and characters" and "are eager to rework the story [...] to their preferences" or "recreate the story their way" (Kirby-Diaz 2013: 39). Awilda's transformative art results in a material object (a knitted scarf or mittens) but its very materiality incorporates its textuality.

Spinning and stitching words

An important point in considering fan handicrafting as narrative transformation is that crafting shares an affinity with writing and storytelling. According to Constance Classen (1998: 99), pens and needles have historically been linked through domesticated, feminine pastimes. In reference to women's art, language links pens and needles—the spinning or the weaving of words for poetry, the fabric of storytelling. Since female fans have so enthusiastically taken up pens to write fan fiction, is it any wonder that they have also enthusiastically taken up needles to do the same? Text and textiles are inseparable. Turney (2010: 42) draws further attention to the connections between knitting and writing, with her discussion of the "correlation between narrative and the making process" in respect of "knit lit," a form of crime fiction set in the world of yarn shops and knitting circles. Cecelia Macheski (1992), whose essay title repeats the "pens and needles" conjunction, quotes Nellie McClung in her epigram making a link between the physical and the emotional: "Women have not only been knitting—they have been thinking." Discussing women's lives during the Second World War, Macheski (1992:170) argues that women encoded feelings into their texts and their textiles. Of course, the pertinent feelings for the knitters Macheski is discussing are those related to the war, including patriotism, loneliness, loyalty, and fear, but it is possible to envisage other knitters at other times and with other concerns similarly encoding their feelings into their textiles. It is not inconceivable to suggest that passions for characters and other affective responses to fan objects (and certainly we already know that these can be intense) are similarly configured and reconfigured in fans' handicrafting projects. Leading on from this, further reworkings of the text are only to be expected. As Jessica Hemmings reminds us (2010: 33), "the idea that knitting is linked to storytelling is far from new."

Indeed, the handicrafters interviewed for this research who are also published writers (they write original—not fan—fiction) often make direct links between these two forms of creative and artistic practice. C.B. Blanchard (female, UK), a knitter and an author of apocalyptic fiction, sees the processes of writing and crafting on the same level: "In simple terms I find all my writing (fiction and articles) AND my knitting a creative outlet for me. Both of them involve taking raw materials and turning them into something more." Echoing this tendency to equate different creative endeavors, BizarreYarns (female, USA), a writer of vampire fiction and a handicrafter, has chosen a Ravelry name that refers to both activities, the yarn she crafts with and the yarns she writes. She describes herself as "a bit of a jack of all trades in the creative realm." She goes on to suggest that the very act of crafting facilitates writerly inspiration:

> Often while spinning, knitting, crocheting, tatting, etc. I will mull over the story in my head and let it wander aimlessly. On many occasions I've had my best ideas while making or working with yarn. When I wrote my novels […] it all clicked while I was spinning yarn, in fact. One minute I was fingers deep in seacell fiber, and the idea just popped into my head of exactly what my characters were, and why it took a whole lot more than a stake to kill them.

Blanchard does not think there is a direct connection between knitting and the genre she has chosen to write in, "except that people who are into apocalyptic media are more likely to enjoy more traditional survival-style skills." But she does see a strong stylistic connection: "It is **very** enjoyable to knit apocalyptic style accessories. Ragged-looking shawls, scarves, gloves and hats with deliberately dropped stitches. It's an aesthetic all of its own." BizarreYarns, on the other hand, incorporates crafting into her novel *Lamia* (published under the name Suzi M 2008). She also describes how:

> [O]ne of the main characters, Nemesis, tries to focus his attention onto things other than mass murder and he takes up knitting. In the process, his lady-love Lamia gets a series of hand-knit items that are of impressive skill.

Thus, for BizarreYarns and C. B. Blanchard, knitting and writing inform each other.

Macheski (1992: 171) also argues that knitting connotes shrewdness, it provides "a virtuous guise [...] for subversive activity, such as thinking, dreaming or harbouring less than patriotic notions." The point is quite telling, especially about the way knitting is not, or not straightforwardly, without a subtext. It highlights the potential for resistance or even subversion in the very act of crafting. In fact, this is not that dissimilar to the acts of appropriation and transformation that female fans do in their fan fiction (often rejecting some elements of the plot and creating new ones, often in order to write unintended relationships between desired characters into the storyworld). In Macheski's account (1992: 171), "the seemingly innocent needles can become weapons to attack the results of war, and to make fiercely concrete and domestic the abstractions of wartime rhetoric." Similarly, although Macheski is speaking about a very specific set of concerns—women's response to warfare and the ideological approaches to war, transformative fan art is by its very nature positioned in opposition to authorship, to the ownership of the text by culture industries, and even to masculine fandom and fan production.

Of course, one has to ask—as Macheski (1992: 175) does—why knitting and sewing? When considering transformative works such as fan fiction and fan vidding, female fans already have well-established narrative avenues in which to challenge the culture industries and remediate the text. Handicrafting, an accessible and widely practiced skill, is even more available to many fans regardless of their experiences of fandom and fan production. Some participants in the study do write fan fiction and produce fan art (as WhoGroovesOn does), and their handicrafting often complements this, as this chapter goes on to explore. But others report that they do not read much fan fiction or particularly seek it out, one interviewee (anon) actively rejects fan fiction:

> There's a side of me that doesn't really like fan fiction because it isn't written by the original author, writing staff, etc. It may be weird, but I guess I'm a stickler that way! I don't have a problem with people who do enjoy fan fiction, or with fan fiction as a general form of expression—I just don't enjoy reading it myself, and I don't write it.

This suggests that some handicrafters are indeed closer to the affirmational fandom of mimetic crafters. But rather more interviewees used to write fan fiction in the past or have tried their hand at it on occasion. Suggesting that some fans prefer crafting to writing, Hannah says she wrote, "A bit of (in the cold light of day, terrible) fanfic, I didn't really do much in it." Samantha says, "I wrote fan fiction in my teens, [...] but nowadays it's just crafting." Another anonymous interviewee suggests that some prefer to keep their writing (semi-)private when she says she writes, "Not so much, and not really for an audience. I occasionally still write drabbles for my friends or for myself." These responses suggest that some fans move on from writing fan fiction, do not want to publish their work in fan fiction archives, or do not feel they have a talent for it. Samantha's comment indicates that crafting can indeed be a substitute for writing.

Fan handicrafting is not obviously a form of narrative fan production in the same way that fan fiction is, it does not tell stories with plot, character, or relationship development. Nonetheless, as shown through the examples discussed in the previous chapters, the social aspects of handicrafting and the opportunities for sociability offered by the Ravelry fan groups open up spaces in which fans can play with the text. As seen with the example discussed in Chapter 3 of the short fictionalized account of homework for a class in the House Cup, role-play—and by extension fan fiction—can be significant components of or accompaniments to fan handicrafting. The link between crafting and fiction evidenced by Susan's Sherlock Holmes designs discussed in Chapter 4 and BizarreYarns and C. B. Blanchard's writing demonstrate just two of the ways in which material-semiotic production in handicrafting can be observed and analyzed. In common with fan fiction that extends and develops narratives with the written word (and this can include visual material in the remix culture of fanvids and photomontage), fan handicrafting can encompass transformations of the text. Fan handicrafters, especially those who take part in fandom outside of Ravelry, do read—and also write—fan fiction. So it is not unexpected that similar kinds of activities observable in the communities organized around transformative works can also be found in the fan groups on Ravelry.

Projected interactivity and transformative works

As Henry Jenkins (1992) asserts, fans involve themselves in the creative process by remediating and rewriting the text. Fan fiction, as well as fanvids and films, are the predominant forms of fan production that have been considered in studies of transformative works. But other forms of fan production, not least fan handicrafting projects, also exist at the heart of an intertextual, transmedial, and archontic relationship with the canonical text. Anne Kustritz (2003: 375) points out that fan writing often serves to make the relationship with the characters more intimate by turning them into real people. Similarly, the processes of parasocial relationships that this involves result in the text becoming manifest for the fans. This has already been noted in Chapter 3 where the sexual appeal of characters is integral to some fan handicrafting projects.

Over and above this incorporation of affective investments into handicrafting, organized activities for fan handicrafters also provide opportunities to construct intricate narratives around their crafting. For a challenge in Nerd Wars involving something useful a player would need at a fan convention, one vampire fan makes a net market bag which she presents in the context of going to a gathering of vampires:

> I know that a good ba[g] is hand[y] at a convention but if I were at a vampire convention I would want it to be more than an ordinary sack. That many blood suckers in one place would make any mortal nervous therefore I would bring my Silver Net Sack. Inspired by a certain silver net used to against a certain vampire in [*True Blood*]. As you can see I have packed my silver ornamented crucifix and my prayer book, just to be safe.

The player thus writes herself and her project into a fictionalized account that references the storyworld (this is not unknown in fan fiction where second-person fics insert the reader into the story as "you").

Such examples are commonplace in Nerd Wars, relating everyday accessories and items of clothing to the text through storytelling. For a challenge related to nebulas, one fan crochets a spider and tells a first-person story around it:

> The strangest thing happened to me last night. Like all my fellow vampires, I was up, looking for some fresh blood and gazing at a beautiful starry sky. When suddenly, I spotted a few spaceships. We were attacked by aliens from the Tarantula Nebula! I immediately picked up my cell phone and tried to call the other Teams to the rescue (you know, those with spaceships, those used to fight[ing] aliens). But no one answered. It seems Boba Fett was having a waffle party at the other side of the universe, and vampires were not invited! Because we do not eat waffles … (and they say, we are selfish!) So the aliens attacked. And look at me now! Could someone please do something??? Instead of eating waffles. I have no intention of eating insects for the rest of my un-dead life!

This example is jokey and light-hearted in tone, as is the one before it, and in this respect there are overlaps with fan fiction, particularly shorter and amusing forms such as crackfic, flashfic, and drabbles.[1] The spider story resembles a crackfic, the conjunction of vampire and alien invasion, the absurdity of Boba Fett's waffle party, and the writer being turned into a vampire-spider are designed for amusement.

In this way, handicrafting remediates the text to encompass the making and the made, and it is worth thinking a little more about the material-semiotic meanings of the yarn (and yarn colors specifically) used in fan projects since these are often used to evoke character and story. Color choices in fan handicrafting are often grounded in and remediate the text. Maura Kelly (2008: 15) maintains that even at a basic level (as when following a pattern) knitting is a creative and highly technical process involving yarn choices, including brand and shade, as well as mastery of different stitches and shaping elements. Jess, who is also an indie dyer, directly connects her yarn dyeing with the act of writing:

> I always thought of my colourways as fan fiction in yarn form. They were a way for me to express an homage to the creators of the stories I loved so much, and the characters within those stories. So, for the people who bought my yarn and knitted with it, those colorways were a way for them to tell a story through their knitting.

This clearly indicates the way color can be an important link between pens and needles. Certainly, color is one of the choices (others are fiber, texture, and drape) of a creative process that reflects the knitter's tastes and desires and is thus a creative outlet according to the model devised by Minahan and Cox (2007: 8). The use of color is an important aspect of creativity for handicrafters, but for fan knitters, color becomes a significant component linking the creative work to the storyworld.

Fans engage in discussion around color associations, and material-semiotic interpretations of colors become part of the fan discourse within the community. In one discussion, the Nerd Wars *Buffy the Vampire Slayer* team talk about the colors they associate with various characters in the series. Reasons for color associations include the physical coloring of hair, skin, and eyes of the actor, costume and makeup designs that the characters are frequently shown in, specific items of clothing that are felt to draw out the particular sex appeal, personality or physical presence of the character, objects or ideas characters are associated with in the narrative, and more amorphous concepts such as emotional responses and gut feelings. Giles, for example, is associated with tweed, brown and gray, signifying his tweedy Englishness and also his job as a librarian. Willow is associated with orange and strawberry red reflecting her hair color, but also with rainbow, a signifier of her homosexuality and relationship with fellow witch Tara. Dawn, on the other hand, is associated with a pure shade of green that symbolizes her role as an embodiment of an occult artifact, the Key, a reading that draws on meanings of the text and responses to it.

In Team Hellmouth's discussion, specific costumes are chosen that reflect affective investments in a character, particular male ones for whom the fans feel desire. "Deep red or maroon" is suggested for Angel as "that silk shirt comes to mind," while Spike is linked to "medium blue because of the shirt at the start of season 7," both suggestions linking to images that evoke desire for the character in the fan. In a similar way, pale blue is associated with Eric from *True Blood*, and purple with Sherlock for a shirt he wore in the recent BBC series—"the purple shirt of sex"—as discussed in Chapter 4. These garments are usually close-fitting, revealing the body beneath, and are deemed to be eminently "swoon-worthy." In this way, projects fill the same function as some kinds of fan fiction in encoding the affective responses to characters and actors much as Plot? What Plot? fiction (vignettes that focus solely on a character's sexual activities at the expense of narrative development) do.

Not all such associations are sexual, however. There is a separation in these discourses between pictorial imagery of sexually appealing male characters and narrative elements associated with the female characters with whom the fans identify but may or may not feel sexual desire for (it is Buffy's independent postfeminist kick-ass persona that is a major part of her appeal). The former is a key dimension of female fandom—emotionality and sexual desire for the physically attractive male actors that often becomes disconnected from narrative pleasures. The latter depends upon the character's status as a role model. Clearly also identification with key characters and readings of them are significant correlations with color associations. Personal responses and patterns of taste can come in to play in this, and indeed color associations are not always agreed upon. Buffy's color associations are split between more Gothic color schemes associated with a vampire series and more feminine colors evoking her blonde, "girly" appearance. Again, fans may make choices based on iconic items of clothing for any character, just as they do for the sexy clothing on their favorite male stars.

In the case of Buffy, this includes character-defining choices related to femininity and the subverting of femininity (Buffy being stereotypically feminine in appearance but also an action heroine in her role as a slayer). The choice of girly pastels for Buffy is influenced by "those baby pink leather pants in Dracula" which were "something else" and "take some serious guts" to wear. This selection of one item from a character's wardrobe that is deemed to stand out or be daring in some way (Buffy's fighting skills and athleticism do not automatically suggest pink leather trousers as a logical wardrobe choice) also recalls Jayne's diegetic response to the hat his mother has knitted him in *Firefly* (discussed in the Introduction): "Pretty cunning, don't you think?" Both clothing items make ironic plays with the character's persona in an amusing way, potentially subverting the stereotype. We would not expect a gunslinger to wear such a garish hat, but—in the words of Wash—by daring to wear it, Jayne signals that he is not afraid of anything. Buffy's clothing, especially in the context of the "Buffy vs. Dracula" episode (2000)—a pastiche of the Gothic text—represents a conjunction of girliness (the pastel pink) and toughness (the leather), and is also the antithesis of the Gothic. In particular, it provides a striking contrast to Dracula's description of Buffy as "a creature whose darkness rivals my own," the contrast being further enhanced by the pink trousers being paired with a black jumper.

Such color choices are intuitive as well as specifically referencing costumes and settings in screen grabs taken from the series. In these various ways, handicrafters make artistic color choices when selecting yarn for their fan-themed projects, and in this way they reflect their personal responses to the text, making the same kind of transformations of the text that fan fiction writers do. In the case of color choices signifying sexually appealing characters, Sherlock's purple shirt makes a useful point. In the context of fan art, it illustrates connections between the handicrafting community and the wider fan community. Projects made from purple yarn linking to the "purple shirt of sex" are common submissions to the Nerd Wars challenges by members of Team 221b, and the link is among the most commonly used in the team tie-in and team unity themes. Gloves and mittens, cat toys, purses and bags, scarves, cowls and shawls, blankets and afghan squares, flowers, hats, phone cosies, hand-spun yarn, cardigans and jumpers, and even a Dalek hat are all crafted in purple yarn. This directly connects to fan responses that have led to a plethora of fan art depicting Sherlock and the purple shirt on sites such as Tumblr.

The fan handicrafting projects thus derive directly from a dominant discourse in the wider fandom. Reinforcing this connection, members of Team 221b also discuss making hedgehogs or red pants for a team project during Nerd Wars. Both these objects relate to significant examples of transformative art in *Sherlock* fandom. The hedgehogs derive from fan art depicting Sherlock as an otter and John Watson as a hedgehog. This came about via a Tumblr photoset by Red Scharlach, "Otters that look like Benedict Cumberbatch."[2] This went viral in 2012, and subsequently otter and hedgehog art proliferated in the fandom. Similarly, the red pants originate with a *Sherlock* fan meme after the fan artist Reaperson drew John Watson wearing red pants in response to a fan art challenge to draw "more bebop!sherlocks or a butt of your choice."[3] The artwork was printed on cards that were distributed offline, and inspired further drawings by other fan artists. The fandom even nominated a day of the week dedicated to John's red pants—Red Pants Monday.

As with the purple connection, members of Team 221b make a range of projects featuring hedgehogs and occasionally otters, both toys and other objects (including hats, socks, purse, and table mats) with hedgehog motifs, or red pants. In some instances, fans actually made pairs of small crochet pants, as shown in Figure 5.1; others simply used red yarn to make other items. These are submitted to Nerd Wars as a team unity building exercise with the theme "Sherlock fandom craziness." These examples of fan handicrafting make direct links to specific instances

Figure 5.1 Crochet version of the *Sherlock* fandom's red pants meme ©Mary Cochran of Etchy & Hooks. (Acknowledgment Sherlock TV Series—™ & © Hartswood Films, BBC, and Masterpiece.)

of fan art, and further they are a significant contribution to it. These examples of artistic interpretations using color and objects drawn from the fandom illustrate how handicrafting forms part of the archontic text (Derecho 2006) associated, in these instances, with *Buffy the Vampire Slayer* and *Sherlock*.

While the examples discussed above might be better classified as fan art rather than fan fiction (though these categories do blur), they are useful in illustrating the ways that handicrafting projects can make explicit links to both fan art and fiction. Such fan handicrafting can be viewed in the light of Derecho's point (2006: 65) that an archontic text "allows, or even invites, writers to enter it, select specific items they find useful, make new artefacts using those found objects, and deposit the newly made work back into the source text's archive." Examples of yarn dyeing linked to fan fiction illustrate how this might work with respect to crafting. When she started out as an indie dyer, Maylin (who works with Awilda on the *Doctor Who* companions patterns, as discussed in Chapter 4) was directly inspired by *Twilight* fanfic. She takes her color inspirations and dyeing techniques from themes or descriptive passages in fan fiction, often those that are popular with (and in some instances written by) other members of the Ravelry group Unicorns Unlimited.

In her Etsy description for Landscapes, inspired by a piece of *Twilight* fan fiction written by a member of the group Lambcullen, she writes:

The colours black, green and shades of brown from gold, through bronze to chestnut are inspired from the following phrases in Chapter 2: "His hair was an amazing mix of bronze, gold and red." [and] "Those green eyes were piercing mine through his trendy black rimmed glasses."

For the colorway Hydraulic, "the blue and blue-green colours of turbulent water evoke the emotions and plot of the story" (in the fanfic Hydraulic Level 5 by Gondolier). Mouse's Autumn Mermaids is rich autumn colors:

Many shades of deep reds, burnt oranges and glowing browns mingle with the merest hint of sombre purple. The colours are inspired by the character of Mouse in the Twilight Fanfic "Poughkeepsie" by the awesome MrsTheKing.

The choice of colors in this instance specifically reproduces the yarn that Mouse (a knitter) uses to make a pair of fingerless Mermaid gloves for the character Rosalie in the fic, encouraging the buyer to knit a similar pair with this yarn.

These links between different versions of the text and the discourses circulating within the fandom, from the original to the fanfic to the yarn to the crafting projects, are evidence of the way the archontic text "is in continuous play, its characters, stories, and meanings all varying through the various fics written about it" (Derecho 2006: 77). While fan handicrafting is not explicitly "fic," it nonetheless exists in a transmedial relationship with the text. The remainder of this chapter explores these relations. Three further categories of the way in which handicrafting intersects with fan fiction and forms part of the archontic text are explored. Two are organized primarily around handicrafting. Firstly, there are narrative pattern books in which a fictional account is created around a pattern or set of patterns or in which the patterns accompany or illustrate the story. This group is not specifically fan fiction since it is not set in existing storyworlds, but it is often linked to genres with strong fan followings such as steampunk, mystery, or paranormal romance fiction. Secondly, there are projects or activities around which fiction is written. These are often related to sociable activities in fan handicrafting communities. The third category is the genre of knitfic—fully fledged fan fiction that involves characters knitting or is about knitted objects of various kinds.

Knit lit and narrative pattern books

There are not a large number of pattern books or collections integrated with a work of fiction, but those that do exist illustrate further the links between pens and needles. The heroine of the young adult novel Grounded: The Seven (Ordover 2013) is a young woman coming to terms with her psychic abilities, but she is also a keen knitter and knitting frequently forms part of the story. There are eight sock patterns that go with the book (these are linked to the seven major characters, with two for the heroine), though these are not included in the novel and have to be purchased separately. This allows the book to be marketed and sold as a novel (as opposed to a pattern book), maximizing the potential readership to include non-knitters. As Turney (2010: 41) points out, knitting in literature has a long history including in the writings of Jane Austen, Virginia Woolf, and Edith Wharton, but it is in contemporary knit lit that it has become an established genre. Turney (2010: 45) argues, however, that while the genre reflects aspects of contemporary femininity, it incorporates "nostalgic yearning" and "reflects the values of the past" (Turney notes that knit lit is read by an older audience).

Grounded, in being generically located within paranormal fiction for the Young Adult market, moves knitting fiction away from traditional concepts of femininity and knitting culture. The heroine is sent away from home after she sets her ex-boyfriend on fire and discovers she has paranormal powers that are a danger to others. Moreover, knitting with a set of five double-pointed needles is for her "like manipulating a flexible ninja throwing star" and she describes herself as a "level five rogue geek" (Ordover 2013: chapter 10), neither of which description evokes a particularly traditional attitude toward feminine handicrafting, but which locates her with respect to craftivism. Ordover's pattern for the character, Rosie's Firestarter Socks,[4] features flames running up the sides to represent her "challenging and unpredictable talents." Story and pattern thus work together to counter patriarchal constructions of gender somewhat more than knit lit does (Turney, 2010: 43), as do examples of narrative pattern books.

The Adventures of Miss Flitt: The Strange Case of the Magician's Cabinet (Hahn 2009) resembles knit lit in some respects, featuring amateur detection. Three young women go to see a magic show and one of them, Lucy, takes part as the magician's assistant. When she later disappears, her sister Emma goes looking for her. In the story, Emma wears a cardigan of her own design and is knitting a shrug for Lucy. Their friend Amity is also enamored of a caplet (a short cape covering just the shoulders) her mother has knitted for her out of the softest wool, caplets being all the rage in Paris. The story makes detailed references to these garments in a way that establishes character, and patterns for all of them are provided. In the second book in the series *Dangerous Ladies and Opium Dens* (Hahn 2010), a wronged woman tells Emma and Amity her story. At one point, she had to resort to picking pockets to survive and describes the gloves she knitted which had a gusset and loop for palming stolen money. A pattern is provided for Sharpers, finger loop gloves that incorporate both the design element mentioned in the story and the act of theft in the name of the pattern (a sharper being an archaic word for a thief). It is important to note here that, unlike *Grounded*, story is subservient to knitting pattern, but this does offer further evidence of the role of crafting as one component in a creative and artistic portfolio. The author not only writes fiction and designs knitting patterns, but is also an artist who illustrates her story with watercolor paintings of scenes.

Despite this imbalance though, characterization is emphasized and women are depicted as independently minded and set against both patriarchal attitudes and abusive men. In the same vein, *Needles and Artifice: A Refined Adventure Story with Ingenious Patterns* plays on steampunk as a maker culture. Within this, the fiber arts are foregrounded; in the story that accompanies the patterns, one of the characters runs a ranch, breeds sheep, and produces acclaimed yarn. Moreover, this book illustrates some of Turney's points about knit lit in that it confronts gender roles and patriarchal constructions of femininity. It draws on the conventions of steampunk, a genre known for its depictions of strong female characters in traditional male roles. The "Ladies of Mischief" (who are both the characters in the story and the steampunk personas of the writers) may knit and drink tea, but they also pilot airships, are inventors, explorers, and botanists, and communicate in code. Photographs that accompany the fiction depict the women with rifles, swords, and scientific equipment, wearing leather corsets and sturdy boots, and posing beside steam trains and industrial machinery (they also model the finished garments from the patterns). One of the Ladies has a punk hairstyle with shaved sides, another swears "in an incredibly loud and verbose manner," and men are either enemies to be vanquished or expected to make the tea.

The only character depicted as being in a traditional Patriarchal relationship is a clockwork woman made to play the role of a wife, a role she rejects:

"I am not your wife!" she snarled at him. "I never was! I was your puppet, your plaything, your pawn! If you wanted me to remain happy with that existence, you should never have given me a mind with the capability to learn."

This contrasts with the women in Knit Fic, a genre in which a "single woman is […] an awkward and out of place entity" (Turney 2010: 43). Patterns in *Needles and Artifice* reflect this, breaking with traditional ways of making garments. One is a shrug knitted diagonally with the patterning spiraling around the arms, another is a mismatched pair of stockings with stripes running vertically on one and zigzagging horizontally around on the other. The generic elements of the narratives and the historical styling in the patterns in these narrative pattern books appeal to fans of historical genres, but the depictions of feminine agency—in which characters are not only independent women but knitters too— offer opportunities for fan pleasures and identification. This is further illustrated in examples of fiction written around projects and activities. In these instances, the fan and her work, and sometimes the group in which the activity takes place, are incorporated into the fiction.

One of the activities practiced widely by Ravelry groups is the swap, where members participate in an organized swap of gifts, usually containing a handcrafted item, some crafting tools or materials, and other small "goodies." In the fan groups, these usually have a fan theme. There are, for example, regular *Buffy the Vampire Slayer* swaps in the Buffy Swap group and Team TARDIS runs regular swaps which respond to the members' areas of interest in *Doctor Who*. The case study discussed here is of a swap in The Knitting Dead group, and a swap package constructed around a fanfic the gifter has written. The core members of the Knitting Dead group form a tight-knit community, as Yvonne says: "We provide lots of moral support for one another. It's really astounding." The members of the group joining in the swap are thus already familiar with each other's tastes and preferences, and this allows for swaps to be intimate and personal. During a swap in 2013, Vicky (female, USA, pilot) prepared a swap package for Sharon, along with a fic "Sharon and Vicky's Great Escape from Atlanta." The swap package includes several individually wrapped items, each referenced in the story.

In the fic, Vicky meets Sharon in a hotel in Atlanta, where both of them are stranded at the start of the zombie outbreak, and they quickly team up in the face of adversity. This underscores Yvonne's experience of moral support provided by the group. Handicrafting tools also feature prominently in the fic and the characters actions are connected to their shared hobby. Vicky has an idea to get to the airport and fly them to Orlando, and they arm themselves with knitting needles:

> I took a moment to go through my bag and grab a pair of knitting needles. I almost went into a fit of giggles when I saw the pencil erasers I was using as needle caps. I actually wanted to have those needles handy in case I needed a weapon. I slid the stitch markers off the needles. I took one needle and handed the other to Sharon.
>
> "Oh, you're a knitter?" She asked. "So am I. You can hang onto those, I actually have a nice pair of aluminum straights I can use."

The story includes photographs of the needles, needle caps (a mace and an axe—both useful weapons against zombies), and stitch markers (knitting dead-themed), all of which are among the items in the swap package.

The needles are used in the story once Vicky and Sharon manage to find a plane:

> All of a sudden we saw a grubby, blood crusted hand reaching toward us. It was the captain I'd been flying with. He must have tried to do the same thing I'd done, only he hadn't been successful. I could tell by looking as his cloudy eyes and gaping mouth. Sharon's quick thinking saved us as she plunged her knitting needle into his eye socket and rammed it as far into his skull as she could get it to go.

This scene replicates moments that are common throughout *The Walking Dead* and places the fans (swapper and swapee) directly into the action. They are depicted as capable, quick thinking, and proactive when under attack by walkers, much as the characters in the television series are.

Moreover, on the way to Orlando, they bond over their knitting, just as they already have in the group:

> We settled ourselves back in the flight deck, this time closing and locking the door. Just in case. On the way to Orlando, we filled the time talking about our mutual love of knitting. Sharon showed me her beautiful skein of Malabrigo and I showed her the pair of Starry Archer Fingerless Gloves I'd made. Funny that we should have the same taste in patterns. We shared some of the candy I'd grabbed from the hotel and a package of chocolate cherry peeps I had in my bag.

The story thus works transmedially, incorporating the storyworld of the series, the transformative work of the fiction, and the posts on the group thread where Sharon displays pictures of her swap package. The package itself provides a checklist of supplies for the zombie apocalypse, taken from the plane, the airport shop, and the hotel in the story, and including snacks, toiletries, first aid kit, vegetable seeds, candle, and instructions on how to start a fire with sticks, as well as the knitting needles with which to kill walkers. While this is related to role-play and performative aspects of fandom, it also forms a meta-textual commentary on the narrative. What is significant in the context of the fan culture of handicrafting is a transformation of the text to include knitters and knitting, not least the fan handicrafter herself.

The way in which the fans write themselves into the text recalls debates about the oft-derided Mary Sue character of fan fiction, an idealized fantasy of a perfect character, often seen as a stand-in for the writer herself, introduced into the storyworld. The Mary Sue fan fic has been interpreted as narcissistic; Jenkins (2013: 173) refers to the character as "autobiographical," Bacon-Smith (1992: 94) suggests she is a "recreation of the adolescent self," and Scodari (2003: 5) says that she represents "a subject position within which the reader-writer projects herself as the focus of attention for idolized and idealized male heroes." Not all introductions of the self into fan fiction might be as problematical as this suggests, however. Chander and Sunder see her as "a figure of subaltern critique and [...] empowerment" (2007: 599), while Ika Willis (2006: 155) frames her own construction of a Mary Sue character in her fanfic within "the complex circulation of desire and gender in texts and subjectivities [...] in which an author's self-positioning corresponds to her identification with characters in canon."

The Knitting Dead swap fanfic is not, of course, an example of Mary Sue, it is rather an invitation to other members of the group to place themselves in the storyworld, just as the Slytherin House Cup players do. Yet the story *is* autobiographical, the self in "Escape from Atlanta" is the writer. She is a professional pilot in real life, and the itinerary of gift packages fit what she knows about the giftee. The fingerless gloves she includes in the package and which both participants are knitting in the story are being knitted in a pattern she has designed to match the interests of the recipient in response to swap questions. Regardless of the fact that the fic does not attempt to fill gaps in the canonical text, or to develop relationships with and between canonical characters (and does not recognize queerness which is Willis's concern), it resembles Willis's (2006) argument that fan stories represent a shared reading of the text that potentially offers fans (in this case, those active participants in the group) new ways to engage with a reoriented canon in a way that valorizes pleasure (the way the fans can imagine themselves into the storyworld directly). An additional factor arising from this case study is the way in which fans feel the desire to incorporate crafting into the storyworld (and knitting needles do seem ideal weapons for killing zombies). Indeed, fan handicrafters have done this in a variety of ways through their fan fiction.

Crafting embedded in fan fiction

Knitfic is a category of fan fiction where the writer incorporates handicrafting into her story. This can encompass either knowledge of handicrafting culture generally (it is usually knitting) or (though more rarely) incorporating handcrafted projects that the writer has made herself into the fic. Fan handicrafting thus becomes an element of the transformative work itself. Knitfic can be found for many fandoms. The online fan fiction archive fanfiction.net (as of February 2015) contains 758 stories tagged with knitting or referring to knitting in the main title. By far the largest group are the *Harry Potter* knitfics (103), but *Twilight*, *Doctor Who*, and *Sherlock* all have significant numbers (around the twenty–thirty range), with a wide range of other fandoms including *Buffy the Vampire Slayer*, *Supernatural*, *Lord of the Rings*, *Hunger Games*, *Walking Dead*, and *Star Trek* also represented. The Archive of Our Own site contains 316 stories tagged with "knitting," featuring fandoms including, among the most popular, *Lord of the Rings/The Hobbit*, the Marvel comic book universe, *Harry Potter*, *Sherlock*, and *Supernatural*. There are also knitfics for single films (*Pacific Rim*), podcasts (*Welcome to Night Vale*), video games (*Kingdom Hearts*), sporting events (the Olympic games, motor racing), and bands (One Direction, My Chemical Romance).

It seems from this extensive list that just about any cult media or popular culture text can be transformed to show characters knitting, learning to knit, or appreciating knitting. Since knit lit is already established as a subgenre of crime fiction, as described by Turney (2010), it is interesting therefore to consider the

Sherlock knitfic, often tagged as "knitlock." It is clear at a quick glance, however, that there is little resemblance to knit lit or to crime fiction generally in knitfic. Knitting is only occasionally framed in terms of Sherlock's role as a consulting detective and his prodigious knowledge of criminality and methods of crime. In "Knitting is Hard" by EnamouredWithSherlolly,[5] for example, Sherlock has "discovered there might be beneficial value to learning to use knitting needles. Murder weapon, self defence weapon…."

Many of the knitlock fics, however, do not incorporate knitting as an element of crime; in fact, few of them contain any mention of crime at all. Sherlock's knitting might occupy him between cases, for example (reflecting the canon of the BBC series in which he is bored when he has no crimes to solve). In "To Interlace" by onereeler,[6] his scarf knitting is interrupted when he is called in to assist Lestrade solve a murder and in "In Which Sherlock Knits and Other Tales of 221B" by Reason to Scatter[7] knitting alleviates the boredom when "no cases demanded his immediate attention"—but knitting is not linked to crime or the cause of crime as it is in knit lit. This is not unexpected, given the usual forms and categories of fan fiction, and criminal investigations are elided in favor of the more usual fanfic concerns of relationships and character's emotional lives.

Knitting is most often written about in the context of Sherlock's relationships, either in "Johnlock"—Sherlock/Watson slash-fiction—or in "Sherlolly"—Sherlock/Molly shipper fics. Short pieces of fiction—such as drabbles, flashfic, and crackfic—are commonplace. Being very short, they do not have much plot, making them easy and quick to write, distribute, and read, are frequently humorous (and therefore entertaining without requiring a great deal of focus on wider fan competencies), and are character-driven (thus serving the fans passions for the character). They express the fans' interests in particular characters and the imagined (and desired) relationships that are not developed in the canonical text. Knitting and learning to knit (often with disastrous effects) are incorporated into the storyworld through characterization and relationships, as well as helping to foreground amusing and endearing qualities in the characters.

This is not to trivialize the importance of knitting in these knitfics. They often present knitting as a sign of love, affection or friendship, or (less often) as stress relief. Knitting is a leisure-time activity, taking place within the domestic environment. There is a sense of authenticity in relation to the culture of knitting here, and these knitfics can thus be seen as projected interactivity with the writers incorporating aspects of their own lives, everyday activities and concerns, into the characters' acts of knitting. In terms of fan fiction writing and projected interactivity, this reflects the fan writer's own experiences (Davisson and Booth 2007) including the sociability of knitting groups (and in the case of fan fiction this takes the form of the fan handicrafting community and the fan discourses found therein). For example, in "Mrs Hudson's Knitting Circle Gets a Fright" by dead air space,[8] a small group of women visit Mrs Hudson for tea and scones, but their knitting is interrupted by loud crashes, creaking floorboards, and alarming cries from upstairs. Going to investigate, they discover Watson and Sherlock in a compromising position, the noises being caused by enthusiastic sex. The point here is that as a piece of slash fiction, the sex (and its discovery) is the central focus of the narrative, rather than the knitting in its own right. The fact that it is Mrs Hudson's knitting circle that interrupts John and Sherlock's coitus underscores the fact this is a light-hearted, amusing scenario and it is the Johnlock relationship that is the payoff for the fans.

However, it is not insignificant that it is Mrs Hudson and her knitting friends who get to play the part of detectives (investigating the alarming noises). As an example of projected interactivity, this writes the knitter/reader into the storyworld. This is important in the context of the Johnlock fandom because Mrs Hudson is seen as one of their own, a fervent supporter of the slashed relationship. When John is first introduced as Sherlock's flatmate in the television series, Mrs Hudson immediately assumes they are a couple. Other knitfic writers use this, whether they are writing a slashfic or not. "In Which Sherlock Knits," for example, has Mrs Hudson assuming John and Sherlock's anniversary is coming up when Sherlock asks her to teach him to knit. This means that these fans already feel a shared affinity or parasocial relationship with the character, both through their knitting and through seeing John and Sherlock as a couple. While this is "an articulation of both the desires of the fan and the fan's perception of the characters' desires" (Davisson and Booth 2007: 36), in terms of the Johnlock relationship this demonstrates that slash need not represent either resistance to dominant meaning or an intervention into the text. Rather, it is "an 'actualization' of a 'latent' property of the text itself" (Willis 2006: 154). The role of Mrs Hudson in these knitfics, and the identification with the character that this builds, permits interactivity with the storyworld. One of the demands of the reader's desiring subjectivity that Willis (2006: 163) stresses in her discussion of Mary Sue is that "the fictional universe should have space for the reader herself, for her desires, her demands, her politics."

Desiring subjectivity is common in Sherlock knitfics where one character learns to knit in order to make a gift to the other; this is often presented in terms of romantic comedy. "In Which Sherlock Knits" depicts Sherlock deciding to make John a new jumper after he has ruined another piece of his flatmate's knitwear. It is not presented as an easy task: "It was rough going at first, the counterintuitive movements and the yarn conspiring to tangle and make him drop stitches." Having persevered, Sherlock "worked hard" to complete the project, but "it was an atrocious piece of knitting." The writer uses all the mistakes that knitters might make (parentheses and italics in the story indicate Sherlock's analytical thought processes as a way to emulate such sequences in the TV series):

(Dropped stitches, places where he'd knit through the yarn—how had he not caught that?—there were holes where he'd wrapped the yarn around

the needle accidentally and broke the pattern, and there were several odd
patches where the tension was off and the yarn was stretched too loose.)
This simply was not acceptable. There was no way he was going to let John
see this. It was mistake-riddled and awful and absolutely not going to see the
light of daylight ever again.

Nevertheless, John retrieves the jumper, and not only wears it during a case
but defends Sherlock against the ridicule that two police officers heap on it
and on Sherlock. The "atrocious" jumper thus comes to signify the feelings that
Sherlock and John have for each other. Returning home after the case, they
laugh at the jumper and then kiss. For Sherlock, "the curious sensations I've
been experiencing since you decided to wear the jumper are magnified by your
touch." And for John, it doesn't matter that he is not gay: "'I'm not,' he said. 'It's
just you, you fantastic, insufferable dick.'" The desired slashed relationship is
thus initiated around an instance of handicrafting. The knitting and the wearing
of the jumper in this example is the means to pleasurably reorient the text for its
readers/writers.

Similarly, detailed instances of knitting tools and techniques provide further
opportunities for projected interactivity. In addition to the desires for characters
and relationships circulating in the fan groups, knitfics incorporate crafting
discourses into the narrative. In these fics, the handicrafter's knowledge and
skills are foregrounded in story. Sherlock is inducted into the realm of the
handicrafter when he is depicted learning to knit, and technical terms well known
to knitters are used. Mrs Hudson has "taught him to backwards-loop cast-
on," for example. Knowledge is displayed through the reference to a particular
technique for casting-on. As with any skill, there are many variations in technique
and experienced knitters know which works best for a particular project. This
is probably of little importance to non-knitters reading the fic (indeed, it may
even be confusing to a reader who is not a knitter), but the writer is clearly
demonstrating their handicrafting competencies in the narrative.

In other examples of this type, it is Molly Hooper, the pathologist at St
Barts who has worked with Sherlock and who helped him fake his death in
"The Reichenbach Fall," who teaches Sherlock to knit. In "You're Using Four
Needles" by random fat echidna,[9] Molly is depicted as an experienced knitter,
using double-pointed needles and knitting in the round. This is in contrast to
the learner knitter fics discussed earlier; rather than the amusement deriving
from failure and ineptitude, it arises in the conjunction of inexperienced observer
and accomplished performer. Sherlock is watching Molly knitting, a pastime she
has been using to occupy herself after work since Sherlock's apparent death:
"A difficult period of time at work concerning Sherlock's death had led her to
knit almost twenty rows every night before heading to bed." This reflects some
personal knowledge of knitting—the regularity of knitting a set number of rows,

implying a set passage of time—and the benefits of knitting—as stress-relief from the pressures of work with the presumption it can help the knitter relax before bed (Corkhill and Riley 2014). Knitting is also depicted as an act that carries forward over a period of time: "she picked up her knitting from the wooden coffee table on her right and continued from where she had left off the night before." Knitting is shown to have regularity—the knitter is familiar with her project that is easily pickupable and putdownable—and be part of the knitter's home life, occupying its own space in the living area. Molly is also shown to be an accomplished knitter, she has "flying fingers" and, as Sherlock observes in some confusion, is "using four needles." The character of Molly thus incorporates aspects of the writer's life into the fiction, as does Mrs Hudson.

The knitfics discussed previously present the female characters of Molly and Mrs Hudson as accomplished knitters, which fan handicrafters often are (or strive to be). This presentation of knitting as a female occupation reflects the gender split in the handicrafting community, with the large majority being women, but one fic does represent the skilled male knitter. In this example, it is John Watson that represents the experienced handicrafter. "Weaving in the Ends" by Freakish Lemon[10] depicts Watson as a knitter, having learnt in childhood and knitted scarves and hats for fellow students in exchange for drinks and pizza at university. Living at 221b, he keeps his box of needles secret from Sherlock until Sherlock's blue scarf is lost in the Thames during pursuit of a criminal and he (Watson) knits Sherlock a replacement. John is finishing weaving in the ends as Sherlock returns and tosses it to him as he walks in the door, much to Sherlock's surprise.

The scarf referred to in this story is an iconic knitted object from the series, which itself forms mimetic projects for the members of the fandom. Projected interactivity takes the form here of mimetic crafting in the knitfic. Sherlock's Scarf Pattern[11] was written by BlushingNewb (female, US) to accompany the fic "The Case of the Disparate Die Lots"[12] that she co-wrote with HiddenLacuna. Both pattern and story were created to celebrate the third season of *Sherlock* and the fic was (as in "Weaving in the Ends") inspired by the blue scarf Sherlock wears in the series and which can be seen prominently in publicity images. The authors thought that "Sherlock might just wear a knitted accessory … if Mrs. Hudson made it for him." In the story, Mrs Hudson (called by her forename Martha) has noticed that Sherlock's scarf is getting threadbare and she decides to make him a replacement, choosing the yarn carefully and cheerfully beginning the project. Her knitting was interrupted, however, when he faked his death and disappeared for two years. Martha abandons the project, rips it from the needles, then tries to repair the work, runs out of yarn, and abandons it again.

When Sherlock does return to London and reveal that he did not die, Martha is cross with him, emptying the waste paper basket filled with news cuttings of his death to show how much anguish she felt. This action inadvertently reveals the discarded project. The knitting is treated as evidence and subjected to Sherlock's deduction techniques. He recognizes how long it has been worked on—"the span of two months, judging by the fading of the colour in the sunlight," that it had been abandoned—"it's got other fibres on it, and there's been no further sunbleach, so it's been stowed away from the light since you stopped working on it," how it has been stored—"with mothballs, common practice for a woman of your means to preserve treasures made with animal fibre. Foul but necessary, often more reliable than cedar or lavender," and for how long—"the bent fibres around the…gaps…shows that it stayed that way for at least a year, untouched." He also reads what this means in terms of Martha's experience of his apparent death, his abandonment of her:

> "You knitted until there was no more of the colour you started with left. And now that it's used up…how do you even go on…now that so much is different…now that the pattern has been broken?" His normally-forceful voice had grown tight and drawn, trailing off completely on the question. Suddenly, Martha felt ropy arms wrap around her and a heavy head rested itself on her shawl-covered shoulder. Messy curls tickled her cheek, soft, just like a small child's. "I…am sorry, Mrs. Hudson." The arms awkwardly clutched her, but then they tightened, squeezing, before Sherlock withdrew to sit at her table once more. With his head bent low, he said into his teacup, "It looks very warm. Most comforting."

Sherlock accurately deduces it was a scarf she was knitting for him and reads the emotions that she went through, leading to an emotional catharsis for him too. This transforms Sherlock, giving the character rather more emotional depth than he is often shown as having in the screen version. Sherlock is softened and made more approachable via the experiences of knitting that are incorporated into the text.

This knitfic reveals the writers' knowledge and experience of crafting, as well as their feelings for Sherlock, expressed through Martha. Martha chooses the perfect yarn, "a pure wool in a lovely worsted weight from her local shop. The fibre had a delicious sheen, and it was both utilitarian and luxurious." Sherlock requires something with these qualities because his designer clothing is treasured but ill-used, she has noticed "the prematurely worn bespoke garments with some frankly alarming stains from dear-knows-what from the streets and that kitchen." Color is also significant, "The store only had one skein of Sherlock's perfect blue (not sapphire like that gem he and John had laughed over, but stormcloud navy) though they assured her more would be in stock by June." This indicates loving attention to the character's taste and coloring—the yarn is not just navy blue, but the exact shade of "stormcloud navy." This incorporates the discourse common in handicrafting culture that the recipient of a hand-knitted gift should be "knitworthy," that is not only someone the knitter loves, but that they know will appreciate the time and effort that goes into hand-knitting and will treasure the gift.

The mention of stock levels in the yarn shop is also a significant detail for knitters, and it is one which will re-emerge later in the story. Yarn comes not just in a color, but also in dye lots—each dyed batch will differ very slightly in depth or tonal qualities. Knitters are frequently warned to ensure they buy sufficient yarn at the start of a project, needing an extra skein later might mean a different dye lot and a noticeable difference in color from start to finish in a garment. The pun in the title of the story, a play on dye and die, thus refers to both Sherlock's disparate die lots—the opening episode of series three revealing multiple possibilities of how he faked his death—and the fact that after two years skeins of yarn from the same dye lot are no longer available. Having deduced the scarf was for him and identified the yarn, not to mention proving his knitworthyness, Sherlock buys Martha the additional skein she needs to finish the scarf:

> The nail of her forefinger caught on it, and she realized she was touching yarn. She grasped around it and pulled it from the bag, then paused in surprise. It was a fat skein of navy worsted wool, about two hundred metres' worth. It hadn't been wound yet, and the label clearly spelled out its brand. Sherlock had found her enough blue to finish. It wasn't the correct dye lot—it had been years, after all, and no doubt the difference in colour would show up … but Martha knew he would wear it anyway. She left the groceries where they were and went to retrieve her nostepinne, already turning in her memory to where she had left off in the pattern—row two of the garter section, if she recalled correctly. There were those irregularities she had left when she picked up her dropped stitches, but she realized that Sherlock would not thank her for ripping back to re-knit the errors. From now on, they would only be going forward.

The scarf thus comes to represent the new conditions of Sherlock and Martha's relationship after the hurt he caused her by faking his death. On HiddenLacuna's Tumblr, the scarf is described as "Sherlock's navy blue scarf of sorrow and redemption!" The emotionality of knitting is thus configured around the emotional journey that Sherlock and Martha make.

The fic is also notable, if not unique in some respects, in that BlushingNewb's pattern for the scarf that Martha knits in the story is available and can be knitted up by fans not just as a mimetic object (it features the alternating sections of seed stitch and garter stitch and the tassels of the on-screen scarf) but to re-enact the knitfic. This offers several layers of interactivity in the text. On the level of the storyworld, Mrs Hudson is already participating in mimetic production by creating a copy of Sherlock's old scarf (as is John in the earlier knitfic). Just as she is a stand-in for the Johnlock slash fan, she also stands in for the fan handicrafter herself. More significantly in terms of participation in the fan fiction community, the scarf that BlushingNewb knitted up is offered as a prize in a raffle for the readers of the fic.[13] BlushingNewb's coauthor also made a crochet shawl to represent Martha in the story. Although this shawl is not mentioned specifically in the fic, Martha is described as a gleeful knitter of all sorts of projects, but in particular, "she wore her own shawls with pride, judging them far superior to mass-produced store garments" (and in this way she is like the *Doctor Who* fan knitter in Chapter 4, who thinks a hand-knitted version of Amy's jumper is far superior to the original mass-produced one). The notes to the fiction stress that the shawl is "rose-coloured (NOT cerise!)" in reference to Mrs Hudson's line, "I should never wear cerise, apparently. Drains me," in the episode "The Great Game" (2010). It is also connected to the emotional heart of the fic in HiddenLacuna's description of the shawl as "a much-needed warm and loving hug (even when you've been naughty and faked your own death)!"

Framing this case study in terms of projected interactivity, "The Case of the Disparate Die Lots" can be considered as an instance of "community interaction with the writer, text, and character" (Davisson and Booth 2007: 39). While the positioning of the fanfic alongside the competition to win the scarf featured in the story is not "feedback" per se, it nonetheless forms an interaction between the writers and readers, constructed around an iconic element of the beloved character's costume. That this also provides a subjectivity for the fan handicrafter, both textually through the character of Martha and interactively through the mimetic scarf pattern made available alongside the fic, is significant. As Davisson and Booth (2007: 38) argue, this creates an identity "beyond the character and the writer, [...] the audience for which the fan writes." In this way, the identity of the fan handicrafter is made clear in the writer, in the text, and in the character.

Making capital

Through these examples of knitfic, and other instances of handicrafting tagged "fannish knitting" on An Archive of Our Own or posted in the I Made A Thing Multifandom, Multicraft Festival on dreamwidth, fan handicrafting is thus becoming more widely recognized within fan culture and archives of transformative works. However, as the prevalence of fic and role-play alongside communal activities, patterns, and projects on Ravelry suggest, it is already well established in handicrafting culture. The fan handicrafters on Ravelry may not often present their work in dedicated spaces for the transformative works produced by fans, but this only serves to illustrate the way in which fannish interests and activities are now just as likely to be found outside of dedicated fan communities as within.

This chapter has explored some of the ways in which handicrafting and writing intersect. But more widely, the examples given here illustrate the forms of prosumption practiced among the wider fan community. The writing of fan fiction, the practices of handicrafting, interactions between fans, fans' desires and pleasures, and the things that inspire fiber artists, designers, and dyers, come together around the archontic text. One further example illustrates the complex web of interactions that can occur. Kaye, a *Doctor Who* fan fiction writer, describes how her viewing of the program, her ideas for fan fiction, a gift from a fellow fan, and the work of an indie dyer combine into an affective experience:

> Christa TOTALLY MADE ME CRY by sending me yarn dyed by Nancy called "Burning Up A Sun" and it actually arrived to me on a day I was being a blubbering idiot while quoting that very line to her. I was spending the afternoon very productively by re-watching EVERY SINGLE SAD moment for the 10th doctor for a fanfic I have been writing and I needed to capture the sorrow. It was so hilarious and serendipitous that the yarn showed up on that very day, like 4 hours later. I'm not like a huge Rose fangirl (I'm a Donna fangirl) but when I was really listening to that line, "I'm burning up a sun just to say goodbye," it absolutely **killed** me that day. [...] Two moments in *DOCTOR WHO* that completely tore me apart that day (as I watched Doctor-Donna as well and cried as I always do when the end of Journey's End happens), in a lovely gift.

This example illustrates the way in which fan activities and affective experiences operate in conjunction with the commerce of handicrafting. A line of dialogue from a cult media text inspires a dyer who then offers her work for sale. This skein of yarn is then bought by one fan and gifted to another. This third fan associates the yarn with her emotional responses to the text, and in turn both are incorporated into her fan fiction. This illustrates the way in which fan handicrafting has developed its own culture and commerce. These contexts are explored further in the next chapter with a close examination of the cultural, social, and financial economy within the fan handicrafting community, and how this has in some instances brought it into conflict with the culture industries.

6

CULTURAL CAPITAL AND THE MICRO-ECONOMY OF FAN HANDICRAFTING

Much has already been discussed throughout this account of fan handicrafting on the importance of cultural competencies and, in particular, how knowledge of cult media texts is transformed into fan art using fiber and textiles. This chapter explores the ways in which this is also framed by knowledge and experience of handicrafting itself. John Fiske's account (1992) of fan cultural capital, from the concept defined by Pierre Bourdieu (1984), underpins this approach. Although Fiske's account is concerned with fan culture in relation to the tensions between official culture (his term for high culture) and popular culture, his discussion of fan cultural capital can also be applied to the practical knowledge of handicrafting that is circulated, shared, and negotiated in the handicrafting community. One of Fiske's (1992: 32) critiques of Bourdieu's mapping of high and popular culture is that it does not encompass factors other than class.

Gender is important in this respect considering that handicrafting is largely a feminine culture. Official cultural capital includes high art of course, but as seen in accounts of handicrafts as part of the arts and crafts debate (already discussed in Chapter 4), handicrafts—or as they are sometimes classified "feminine handicrafts"—have often in the past been elided in the canon of art. Yet as Karin Peterson (2011: 99) states, traditional handicrafts such as quilting has been reappraised as art (itself evidence that cultural artifacts can change location on the map), and fiber artists are now recognized for work that incorporates quilting, appliqué, crochet, knitting, and embroidery. Since the late twentieth century, there has been a movement toward art encompassing crafting as a medium, as Evelyn Payne Hatcher (1999: 245) outlines:

The eclecticism of the Post-Modern period makes for an extraordinary diversity in the art scene. The craft arts that had been largely ignored by the purveyors of Fine Arts are now displayed, including quilts and other fibre arts, even knitting, multimedia works and works in glass.

Female crafts such as quilting and knitting thus resist their location on Bourdieu's map much as fan culture does according to Fiske. Handicrafters, like fans, "are active producers and users of such cultural capital," and handicrafting "fill[s] the gaps left by legitimate culture" (there is clearly a feminist issue here in relation to patriarchal culture that subordinates women's and domestic work) and "provides the social prestige and self-esteem that go with cultural capital" (Fiske 1992: 33).

It is important then to consider the culture of handicrafting in general (as opposed to fan handicrafting specifically), particularly in terms of the tensions that might be created with respect to fan cultural capital. In fan handicrafting, cultural capital is important in respect of both elements implicit in the term, that is, fandom and crafting. The cultural capital of handicrafting is an important consideration, not least since the larger amount of fan handicrafting—and the community producing it—operates within the handicrafting community. Moreover, in respect of the fiber arts, economic, social, and also artistic or creative discourses come into play. With the latter, symbolic capital, in respect of fame or accumulated prestige, is also relevant, not necessarily in respect of fan status per se, but in conjunction with highly respected skills in dyeing yarn and designing patterns that take inspiration from the fan text. And given Ravelry's inclusiveness in terms of fans from many different and multiple fandoms and on many different trajectories of fannish behavior coming together, fan cultural capital is highly varied. This can of course result in tensions within the fan community, leading to the situations where social capital is accorded higher value than cultural (it is the friendships within the crafting community that count, not fan competencies) and where creative and artistic talent are the basis of symbolic capital (cultural competencies are often outweighed by crafting skills). This chapter, partly responding to Hills's (2002, 30) call for further work on fan social capital, explores aspects of cultural capital expressed in the handicrafting community in conjunction with the social, symbolic, and artistic capital of fan handicrafting.

Handicrafting knowledge and fan cultural capital

Given that "the accumulation of knowledge is fundamental to the accumulation of cultural capital" (Fiske 1992: 42), it is only to be expected that fan handicrafters with high levels of handicrafting knowledge are valued within the community.

Furthermore, knitting, as Sal M. Humphreys (2008: para 3) states, "can be included as a category of the creative industries: it generates economic activity and cultural capital." Creativity is widely expressed in the Ravelry community and many members freehand or make up their own patterns, many writing them up and self-publishing them (Ravelry's pattern database allows members to upload patterns and sell them or allow them to be downloaded for free through the site). As Humphries (2008: para 4) recognizes, "knitting and yarn spinning and dyeing are activities where there is creative input, design, and modification done by a large percentage of the users." This is no different for the fan handicrafters, who additionally express their fan competencies in their creative work. For example, patterns designed by fan handicrafters (which already demonstrate skill and knowledge of how knitted or crocheted objects can be engineered or how stitch patterns can be used to produce aesthetically appealing fabric) provide evidence of the accumulation of fan cultural capital. Handicrafters value the ways in which such patterns relate to the original text, and while many such patterns are free, they nevertheless generate fan cultural capital.

Several of the case studies discussed earlier in the book illustrate the ways in which the cultural capital of handicrafting works in conjunction with fan cultural capital, both communally—the members of the *Doctor Who* groups analyzing screen grabs and sharing their knowledge of stitch patterns or reference skills in locating patterns in knitting compendiums for Amy Pond's scarf—and individually—Rebecca's adaptation of a Fair Isle yoke pattern for her Paper Daleks jumper. Insider knowledge (and this also brings a degree of symbolic capital) can also be a factor: as Witty Little Knitter has having obtained access to one of the original scarves worn by Tom Baker in the series *Doctor Who*. Conjunctions of handicrafting skills and fan cultural capital can thus be extremely varied. A significant point here is the function of authenticity. This has already been discussed in relation to mimetic fan production in Chapter 4, but here it further relates to knowledge of crafting. These negotiations between fan cultural capital and handicrafting knowledge are illustrated by the tensions that emerge between fans' mimetic crafting of knitwear seen in historical dramas and knowledge of the history of crafts.

Historical and heritage dramas (*Downton Abbey*, Jane Austen adaptations, and *Outlander*, for example) have active fan followings on the Ravelry forum, and one interesting aspect of cultural capital at work within the fan handicrafting community can be identified in the discourses prevalent in relation to period authenticity in these historical dramas. For many fans of such dramas, accuracy of historical detail in representations of the past is not considered of high importance when measured against narrative elements such as plot development, characters, and relationships, or the aesthetic appeals of costume or set design. But some handicrafters (also) have an interest in the historical period in which a series is set, or—more pertinently with regard to filmic or televisual representations of crafting—the history of textiles and crafts. Some of these are informed amateurs, but others have investments in terms of cultural and even economic capital, they participate in re-enactments or living history, or they are historians, curators, or conservators working in academic and other professional fields.

Authenticity is considered by members of these groups in a very different way to that of the mimetic fan handicrafters. The concern here is mainly focused around what research into the historical record or re-enactment of the crafting methods as a form of living history can tell us about making and the made in the past. Cultural capital pertains to the history of crafts and crafting, and the record we have of handicrafting's origins and historical developments. With more recent history, and particularly the early nineteenth century onward where patterns and garments are readily available, knowledge is widely disseminated. Vintage patterns from this period onward are reproduced and circulated via archives such as the Antique Pattern Library and patterns are updated for contemporary knitters in books such as *A Stitch in Time* (Crawford and Waller 2008). In general, handicrafters with an interest in retro and vintage fashion, as well as re-enactors and amateur historians, value such patterns. These handicrafters, especially where they are fans of historical dramas and heritage cinema, might well seek out historical patterns (whether updated for the modern knitter or not) and craft reproduction vintage garments. Several publications also cater to this interest, including the *Jane Austen Knits* and *The Unofficial Downton Abbey Knits* magazines, and the book *Austentatious Crochet* (Horozewski 2011). The difference between these publications and the vintage patterns is that the former offer contemporary patterns inspired by the films and TV and the periods portrayed. Authenticity is not a key consideration, though they do recreate period details and styles. For those with a stronger interest in history, inauthentic representations of crafts and crafting in contemporary film and television become a point of tension in the community.

There are several groups related to historical and vintage crafting on Ravelry, and although these are not directly relevant to fans of historical dramas, discussion sometimes overlaps. For example, Susan Crawford's group (Crawford is the professional designer who updates vintage patterns for the *Stitch in Time* collections) contains a thread where members identify possible patterns for knitwear they have seen in historical dramas. There is a connection here between interest in retro-fashion and lifestyle (Crawford's designs from the early- to mid-twentieth centuries are closely linked to retro fashion trends), and this underscores links between style cultures and fan culture (it is related to the shabby chic trend discussed in relation to the *True Blood* Water Lily Blanket in Chapter 3). More significantly, this illustrates the way in which authenticity can be related to mimetic crafting and the ways in which fans seek to reproduce knitwear seen on screen by incorporating authentic designs from the relevant period. Crawford herself is regarded as an expert in early twentieth-century knitwear and has made historically accurate jumpers for the BBC's *Wartime Farm* (2012), a documentary that recreated farm life during the Second World War. In this instance, the production team were striving for period authenticity. Knitwear in other historical series may not be so period authentic, for example where costumes are designed for purely aesthetic reasons.

Interesting discussions around such examples of knitted costume elements seen in historical dramas, often with close analysis of the costume design, arise in both the historical and fan groups on Ravelry. The costumes in the historical fantasy *Outlander* (2014–) are a case in point. The series is based on the highly popular novels by Diana Gabaldon about a woman from the 1940s who is thrown back to Scotland of the year 1743 when she steps into a stone circle. The narrative thus incorporates two historical periods which the fans of retro styles and historical fashions might be interested in. There was already a fan group for the books on Ravelry, but the television adaptation attracted a large audience. This bought in a lot of new fans who had not read the books, many of whom talked about it in a newly formed Outlander TV series fan group, but also strayed across several other (non-fan) groups including Lazy, Stupid, and Godless (an adult-only group for handicrafters with liberal views), an indie dyer group The Unique Sheep, and Needlework News—itself indicating that fannish interest in the series was widespread. The costumes in the series attracted a lot of interest, especially the heroine's shawls, cowls, and mittens. A significant proportion of the discussion was in relation to mimetic fan handicrafting in order to recreate these garments (and followed a very similar pattern to that observed among the *Doctor Who* fans discussing Amy's scarf and jumper—see Chapter 4). However, the fact that the knitted items were anachronistic, running counter to our understanding of the history of crafting, meant that some viewers felt their overall responses to the series were invalidated. They could not take it seriously when the representations of knitting were so inaccurate and this affected their responses to the text and the pleasures they got from investments in the storyworld.

The knitted items that attracted the most attention, both positive and negative, were an oversized, bulky knit cowl (known as Claire's cowl), a shrug, and a garter stitch capelet. Members of the Outlander Fans group referred to the "pretty, pretty knits." Among the many comments made were: "LOVING the costumes in this show!!!:D"; "It has a very nice knitted shawl in it, geeky with black stripes"; "[I] have a feeling we're going to see some lovely knitted items in the show"; "I can't wait to get a look and start recreating them"; "the shrug had my heart beating very fast—I hope we do have patterns at some point—it would be just lovely"; and "Yeah, that shawl is flipping beautiful! I want to get some closer pics and make one." The oversize cowl caused quite a bit of discussion about what size needles might be required, with comparisons to other bulky knits on size 19 needles being "nowhere near as loose." Size 50 (or 25 mm in European sizing) needles are mentioned, with one member referring to something that large as "broomsticks." Some of the knitters were unaware that needles that big were even made[1] and others cannot imagine being able to even hold them. One states that she is unwilling to buy expensive needles (the unusual size and low demand making them so) just for one project. The desire expressed here to undertake mimetic production is related to the aesthetic appeal of the costumes for these fans.

This discussion is, however, interrupted by posts pointing out that such garments would never have been knitted in eighteenth-century Scotland: "I think it is cool that everyone is loving all the knits in the show, but I am a little sad"; "I'm disappointed in the knitted garments, not period accurate at all"; and "None of it is authentic. Sorry." These posters pointed out that "great chunky yarns" would not have been spun then, knit shawls do not appear in the historical record until the mid-nineteenth century and shrugs are not found till probably the twentieth. The problem for some is that it pulled them out of their engagement with the narrative: "I get all sucked in by a scene and then someone walks out in a chunky lace and cables cowl and boom, I am watching a twenty-first-century show in the twenty-first century." This interrupts their pleasures in viewing the series, providing evidence that their affective investments in the storyworld are disrupted.

Other fans interpret the text in a way that tries to make sense of the disconnect between the aesthetically pleasing (to a twenty-first-century eye) knitwear and the historical record. One fan who describes herself as a "costume snob" and has done "pretty extensive research" for eighteenth-century re-enactment finds a solution: "I tell myself that this really isn't 18th c. Scotland, but rather a parallel universe (where time travel exists) and someone figured out knitting (and circular needles)." Similarly, the fact the series is about characters living in a different time to the one they were born in is given precedence:

I remember that time travel isn't real too and that this is a fairy story after all. Maybe Geillis Duncan brought her twentieth-century ideas back with her and held knitting fashion design classes in the loft? I did notice her funky 60s hippy mobile of crystals and bits of glass.

Others think that the anachronistic knitting creates a historic milieu: "I think chunky knits may have been chosen because to most twenty-first-century eyes they look more rustic. Therefore more handmade and old fashioned."

Though historical knitters and re-enactors might still be annoyed by the historical inaccuracies, this does not put others off enjoying the program or the mimetic fan handicrafters from being inspired to knit. Among the comments are: "It niggles me a bit but not enough to spoil the show"; "As long as the costume designers know they are making choices, I'm fine with deviations"; "It's a TV

Show, not a museum"; and "It's really best if we just enjoy the show and let it inspire us to make something that makes us happy." These comments suggest that for *Outlander* fans, their fan handcrafting has status if it closely reproduces costumes seen on screen, whereas handicrafters with a primary interest in historical crafting are annoyed by the fact that knitted garments are historically inaccurate. The historians criticize and even reject the program because of this, whereas fans—who are more invested in the storyworld than real-world history—gloss over it. In fact, the interest in mimetic *Outlander* crafting is high (the historians who are unwilling to put aside their historical competencies forming a small minority). There are over 100 patterns in the Ravelry database that recreate knitted costume pieces, several other interpretive patterns are inspired by characters, and several indie dyers sell *Outlander* colorways, kits, and themed-clubs (including Bijou Basin's range of "Outlandish" colors, and the Unique Sheep's "Colours of Scotland"). It should also be noted that the mimetic crafters are not making the cowl or shrug with the illusion that it is historically authentic, but because it is a warm and cozy accessory, they can wear in chilly weather or when leaving the house on cold nights.

These points, reflecting both textual and historical competencies, are organized around three issues: the historical records of textile crafts and crafting; concerns about costume authenticity; and how to make the knitted costume items. This clearly expresses the delineation between history and popular culture in the minds of these knitters, regardless of their own backgrounds and interests. Historical re-enactment and vintage handicrafting remain significant factors for some, but for many it is the focus on objects seen in their favorite texts that dominates. One point this does illustrate is that there has to be a perceived fit between the strong expressions of fan and historical knowledge, and moreover that social capital is often quite significant. One member of the Outlander Fans group stated her intent to leave the group because she felt that the community did not welcome her historical knowledge. The discussion did not reveal any attacks on her knowledge (nor any personal attacks), but fans who liked the knitwear and wanted to recreate it were not overly concerned by the historical inauthenticity and just wanted to get back to discussing the costumes seen in the program. She nonetheless felt uncomfortable expressing her point of view, and one point this underlines is the importance of the social aspect of shared fan cultural capital. In a historical group, expertise or status in a historical field (such as doing research for re-enactment) brings symbolic capital, but the shared cultural and social capital of the fan group might not value this expertise.

I do not present this case study of divergences in viewpoint, which can result in some members feeling they do not fit into a specific group, in order to suggest that fans necessarily set themselves up in opposition to others with (slightly) different sets of competencies. But it does underline the fact that those with more intense investments in one form of knowledge over another oppositional one might privilege that set of competencies. As Fiske (1992: 36) argues, modes of taste and discrimination can be identified, and moreover these appear to be linked to social factors. Among those with fannish interests in *Outlander*, those closer to official culture (i.e., the historians, curators and researchers, often with an educational background to degree level and higher) stress the inauthenticity in respect of craft history, whereas those with higher levels of fan cultural capital (e.g., fans with affective investments in the relationship between Claire and Jamie, and the physicality and sexual appeal of the hero—in other words, those who are subordinated in Fiske's model by their fangirling) are not so much concerned about authenticity (at least in respect of the anachronistic knitwear).[2] Their main focus is simply on the possibilities for mimetic crafting.

Social and symbolic capital: The celebrity fan handicrafter

These debates, which draw on crafting knowledge to recreate garments from publicity shots or screen grabs, extra-textual knowledge of the production (*Outlander* fans discussed the costume designers blog and the work of the fiber artist Inner Wild who designed the knitwear[3]), and knowledge of crafting techniques and history, illustrate the tensions that can arise in the community. However, as Hills (2004: 29–30) argues, fan social capital is as important as cultural capital. Its significance should not be overlooked in fan handicrafting. The use of Ravelry groups is telling in this respect. The fans groups are used in ways that encourage sociability, with group moderators (those who set up and administer the group) and others seen as highly active or knowledgeable gaining status.

One thing that is clear from this research is that fan social capital is highly variable and does not correlate with handicrafting competencies. Some of the fans taking part in the study are highly active in fan communities outside Ravelry. WhoGroovesOn is famous for her wallpaper and bee scarves, as well as her goldfish art, in Sherlock fandom where she models her scarves at Sherlock conventions. Similarly, Ashley's (female, 30s, USA) amigurumi are renowned within the *My Little Pony* fandom where she sells her crocheted ponies at fan conventions. Voice artists for the animated characters have posed for photographs with their respective amigurumi ponies and patterns for her designs sell strongly on Ravelry. Both fans have high levels of fan social capital, but different levels of social capital in the crafting community. WhoGroovesOn is not particularly active on Ravelry, her fan activities, including exhibiting her fan art, are focused on her Tumblr. Ashley, on the other hand, has a high level of social capital in the crafting community. She is a prolific designer with many patterns in the Ravelry database, including Power Puff Girls and Totoro as well as generic toys, and has her own group in the forum, Nerdy Knitter Designs, with over 800 members. She has worked professionally with a commercial yarn company designing toys and participates in fan groups, including in Nerd Wars.

More widely, however, many of the fan handicrafters have low levels of fan social capital, at least outside of Ravelry. These fans participate wholly or predominantly in the Ravelry fan groups, some having been more active in fandoms in the past but no longer, or now merely lurking, others not participating in wider fandom at all. David, for example, is typical of this group. He describes himself as:

> an all around geek with fairly broad interests in popular comics (i.e. DC and Marvel Universes) and their TV/movie incarnations, video games (we have a Wii and I recently bought Minecraft for the PC), some sci-fi TV (*Doctor Who*, the various incarnations of *Star Trek*), supernatural TV (*Buffy, True Blood, the Walking Dead, Supernatural*) and cop/detective dramas (*Sherlock, the Closer, the Killing, Luther*). Before I started knitting, I was an avid reader and would read one or two books a week (because of the commute); mostly gay fiction with a heavy leaning toward mysteries, but also more standard stuff (the *Harry Potter* series, the *Wicked* series, almost anything Anne Rice wrote).

He considers himself a fan of these texts "because of their inherent ability to offer an escape from 'real life'." He does have a well-developed knowledge of his fan interests and possesses fan cultural capital—he has been as an active member of Nerd Wars on several teams, Jazz Hands (for musicals fans), Bite Me, and TARDIS, but he is otherwise relatively non-participatory, describing himself as a lurker, and has never been to a fan convention (although he would like to go to a *Doctor Who* one).

In general, David does not become involved in outward displays of fan cultural capital. He explains that while:

> there is a group for every flavor of every nerdery on Ravelry, and I'm a "member" of many of them, I don't usually participate in fan related discussions regarding a nerdery. I find the fan groups tend to speculate a lot about the direction of the stories and, sometimes, are a little more vociferous than I about their love/ devotion that I tend to feel I don't quite like something "enough."

This exposes the way in which fan communities—and the intense discussion that takes place—can work against fans like David. Where semiotic productivity is well-developed, but enunciative and textual productivity are comparatively less-developed, fan social capital may be low. Nonetheless, fans like David are participating in groups of fans and making fan handicrafting projects that can be considered in terms of material/textual productivity. David's singular fandom illustrates Hills's (2013: 143) point that semiotic productivity—which Fiske (1992: 37) sees as "essentially interior" and not therefore specific to fan cultures—"shifts […] into textual productivity in a series of (hybridized) ways."

David dates his fannish interest with "stories of the fantastic and the extraordinary [that] always seemed more fascinating than reality" to "a very young age." His comments suggest that his form of fandom is a lifelong affective investment that indicates a fannish disposition (Pearson 2007). But his use of quotation marks around "member" and measuring himself up against vocal members of a fan group in terms of that being evidence of how much he likes a text—and failing this test—are indicative of ways in which participatory fan culture might work in some instances against some fans. Other fans interviewed for this study had other reasons for not being involved socially, from one who was a carer for an elderly relative and lacked the time or resources to do so to social barriers such as "not being comfortable in large groups." These fan handicrafters might not be involved to any great extent in participatory fan communities but nevertheless participate as fans in Ravelry groups, and more to the point are fan producers. Some find ways of sharing their fan handicrafting within other social groups to which they belong. For example, Carol displays her fan handicrafting in her local community:

> I have had great reaction to my fan crafts. I showed them at a recent Lace Event. I also put items in the local Fair. The reactions from the Fair range from happy to "What IS that? Haha." There typically are not many fandom related items in the Fair … except for mine. Sometimes I get a judge who just GETS it. Sometimes … not so much. But, it is always fun to enter to expose everyone to the possibility of something different being displayed.

This illustrates how fans might find ways to confirm their fan identity and fan cultural capital through the sharing of their fan production with those who are not fans within the wider handicrafting community.

David's participation in Nerd Wars (which is both a fan and a handicrafting group) and Carol's at craft fairs (where the social group is her local community) provide "cultural validation" (Hills 2013: 141) for their creativity on the fringes of and outside of fan culture. In this way, handicrafting itself creates social capital. Maria Elena Buszek (2011: 1) draws attention to why knitting and social networking might be strongly connected:

> It is unsurprising that such old-fashioned, handmade images and objects should resonate with artists and audiences in our high-tech worlds. In today's information age the sensuous, tactile "information" of craft media speaks […] of a direct connection to humanity that is perhaps endangered, or at

the very least being rapidly reconfigured, in our technologically saturated, twenty-first-century lives—thus demonstrating the extraordinary potential of these seemingly ordinary media and processes.

Social capital is an important factor in the design of Nerd Wars, which facilitates team building and social interactions around handicrafting as much as around the fandom. Many players comment that the social side of Nerd Wars is important to them, for example with Kiki (female, 30s, Australia, partnered, full-time fiber artist) saying, "I had found my people!"

The sharing of fan knowledge also raises important points in this respect, facilitating the flow of fan cultural capital not only within the handicrafting community but also into and out of the wider fandom. Ravelry provides an important platform for the sharing and discussion of fan handicrafting, especially perhaps for the fans not involved in participatory fan communities elsewhere. The Nerd Wars teams are an interesting case in point. Some players who have fannish interests but have no experience of fan culture gain access to information about the fandom through shared documents on the "pages" tab for the group, threads in the group listing useful information and links to episode guides or program wikis. One member of the Brass Octopus team developed a Pinterest board where players could find steampunk images, book covers, and cosplays.[4] A player with less knowledge might post a photo of a project in the team group or thread and ask their teammates for help in finding a team tie-in.

In Team Impala, for example, the team captain writes:

If you ever make something but can't find a way to tie it to a challenge or back to Impala, just throw it to the team. Just post a "I made this, I need to tie it in to X challenge/need team spirit tie in, halp!" Impalitos can tie pretty much anything to any challenge, or make things work for team tie ins.

When a member posts, "I'm gonna need some help tying in a Captain Hammer[5] blanket square to [Supernatural]," she receives several suggestions (in addition to a lot of joking about the male anatomy): Thor's Hammer (a supernatural artifact found in season 8), the episode "Hammer of the Gods," Dean using a hammer when making repairs to his car, and the captain of the boat Sam and Dean investigate in the episode "Sailor's Ghost." This is an example of the "processes of verification" that require "a degree of expert knowledge in the relevant field of (fan) cultural practice" (Hills 2013: 141) and is similar to the mentoring of novices by experienced vidders in the fanvid communities that Hills cites as an example (2013: 141–142). The players getting help in the team group are often fans with high levels of fan knowledge who just need reminders to help them making team connections, but this form of discussion potentially allows all the fans opportunities to acquire knowledge. More importantly, it builds social cohesion.

The sharing of fan handicrafting projects, primarily through the Ravelry fan groups and events but also as Carol's experiences illustrate outside of fan communities, is significant. Handicrafters in general find many ways of sharing their skills and experience, designing patterns, writing for knitting and crafts magazines, teaching in local yarn shops and community organizations, writing blogs, and making instructional videos to share on YouTube. In respect of symbolic capital and celebrity, these handicrafters may become well-known content creators on the social web (as bloggers, making videos for YouTube and podcasting) or run micro-businesses to sell their patterns or yarns. Many of them set up their own groups on Ravelry specifically for their consumers or customers. A case study of a fan handicrafting podcast illustrates how this contributes to symbolic capital specifically within the fan communities on Ravelry.

Brass Needles,[6] the podcast by Miss Kalendar (female, USA), is "Devoted to the wonderous arts of knitting, sci-fi, steampunk, cosplay and random geeking." Even the title of the podcast has a doubled meaning, referring to needles as the tools one knits with and the material that personifies steampunk (as in brass goggles, which is also the name of the foremost steampunk online community). She aims for a wide audience for her podcast: "Knitters, cosplayers, sci-fi and steampunk enthusiasts, gamers, larpers and other people who might classify themselves as dorks, nerds, geeks, etc." The podcast thus differs from many fan podcasts which are aimed at specific fandoms. Rather, she positions it as a crafting podcast that crosses over many fan interests, but which focuses primarily on handicrafting: "I talk about my knitting [...] because that's what this is about for me, that's how I got into crafting and cosplay." She adds that "Brass Needles, my sci-fi and knitting podcast is currently giving me an outlet for my crazy cosplay fantasies and ideas." In episodes of her podcast, Miss Kalendar talks in depth about her fan interests: her core fandoms are *Farscape*, *Star Trek*, and science fiction literature, mainly steampunk, while the fan activities she discusses are cosplay and the fan convention attendance that goes along with this. In this way, she addresses herself to like-minded fans, and this may facilitate movement across media—fans might find her podcast and then be directed to her Ravelry group, or vice versa.

Many members in the Brass Needles group share Miss Kalendar's interests and have a liking for steampunk or *Star Trek* in particular. These listeners are then able to enter into a dialogue with the podcaster, as well as join in with other activities she initiates (extending the episode with members' contributions, knit-alongs, and competitions), as well as give feedback or responses on each episode of the podcast. The Ravelry group gives the podcaster status among her peers, but at the same time develops a sense of community among the members of the group. One important aspect of this effacing of hierarchy is that the fan handicrafter podcasts analyzed during this study—this also included

The Dark Knit and Geeky Girls Knits podcasts[7]—are not focused on expertise or the passing on of knowledge and skills to those less expert, experienced, or skilled (as are the handicrafters who film themselves demonstrating particular stitches or techniques for their YouTube channels). Rather the fan handicrafters' podcasts are about shared handicrafting interests relating to the pleasures of being a fan.

The Brass Knits podcast clearly differentiates between handicrafting and fan interest, being divided into two segments, a sci-fi segment, in which Miss Kalendar talks about her favorite programs, and a segment in which she discuss her current crafting projects. However, there is a lot of exchange and fluidity between these two areas. In the crafting segment, she frequently references the ways in which her fandom intersects with her crafting (including a friend making a *Star Trek* jumper for her baby), with several concrete and direct links related to cosplay. One of her cosplay outfits included knitted steampunk gauntlets and she wrote up the pattern for these to sell on Ravelry. Crafting flows over into the fan segment of the podcasts too, and in this respect, it often illustrates the ways in which fan handicrafters view programs with an eye on costumes and sets (as the *True Blood* fans narrow in on the blankets that are part of the set dressing). In early episodes, Miss Kalendar also includes guest spots from Gail Carriger, the author of the *Parasol Protectorate* novels, talking about knitwear in high fashion catwalk shows and how this could be incorporated into projects. This also adds symbolical capital through access to a widely enjoyed author with a fan following of her own.

There is also discussion of handicrafting for gallery exhibition in some of the segments. Several of Miss Kalendar's fannish crafting projects are not designed to be practical, but rather to illustrate the artistic possibilities of crafting and fan art. In episode one, she talks about an idea (or a dream as she calls it) to knit a period-correct Victorian outfit in its entirety, admitting that this raises a number of challenges. She is specific that it would not be for wearing—in fact she defines it as "sort of an art project" and "an installation art piece"—and recognizes that such a garment would be non-period authentic in any case, since knitted dresses did not exist in this era. She thus taps into the discourses around authenticity of knitting in historical contexts, but it also serves to demonstrate her knowledge of Victorian fashion. This is quite different from the usual conjunctions of contemporary technology and Victorian aesthetics seen in steampunk (her main fan interest), but rather highlights an improbable garment as a signifier of the tensions around fan identity, harking back to Mark Newport's knitted superhero suits discussed in Chapter 4.

Moreover, in discussing her binge viewing of the DVD box set of *Farscape* (itself indicative of a particular fan trajectory), Miss Kalendar also makes connections to the tensions between artistic desires and the practicalities of crafting for cosplay:

I've been able to meander through it at my own pace, maybe one episode a night, or a few more like five (coughs) six (cough) seven eight ten episodes a night, whatever I have time for. It's a great series for sitting in front of with your spinning wheel or your knitting. [...] *Farscape* is actually pretty cool because of a couple of reasons and one is because Zhaan wears this wrap throughout the first season that kind of looks like its made out of fun fur. So I've been sitting here looking at it going [...] it looks like someone skinned a Muppet, which kind of makes me wonder what animal that came from in that 'verse since there's all sorts of Muppets being used. Maybe it's some other version of Gonzo or Fozzie Bear or something she's skinned. The use of Muppets in there is pretty cool regardless even though she's got her Muppet skin wrap. I think that'd be really fun to make out of fun fur. It's probably woven, fair enough, but I think that you could probably grab your size 16s [referring to needle size] and twelve or fourteen strands of fun fur—I don't know, maybe three strands of fun fur, and just go to town and maybe do a linen stitch or something that looked woven and cosplay Zhaan. Although I'm never gonna cosplay Zhaan because that is a lot of makeup. I love the colour blue and I love her makeup, it's awesome, but yeah, that's a lot of commitment, that's a lot of commitment for your cosplay. It'd be a lot easier to cosplay someone like Aeryn, right?

This commentary suggests a train of thought involving patterns of fannish consumption (watching box sets in single sittings), the simultaneity of handicrafting and viewing, fan competencies (the extra-textual link between *Farscape* and the Muppets[8]), crafting knowledge (of yarns and needles), and the range of possibilities for mimetic crafting and cosplay (or its impracticability). In this way, the podcaster invites the listener into her life in an intensely personal way, and shared fan experiences can be identified. Moreover, this extract ends with an address to the listener—that, they too, will think Aeryn a much easier character to cosplay (she is human in appearance and her costume is a relatively straightforward military style).

The podcast thus functions as interaction between Miss Kalendar and her listeners, and this extends into chat in the Ravelry group. In the crafting segments of the podcast, Miss Kalendar encourages participation by making direct links to various craft-alongs and other activities in the group. Such podcasts can be consumed as stand-alone entities (without being part of the associated Ravelry group), but in respect of the fan handicrafting community and social capital, the dialogue is continued over into Ravelry group. Miss Kalendar hopes that fans will

[t]ell me what your making and what inspires you, and show me your pictures of cosplaying, show me the pieces you made yourself or the clothes that you

altered so you could be that character, [...] show me the pattern, show me the pattern you made up yourself, ... I want to explore what we [fans] can do, and what we can make and what we can put out there that isn't out there yet.

In her Brass Needles groups, she runs knit-alongs, competitions, and encourages discussion that facilitates sociability. One member of the group giving feedback on an episode says, "You kept me company while I mopped my floors and then walked a 5 km route." Such chat can facilitate a sense of companionship.

For example, episode 14 includes a segment on the Who is Spock? game (where characters on other series are equated to characters on *Star Trek*) and asks the listeners to make their own suggestions. These include Gonzo (from *The Muppets*) who is Barclay (from *Star Trek: The Next Generation*) and Joey (from *Friends*) who is Captain Kirk. But then a group member asks which character Miss Kalendar resembles, thus bringing the discussion onto a much more personal level. She declares herself to be Deanna Troi (making a joke about the fact that the character is an empath) as, "I am sensing that this lace pattern is difficult!" This illustrates the way in which the podcaster's personality and sense of humor—important in terms of the presentation in the podcasts and in attracting her listeners—is also important in connecting the group.

In return, the members of the group also provide encouragement for the podcaster, for example when she talks about never finishing a project and thus being a quitter. Among the responses is, "Setting unreasonable expectations for yourself only sets you up for failure." Another, her encouragement reflecting her status as a regular listener, says,

Okay, reality here: you are withdrawing from something that doesn't fit the way you knit. And you said, from the beginning, that you didn't know if the challenge was right for you! You're not a quitter—you're sensible.

There are thus mutual benefits in terms of social capital, with the group providing a close-knit and personal milieu more like a group of friends than a fan forum, as well as symbolic capital for Miss Kalendar.

This provides an interesting illustration of the way celebrity culture can be reframed in terms of fan culture (Hills 2006), extending—as here—within small groups organized around web content creators. Miss Kalendar's status fits within Hills's (2006: 102) observation that "the Internet has offered a potentially liminal cultural space where the usual mechanisms of media-industry celebrity cultivation can be supplemented or even side-stepped." Her knowledge of cult media, her collaboration with a steampunk author, her handicrafting, all position her as a celebrity, someone who is recognized within the fan handicrafting community, but remains outside media constructions of celebrity. What is perhaps more interesting here is that this differs from Hills's (2006: 104) point that recognition might be "non-reciprocal," thus creating a hierarchy of fans. Rather, many of the pattern designers, indie dyers, and podcasters among the fan handicrafters, like Miss Kalendar, incorporate degrees of reciprocity into their associated groups, thus eliding hierarchy. This, then, serves to create a sense of sociability and moves the member/celebrity relationship into the area of mutual benefit and potentially friendship.

It is also important to consider how some fan handicrafters in this segment (those with higher levels of symbolic capital) achieve economic capital alongside higher status in the community and celebrity both as fans and as fiber artists. In the case of designers, monetary gain is achieved through selling their patterns via Ravelry and for indie dyers by advertising their micro-businesses on the site. Fan handicrafters in both categories generate economic capital by encouraging interactivity on the Ravelry forum, both via their own e-commerce or designer groups and through fan groups in the wider community.

The micro-economy and commodified fan production

Fiske notes that popular cultural capital is not typically convertible into economic capital, though he proposes a range of exceptions. The kinds of material production undertaken by fan handicrafters might be considered among these exceptions, playing a part in the micro-economy of fan handicrafting. For example, vampire fans can search the pattern database and choose from over 90 generic patterns tagged as vampire related, with around 20 for *True Blood*, 15 for *Buffy the Vampire Slayer,* and over 150 that are *Twilight* inspired. Where not available to download for free (and there are many such patterns suggesting that an exchange economy operates within fan handicrafting just as it does with respect to fan fiction), these are available to buy for between $3 (for the Jardin Sauvage Vampire Mitts, for example) and $12 (for Dracula's Bride, a complex lace shawl). However, it is knitting materials and notions—especially yarn—that primarily contribute to a micro-economy of fan handicrafting.

Of more significance in terms of commodification then are micro-businesses. Peer-to-peer e-commerce sites (Etsy, for example) are used to convert fan cultural capital into economic capital by allowing entrepreneurial fans to sell handcrafted fan-themed objects, or the tools and materials used in crafting. Fan handicrafters make and sell knitting bags made from fan-themed fabrics[9] such as those shown in Figure 6.1, stitch markers and other tools or notions as examples in Figure 6.2 illustrate, and hand-spun art yarns. By far the most significant way that fans convert fan cultural capital into economic capital, though, is through setting themselves up as a micro-business dyeing and selling their

Figure 6.1 Project bags made from *Doctor Who*-themed fabrics © Brigid Cherry. (Acknowledgment Doctor Who — ™ & © BBC.)

Figure 6.2 *Doctor Who*-themed stitch markers, pattern guides, and notions tin © Brigid Cherry. (Acknowledgment Doctor Who — ™ & © BBC.)

own yarn. The volume of fan-themed yarn available from indie dyers underpins the thriving micro-economy of fan production and allows fan handicrafters with the time, space, and equipment to supplement their income or branch out into self-employment. This recalls Fiske's example (drawn from D'Acci's study of *Cagney and Lacey* fans) of the fan who gains the self-confidence to start her own business through her fan interest, and Sarah Thornton's (1996) examples of how subcultural capital can lead to economic capital through music recordings and running nightclubs.

Ravelry facilitates the micro-economy of fan handicrafting by offering opportunities for micro-businesses to advertise to niche markets of like-minded fans. Frequently, ads for fan-themed patterns, yarns, and sock clubs will run in the relevant fan groups in the forum—an ad runs on the foot of each page in forum threads and these are frequently tailored to group interest.[10] The owners of the micro-businesses select which groups they want their ads to appear in, thus catering to niche fan audiences. For example, *Sherlock* fans reading the discussion threads in the 221b group might see ads for indie dyer Gnome Acres (who produce the 221b Baker Street colorway discussed in Chapter 3) and other indie dyers who produce a wide range of fandom-inspired yarn including Nerd Girl Yarns and Soft 'n Shiny (dyed by Kaye), for Slipped Stitch Studio who offer monthly limited ranges of knitting bags and notions in fan-themed fabrics, and even for an *Outlander*-themed yarn club.

A number of different models are used for establishing and running the micro-businesses advertising in this way. Many such micro-businesses start out on Etsy (or its equivalents such as Patternfish or Craftsy for designers). Such sites are a popular choice, providing a marketplace (including shop front and sales tools as part of its package, the handling of shopping carts and checkout systems) and offering advantages to a seller such as a broad customer base—a fan handicrafter can search on terms such as *Game of Thrones* yarn, *Walking Dead* fiber, or *Doctor Who* stitch markers. Some micro-business reach the point where they have the resources and demand (having built up a loyal customer base) to develop an independent website (apps for checkouts and shopping carts make it easy for micro-businesses to produce customized online shop fronts). Since these are micro-businesses, often run out of the home, they tend not to produce or carry large quantities of stock (unlike local yarn shops, larger crafting chains, and department stores with craft departments and the mainstream yarn companies which supply them). Nevertheless, they can become hugely popular among fans. In some cases, the dyer's yarns develop a cult status in their own right and become highly sought after, with stock selling out within a few hours or even minutes of a shop update.

Nerd Girl Yarns was selected to illustrate this as it offers a broad range of popular fan-themed yarn. Fandoms catered to by Nerd Girl Yarns include current and recent programs with large followings such as *Doctor Who*, *Warehouse 13*

(2009–2014), *Sherlock*, *The Hunger Games*, and *Supernatural*. But the fact that more niche cult media are also included—there are colorways inspired by the podcast *Welcome to Night Vale*,[11] classic comedy *Monty Python's Flying Circus*, cult horror *Army of Darkness*, the canceled series *Firefly*, video games including *Halo* and *Bioshock*—reiterates the qualities of nerdiness that is conjured up by the dyer's business name. This is further underscored by other geek or nerd-related themes—science, art, hashtag acronyms, and memes (yolo, trufax, selfie, lolwut). The dyer Christa is highly respected for her dyeing skills and her sources of inspiration, making her business very successful.

Nerd Girl Yarns offers a large catalogue: 148 colorways of yarn and 84 of fiber on the day the shop site was surveyed.[12] This offers a limited range of in-stock yarn on the "Instagratification" page, the title signifying the pleasures of consumption and impulse buying. Handicrafters clearly fall into patterns of consumption observed by Juliet Schor (1991: 10), who defined shopping as "a primary pleasure principle." Indeed, references to stashes and enabling are a dominant discourse on Ravelry. Alongside this, the Nerd Girl Yarns website (and others like it) offers shopping for pleasure, but more specifically enable fans to purchase yarn which is exactly tailored to their interests. The full range of colorways can be bought as "dyed-on-demand" yarn where the customer orders and pays for the yarn, and it is then dyed specifically for that customer. Under this model customers are required to wait for the yarn to be dyed; it is delayed, rather than instant, gratification. The dyeing process can take around two weeks, sometimes longer if there are a large number of current orders. As suggested, the customers (who are often dedicated ones—they are fans of Nerd Girl Yarns and are members of the dyers Ravelry group) are willing to commit themselves to the wait (and to the small risk of having to pay in advance[13]).

There are benefits to this model for dyer and customers. The dyer does not have to invest in large amounts of stock, but more importantly the customer can choose the base yarn on which their selected colorway is dyed. Nerd Girl Yarns offers thirty-one bases across the weight range from lace weight to super bulky. This means that the customer can tailor their purchase, choosing the exact yarn and colorway for a specific project. Yarn weight can be selected as required for the pattern and the fiber content of the base yarn to give the required stitch definition or drape for the project or for personal preference (which may entail allergies to specific fibers). Different fiber content and combinations of fiber also dye differently. This allows for further customization and artistic choice on the part of the customer, feeding into Kelly's (2008) model of creativity. One-of-a-kind colorways are also offered in shop updates, attracting customers with the idea that they will have a unique skein that only a small number of other people will have. This again taps into the idea that handcrafted objects are one-offs and highly personal. There is often high demand for these, with the yarn selling out quickly. Indie dyers notify customers of when updates will be (to the exact time of the update as well as the date) through e-mail newsletters, blog sections of the shop site, ads on the shop home page, and their Ravelry group. Eager customers will be online, refreshing the page frequently, in order to catch the update at the earliest moment and "snag" a desired skein (again, tapping into pleasures of consumption). This situation may be counterproductive, putting off some customers who do not want to participate, disappointing others who fail to get the yarn they wanted, or excluding customers in different time zones.

Fan-themed yarn clubs provide another way of making exclusive colorways available to fans, such clubs contribute in a major way to the micro-economy of fan handicrafting. Fans joining these clubs pay an upfront fee (or commit to recurring payments) for a skein of yarn that is sent out every month or two. Commonly, the members do not know what colorways they will receive, but these reflect the theme of the fandom. Kiki (female, Australia) of Yarn versus Zombies ran a twelve-month long *Doctor Who* club in 2013 to mark the fiftieth anniversary of the program. During this club, the members received a skein of self-striping yarn representing each Doctor, one a month, though not in order of regeneration so the members got a surprise every month. For example, the fifth Doctor yarn, shown in the process of being knitted into a sock in Figure 6.3, consists of beige, rusty orange, and soft green stripes representing Peter Davison's Edwardian cricketing outfit and the celery pinned to his lapel. Nerd Girl Yarns offers Who's Your Doctor (*Doctor Who*) and *Warehouse 13* clubs as well as the Random Fandom club (where each month a different fan-themed skein is sent out to members, thus catering to the nomadic fans with multiple interests), these being released and selling out equally as quickly as her shop updates. Yarn clubs often reinforce the connection to the fandom by including small extras (a TARDIS needle gauge, for example) or in the way they are packaged. The yarns for the *Warehouse 13* club shown in Figure 6.4 were in sealed bags similar to those the characters in the storyworld use to neutralize the paranormal energies of the artifacts they collect. All of these points suggest that fan handicrafters exhibit similar patterns to other fan collectors, as for example when *Star Wars* fans queue for long periods of time to buy the latest merchandise release.

As Hills (2004: 44) also points out, fan culture, despite being distanced from commodification, is bound up within it. A "suspensionist position" can accommodate a both/and situation in which fans can be "simultaneously inside and outside processes of commodification." Some fan handicrafters are eager consumers. For example, David is a keen customer of Nerd Girl Yarns:

> I do buy fan yarns! *Love* Nerd Girl Yarns' selection of fan based fiber and have bought (for myself) yarn based on Narcissa Malfoy (from the Harry Potter fandom) and (for a friend and fan of *Walking Dead*) a zombie colored yarn. I've got quite a few NGY fan colorways on my Amazon birthday list.

Figure 6.3 Yarn vs Zombies self-striping yarn representing the fifth Doctor © Rebecca Spry—GenYKnittingNanna. (Acknowledgment Doctor Who—™ & © BBC.)

Figure 6.4 *Warehouse 13* club yarns in neutralizer bags © Brigid Cherry. (Acknowledgment SyFy series *Warehouse 13*—™ & © SyFy.)

Fans are aware that there is a paradox in buying yarn simply for a name. Jess describes herself as "a sucker" for doing this, but says, "If someone dyes yarn or fiber inspired by my favorite characters and stories, I'm a lot more likely to buy it than I am to buy a pretty yarn with a more general name." Nerd Wars also exposes this irony, players are not allowed to use the name of a yarn colorway alone as a team tie-in. Nonetheless, using a fan-themed yarn does afford additional meaning and pleasure to the fans as it allows them to express their affective investments in the text in their crafting, just as it inspires the fiber artists in the dyeing process, as explored in Chapter 4.

There is obviously economic capital and exchange built into this, and this does exclude some fans. Carol, for example, cannot buy such yarn because she cannot afford it, saying, "I have received some in swaps, and they are fabulous, but in my current situation, money is tight and $25 for a skein of yarn…is way out of my price range." Other fans simply do not have easy access, Samantha saying, "I tend to buy my yarns at [local yarn shops] so I don't really get exposed to fan products." Nevertheless, despite such barriers between producers and consumers, it is possible for fan dyers to generate economic capital. In terms of women social situations and financial independence, dyeing and selling yarn from home offer opportunities for generating income. Many of the dyers are mothers with young children who are not working outside the home or are women wishing to supplement their income while using their artistic skills in an enjoyable and potentially profitable way. In this way, micro-entrepreneurs can tailor the business model to suit their own needs and requirements. They can progress the business at their own pace and only expand if and when they want to. The business models used for selling yarn are of course available to all indie dyers, there is nothing in this that is particularly specific to fan handicrafting. What is different is the interaction between indie dyer and customer/fan base that breaks down the usual barriers between producer and consumer.

For example, Carrie (female, USA) was inspired to experiment with dyeing after being unable to obtain other fan-themed yarn:

I first started dyeing because though another indie dyer was producing the yarn I wanted, they were never available. That was a fan-based yarn: Harry Potter self-striping House Yarns, so even my first inspirations were from fandoms. From those first four yarns, I started to get inspired by *other* pop culture references. I've always been into the more macabre end of things as an artist. Yarn and fiber have been the mediums I've really fallen in love with and dyeing is another way of expressing that passion and enthusiasm. Now, when I see something I enjoy, I envision how I could make a yarn from it. It gives me a place to focus. And as a business, I get to geek out with my customers/friends about these secret things we both enjoy, as well as having a niche market—anyone can dye a Hydrangea yarn, but not everyone can research and apply blunt force trauma blood splatter.

Carrie's comments thus frame yarn dyeing as a form of fan art; as a fan of *Dexter*, she is remediating his role as a blood splatter expert in police forensics and as a serial killer. As an independent dyer, she can incorporate her fan interests into her business, but as a fan she can "geek out" with the other fans, not least those who buy her yarn. The sense in which the two sides are both part of a shared fan community (be that as fans of a popular culture text coming together or as a celebrity dyer with a fan group of her own) can lead to the dyer and the customers feeling as though they share the bond of the fan community rather than it straightforwardly being a commercial transaction.

It is appropriate here to consider the fact that the loyalty of the customer base can be explicitly tied to a shared fan status or particular fan interests between seller and customer, and how these might be encouraged. The independent dyers' Ravelry groups, like the podcasters' ones, reflect fan interests and create fan social and symbolic capital. GnomeAcres, for example, offers *Sherlock*, *Harry Potter*, comic book superhero, Tolkien, zombie, *Firefly*, and *Supernatural*-themed colorways. These she describes as "nerd flavoured," and she also refers to her yarn as "gnomemade." The punning play on homemade also facilitates a less than serious approach among the members in her group, which Rachel, the blogger who took her 221b yarn on a tour of Sherlock sites discussed in Chapter 3, is playing along with. Both Nemoidia (the owner of GnomeAcres) and Rachel achieve celebrity status for their blog and business within the group. Similarly, when Carrie dyed yarns inspired by each new episode of *True Blood* (which could be pre-ordered from her Etsy shop in the week before transmission), some of her customers would guess which line of dialogue she would select as the colorway while they are watching the episode.

Maylin (who, as discussed in Chapter 4, dyes custom colorways for Awilda's *Doctor Who* companions patterns) employs a different model to sell her Tri'coterie yarn. This is based on sociability in that she sells limited edition colorways, inspired by characters and events from cult media, only through her Ravelry group (though she began as an Etsy seller and still maintains an Etsy shop front to sell leftover skeins that have not sold in her updates). Customers are thus bound in to the dyer's Ravelry group, building customer loyalty, but also further breaking down the customer-fan boundary. Such shared love of the text between the dyer and her customers is indicative of Humphreys's (2008) hybrid market environment in which there is no clear distinction between social and commercial economies, they coexist in the same space. As she suggests of the social network market, the social matters here as much as the commercial and financial. Furthermore, the social network influences both production and consumption within the fan-knitting community.

One important thing to note from these groups is while they are set up as yarn company groups, run and moderated by the indie dyers, they are not focused solely on the yarn. Whereas the topics in the groups for commercial yarn companies are all concerned with yarn and patterns from that company (the Rowan Love and Red Heart Lovers groups were observed for this study, Rowan Love's members organize knit-alongs of Rowan patterns and Red Heart Lovers organizes a project bag swap, but otherwise the discussion is restricted to these companies' products), topics in fan indie dyer groups take in discussion of cult media and fan activities. The group associated with Nerd Girl Yarns, for example, is a very active one, with prolific posting on a broad range of topics and activities. The group has threads on "What are you watching?," "Nerd Girl House Cuppers" (for members participating in the Harry Potter Knitting and Crochet House Cup), "lolwut? ANOTHER GIF PARTY" (for posting memes and gifs), "Sailor Moon Mondays" for a watchalong of Hulu's screenings of the *Sailor Moon* anime series (1995–2000), a monthly book discussion, and a "Nerdy Octopus Brigade" thread for the steampunk fans.

The latter represents a unique form of customer involvement. Often Christa designs a limited colorway based on the current read-along. When the group read *Soulless* (Carriger 2009), there was a great deal of interest and discussion around their liking for steampunk and the concept of the Parasol Protectorate, a group of women in the novel who investigate nefarious activities and secret societies. The thread that continued after the read-along referenced the Order of the Brass Octopus from the novel. With the interest in steampunk high among these fans, and with steampunk culture already based around the adoption of a steampunk persona and "nom-de-steam" (Cherry and Mellins 2011), they formed themselves into the Nerdy Octopus Brigade and participated in imaginative play around the characters in the novel. They gave each other the Parasol Protectorate code names mentioned in Chapter 3. The members who joined in the naming before a cut-off date were given an opportunity to provide the dyer with inspirational pictures reflecting their code name. Members posted pictures of Victorian bloomers, brocade fabrics, octopods both real and mechanical, pictures of steampunk cosplay, patinaed metal surfaces, watch and clock mechanisms, steampunk-style jewelry, and dieselpunk aviatrixes. Christa then dyed up personal colorways for them, a selection of which are shown in Figure 6.5. This example of niche marketing was thus embedded in the imaginative play and affective investments of the fan (in this case, incorporating responses to the steampunk aesthetic).

Of course, on one level fan-themed yarn could be seen as primarily a marketing tool aimed at selling the products of the micro-business to a niche audience. Rebecca whose steampunk designs were discussed in Chapter 4, says: "I will also admit that I'm aware that steampunk is popular, and would be a positive selling point for the patterns." But the fact remains that the indie dyers

Figure 6.5 Nerdy Octopus Brigade yarns for the Exquisite Orchid, the Clockwork Muff, and the Emerald Gaiter © Brigid Cherry.

who produce such fan-themed yarns are inspired by their own fan interests and this was often a key factor in setting up the micro-business or selling their yarn to fellow fans. This reinforces the notion of the peer-to-peer micro-economy. Fandom and specific fan communities—and the niche fan markets associated with them—are already established as a niche consumer group. Moreover, they offer something that the commercial sector with its official merchandise does not offer, unique products, engagement with the affective investments of fandom, and the opportunity to own unique collectables.

The acquisition of fan-themed yarn also represents, for the customers of these indie dyers, an expression of fandom in the form of collecting. Handicrafters in general already have the concept of a yarn stash as a collection of yarn that the crafter has bought on a whim, received during a yarn club membership or picked up in the sales that they do not necessarily have in mind for a pattern. Collecting, undercutting the sense that this is an obsessive trait of male fandom, is an important factor here. Many fans are already collectors of action figures, models, and toys, and this is part of a commodified fan culture–culture industry relationship. Although collecting is part of the commodification of fandom, and fans are increasingly seen as consumers of material objects sold by the culture industries (Geraghty, 2014), for fan handicrafters this is simultaneously embedded into prosumption. The yarn they collect as consumers is also the raw material of their fan production, just as molding clays, paints, and modeling tools are for those fans building customized action figures described by Hills (2014).

Amigurumi are a case in point here. As scale models of characters, amigurumi are the fan handicrafters equivalent of action figures and models (though fan handicrafters do also collect authorized action figures and other merchandise). As discussed in Chapter 4, fan handicrafters often value the material objects they make themselves more highly than merchandise that is mass-produced. In doing it for themselves, they are not beholden to the whims of the culture industries. For example, amigurumi can be made in any desired form the fan wishes, without having to wait for the release of an action figure of a favorite character or character in a favorite costume, for example, or even in the absence of any merchandise at all for a long-canceled or less popular series. There may also be other benefits of such prosumption, with the fan handicrafter preferring to use up small scraps of yarn leftover from other projects (for reasons of thriftiness or environmental concerns), or to spend their money on goods produced by the handicrafting micro-economy (fan-themed yarns, for example) rather than on mass-produced authorized or licensed items. Or in the latter case, it may be that the handicrafter simply prefers to own a unique object made by her hand than the mass-produced one.

For instance, Hanka, a fan of original *Doctor Who* as well as the post-2005 series, is creating a complete set of Doctors and their companions, part of which is shown in Figure 6.6. She can thus set up tableaux of any TARDIS crew she desires; Figure 6.7 shows her amigurumi of the Peter Davison Doctor with Nyssa, Tegan, and Adric. Kati started making amigurumi when she wanted to give a unique and personalized gift to a fellow fan:

> I couldn't say how I stumbled upon the picture of an amigurumi Dalek, but my first thought was that it could make a fun gift for a friend. She has been collecting the murderous pepperpots for many years (and lives in a country where they are easy to find), so no chance with a commercial one, but a handmade Dalek would be new to her collection. So I looked up tutorials online and dug up some old yarn and crochet hooks my mother had used decades ago. It all started as a one-off project but by the time I finished it, I wanted to do more, and do better (the pattern was originally for a bottle cover I think, cool but not perfect), and never looked back since.

These examples demonstrate the ways that fan handicrafting projects can, on the one hand, be a form of collecting in their own right and, on the other, provide a way of adding to a collection of official merchandise that a fan already has. In terms of fan economic capital, handcrafted items can also have exchange value. Lotta (female, 20s, single, Germany), who also makes amigurumi figures of Doctors and companions, as well as having made several adipose, a scarf, and "10(!) Daleks," says, "I swapped most of my Daleks and Adiposes for DVDs of *Doctor Who*." Not only does this indicate that fan handicrafting can build status and social capital, it can be a form of fan trade or barter.

Figure 6.6 Part of Hanka's *Doctor Who* amigurumi collection © Hana Jaroňová. (Acknowledgment Doctor Who—™ & © BBC.)

Figure 6.7 Tableau of fifth Doctor amigurumi with his companions © Hana Jaroňová. (Acknowledgment Doctor Who—™ & © BBC.)

The micro-economy of handicrafting is at the heart of these negotiations of social and symbolic capital, yet this is not without its difficulties in relation to the culture industries. Yarn dyers and pattern designers who are building economic capital through their interpretive fanwork—this is transformative and therefore falls under fair use as discussed by Schwabach (2011) in relation to fan fiction—

are unlikely to infringe on trademark, intellectual property, or copyright ownership help by the culture industries. Mimetic and emblematic crafting can be rather more problematical, and this is a concern for some handicrafters.

Copyright and intellectual property

The situation described earlier can be seen as an idealized fan marketplace, one that exists outside the culture industries that positions fans as an exploitable market segment. Though the micro-economy of fan handicrafting does work in ways that commodify fandom, its business model is often designed to deliver the raw materials of fan production—patterns and yarns, in this case—directly to the fans. The dyers and pattern designers are fans themselves and interact within the fan community as fellow fans, their peers who are also their customers in other words. According to Humphreys (2008), the dominant mode of practice of feminine handicrafting has shifted from domesticity to commerce, so this falls in line with what may be happening in the handicrafting marketplace generally. Humphreys goes on to discuss how the issue of intellectual property for pattern writers can become a challenge. Her argument is focused on wider issues of publishing and copyright law, and certainly the Ravelry community is largely critical of any patterns being stolen or copied, but it is clear that fan knitting-as with other "poaching" (to borrow the term from Jenkins) of the cultural text in fan production-can be in opposition to the culture industries that own the text. It is the category of mimetic fan handicrafting that is of most concern here.

Two instances of what results when this opposition occurs are the BBC's action against handicrafters making knitted adipose and 20th Century Fox's against knitters of Jayne hats. In both cases, sellers on Etsy and eBay were the target of cease and desist notifications when each company licensed the respective objects as official pieces of merchandise (Woerner 2013). In the case of the Jayne hat, this embodies a disjuncture between the fact that in the storyworld the hat is handmade and unique, which the fans' hats mimic, whereas the official merchandise is mass produced, uniform and clearly machine made. The problematical dilemma for the fans was exacerbated in this instance because the program had been canceled after only ten episodes of the fourteen episode series had aired. It was almost ten years later that 20th Century Fox licensed a hat made by Ripple Junction and sold through ThinkGeek (Hall 2013). In the interim, the flourishing cult fandom, ignored by the TV network, had adopted the iconic hat as a symbol of their fan status. Quoted by Hall, the Etsy seller Ma Cobb's Shoppe stated that "it's the fans of the show who have propelled the hat into the iconic symbol that it is. The hat itself had only a few measly minutes of screen time in one episode—an episode that Fox didn't even air." The situation with the knitted adipose was also complex.

The BBC forced the designer to remove the pattern that fans could download for free from her website only after the TV company learnt that sellers on eBay were selling completed adipose knitted up from her pattern (BBC 2008).

The issue in both these cases, of course, is not the individual fan making herself or a fellow fan a Jayne hat or an adipose toy, it is that non-licensed producers are making profit from the finished items. They each illustrate that in the micro-economy of fan handicrafting, mimetic production can bring the fans into conflict with the culture industries. However, many fan handicrafters do see trademark and intellectual property protections as something they should respect, and they are careful not to breech them when it comes to downloading of film, music, and TV programming. This contrasts with the perception that fans are "poachers" stealing from the culture industries. In fact, this is not a straightforward position as discussions about transformative works and fair use illustrate (Schwabach 2011). Like fan fiction writers, the large majority of fan handicrafters make mimetic projects for their own use or pleasure only or to share with fellow fans, not to sell and make profit from. In part, the general discourse that handicrafters should be careful to avoid infringing intellectual property, copyright and trademark rights is related to the fact that many handicrafters write and publish their own patterns.

The concern around the illegal copying and distribution of patterns is, according to Kirsty Robertson (2011), creating a scenario in which infringement and protection are being increasingly emphasized. Robertson rightly points out that this discourse is heavily American-centric and is not based on case law, but "appears to be much more organic, coming from makers themselves" (2011: 88). This creates a situation for fans where, in some instances, mimetic crafting is seen as problematical. Ravelry does not allow charts to be uploaded to its pattern database where these are straightforward scans of images that the member does not hold the rights to. This has resulted in a situation where charts for projects such as a Firefly scarf taken from a 20th Century Fox publicity image of the Serenity spaceship or one with the BBC's image of all the Doctors for the fiftieth anniversary of *Doctor Who* have been removed from the database. Rightly, of course, this is the correct approach for Ravelry to take as a company concerned to protect itself from the risk of legal action. In terms of fan culture, however, certain fans at certain times might feel subordinated by the culture industries due to these prohibitions.

In the case of the Jayne hats, *Firefly* fans felt exploited by 20th Century Fox after they had turned the hat (which was in any case a commonplace hat design recognizable for a not-uncommon color scheme—it resembles a piece of candy corn) into an iconic signifier of the text and of the fandom. In respect of fair use, such cases raise a question as to the extent to which mimetic and emblematic crafting can be considered transformative works. Rebecca Bley (2009: 47) points out with respect to fan fiction and vidding that fans continue to include legal disclaimers at the start of their fics even though a legal precedent has not (yet) been set. Fan handicrafters similarly negotiate these positions with care. Lattes and Llamas, the designers of the Geek-along blanket squares, for example, are careful only to use logos and images that are part of the creative commons, not trademarked or copyrighted, or constitute fair use,[14] saying that their patterns "are carefully crafted to adhere to federal guidelines regarding copyright and fair use of licensed material." Furthermore, the designs on their squares are always drawn from their own artistic interpretations; they do not scan any copyrighted art or trademarks to produce pattern charts using charting software.

The fact that the Lattes and Llamas patterns are free also illustrates the gift economy that is important in the fan handicrafting community. Suzanne Scott (2009) argues that a gift economy is ideally suited to fandom. Indeed, the group swaps, sharing of projects and ideas through the Ravelry forum groups, and Lotta's bartering of crochet Daleks for DVDs, not to mention the fact that knitting is often for gifts for the knitworthy, all fit within the prosumption model of fan handicrafting. Scott also argues that the free exchange of gifts has with it the potential to evade copyright restrictions, though as the BBC's actions against a pattern designer who was sharing her work for free illustrates, this does not necessarily bring immunity. The situation within fan handicrafting is somewhat different and more problematical that Kirby-Diaz's account of fan fiction (fan fiction is generally not sold, either by the creators themselves or by others using their work without permission for profit). Within the dominant discourse on Ravelry that copyright and intellectual property rights should be observed, independent dyers and designers are also counseled not to use character names when selling patterns through the Ravelry database, even where these are examples of interpretive projects. Scott also suggests that the gift economy can create a closed social network, and this is certainly true of the dyer and designer groups where the owner has high symbolic capital.

Furthermore, other instances of the gift economy also allows fans to participate in charitable acts. The fan handicrafters making the Geek-along blanket also raise money for charity. The designs for the Geek-along squares can be downloaded for free on Lattes and Llamas website but they suggest that anyone making the squares make a donation to the Child's Play charity, providing a link to their donation page on the charity website. In 2014, they raised $1,215 from Geek-along members' donations and their original blanket was auctioned for $2000 at a charity event. These handicrafters find ways to create economic capital as well as build social and symbolic capital from their crafting, but this might well be in terms of the gift economy and charitable donations as much as for personal financial gain. This creates a sense of altruism among the fans. Moreover, even where the micro-economy of fan handicrafting involves commercial purchases of yarn and notions fans can feel that they are supporting their fellow fans to create successful micro-businesses. These aspects of economic capital thus work to challenge the relationship between fan culture and the culture industries, complicating the question of who owns cult media texts and in some cases rendering it negotiable.

The culture of fan handicrafting

The various levels and degrees of capital explored in this chapter form a framework in which fan handicrafting—the makers, the making, and the made—operates. Fan cultural capital is, in many respects, inseparable from handicrafting cultural capital, and both are integral to social and symbolic capital. And while these can work against each other on occasion, in the main these factors together serve to underpin the thriving material culture and also the micro-economy of fan handicrafting that provides pleasures for fan producers. Moreover, taken in conjunction with the accounts of fan identity, material production, and fan narratives that proceeded this chapter, this is illustrative of how the culture of fan handicrafting is distinctive in its own right, connected with but clearly delineated from both fan culture and the culture of knitting and crochet. As fans and as handicrafters, these individuals are forging their fan identities and participating in wider fan communities in innovative ways. Through online craft forums, blogs, podcasts, fan fiction archives, and social networking sites, they can showcase their knitting, crochet, spinning, and dyeing projects as fan art. This culture of fan handicrafting is one in which fans of films, novels, and TV shows are increasingly engaging with textile crafts as a way of reworking, reimagining, and transforming cult media texts.

CONCLUSION: CASTING OFF

In bringing this account of fan handicrafting to a close, I want to revisit my autoethnography for a moment. The account of fan handicrafting presented in this book is refracted through my own fandom and my own handicrafting, and I have interrogated those experiences as I have identified and analyzed many different examples of fan handicrafting and the interactions between fans (the social elements of fan handicrafting) that take place on Ravelry. I have come to recognize that fan handicrafting is not coexistent with fan culture as it has often been described in past studies, but rather is embedded in handicrafting practice and communities. Nevertheless, it shares much in common with fan production (it is transformative work incorporating imaginative play, fan fiction, and fan art) and other activities observed in fan communities (not least, chat, sociability, and communal events).

In summing up, I therefore want to stress that the profile of fan handicrafting presented in this book represents a group of fan producers who are remediating and transforming the text through their projects just as fan fiction writers and artists do. Through their fan work and social groups, they draw on their affective investments in the text and participate in identity role-play, even though fan handicrafting largely exists outside of participatory fan communities. The fact that fan handicrafting is predominantly contained within the Ravelry handicrafting community is important in illustrating the spread of fandom and fannish activities across the social web. I therefore conclude the book by discussing the findings in terms of what fan handicrafting tells us about a largely female fan community and thus feminine fan culture. This focuses on the implications of the findings with respect to our understanding of fans' relationships with fan culture, particularly where they exist outside of established fan communities, and for our understanding of the fan audience in general.

A number of points of opposition emerge from this study that might serve to shed light on how we understand fans and fandom in the era of the social web, one in which we are all fans now. The fan handicrafters do form an online community, at least they form social groups within the Ravelry handicrafting community, but they are not a homogenous one. Nor are they necessarily contiguous with established media fandoms. Some fan handicrafters are active in fan forums and attend conventions or other meetings of fans. And some are participatory fans, producing handcrafted material objects alongside other forms of fan production such as fan art and fan fiction. But equally, many have little or no experience of fandom—either online or in face-to-face situations. Some might have done when they were younger but they now channel their creativity and desire to transform the text into their handicrafting. Some are put off by the fan communities they have joined or looked at in the past, some would like to participate in the future. But there are no particular patterns of participation in the dedicated spaces of cult media fandom. What does emerge from this study is that fans on many different trajectories of fandom, with widely different levels of experience in fandom, and with varied levels of fan competencies, are actively engaged in a form of fan production that shares similarities with but is distinct from fan fiction writing, mimetic prop building, and cosplay or costuming.

The snapshot of fan handicrafting emerging from this research reveals that viewers of cult media and other popular culture texts participate in activities and exhibit behaviors that can be classed as fannish; in other words, they possess a fan disposition. What is clear is that the common pastime of handicrafting has been co-opted into the service of expressing and sharing fan interests and affective responses. While some fan handicrafters are cult collectors and consumers of official merchandise, all are prosumers of handcrafted objects that stand in for that merchandise. Similarly, just as handicrafting and handcrafted objects have become a form of fan production, the handicrafting community now stands in for the traditional fan community with fans often opting into the former and out of the latter. Moreover, this is often in the context of the social spheres of the handicrafters, rather than a specifically fan space. Fan handicrafting takes place within and without fan culture, but most significantly the acts of crafting and the material objects produced are firmly embedded within everyday life, domesticity, and the social situation of the handicrafter. Some fans undertake handicrafting projects for costuming and cosplay, for example, but the majority make clothing or accessories for everyday wear, incorporating mimetic (as well as emblematic) projects into their casual wardrobe. Some do not read fan fiction, and one interviewee even rejects it, though the material culture of fan handicrafting is clearly transformative work.

As the case studies in this book indicate, even mimetic production is subject to transformation. Material objects can be steampunked, feminized (as in Fem!Doctor cosplays), and hard technologies reproduced in yarn. Authenticity is valued in mimetic crafting, but not always in ways we might expect. In particular, the handmade is valued over mass production with fan handicrafters often deciding that a handcrafted version improves on both costumes as seen on screen and commercial merchandise, often in obvious ways that diverge from the original. Colors and designs can be imported from other examples of cult media for crossover projects (a pair of socks in *Doctor Who* scarf colors, a *Doctor Who* scarf in colors inspired by a video game). Moreover, all kinds of projects can work as narrative additions or remediations of the text. Projects of all kinds, however loosely they are connected with the original text, can be imbued with material-semiotic meaning through stitch patterns, choices of yarn, and the pattern selected for the project. Projects can even be given narrative connections to the text by working on a project while watching episodes, reading novels, or listening to audiobooks and plays. Handicrafting is at heart a creative activity and fan handicrafters carry this creativity over into their fan productivity, customizing their work in artistic and innovative ways. Handcrafted objects thus transform cult media texts.

Hybridity and fluidity of fan interests and identities thus emerge as a key finding in the study of fan handicrafting. A very small number of fan handicrafters belong to a single fandom on Ravelry and produce work only in response to that text. The vast majority belong to multiple fandoms and freely move back and forth between them. Events such as Nerd Wars facilitate these nomadic and crossover interests. There is a sense here of fluidity and a mixed-fannish community, the fan handicrafters exhibiting a wide range of the trajectories of fannish behavior that Kristin Busse (2006) describes. This also suggests that in the era of the social web, segmentation of audiences and responses to texts break down. Within the handicrafting community, divisions between categories of semiotic, enunciative, and textual productivity (Fiske 1992) and distinctions between fans and enthusiasts (Abercrombie and Longhurst 1998) are to a large extent effaced. This illustrates the points that Matt Hills makes about digital fandom's fluidity (2013: 130) and the leaky borders between material and textual production (2014: 1.1). Fan handicrafting is both material and textual; as material-semiotic production, it encompasses both mimetic and transformative art and both affirms and remediates the text.

Fan handicrafting also represents fluidity in terms of gendered fandom and fan practices. The large majority of fan handicrafting projects can be classified as belonging to the transformative/feminine categories of fan art and fiction writing. And while some notable instances of fan handicrafting can indeed be categorized as similar to the mimetic fan work of prop builders and thus the affirmational/masculine practices of fan culture, it is also clearly embedded in the domestic sphere. Furthermore, fan handicrafters often eroticize the text in ways that resemble the underlying discourses of transformative works such as slash fiction. Fangirling is to the fore when the actors and characters of cult media are discussed, and even when some fans participate in mimetic crafting for cosplay they might reassign the gender of male characters through crossplay. Moreover, as a body of work, fan handicrafting is not always respectful of the text; it is also light-hearted, quirky, and sometimes subversive (as with crossplay). This reflects the fact that fan handicrafting is firmly anchored in the culture of the fiber arts and the craftivism approaches of the knitting revival as much as it in popular culture and media fandom. Appropriately, the qualities exhibited in fan handicrafting—fluidity, hybridity, and mobility—are also the qualities of the materials fans handicrafters use—yarn and fiber, and in the objects they produce—the drape and softness of fabric, and the malleability of stuffing.

While I have focused mainly on cult media fandoms in this book, this was not to deliberately ignore fans of mainstream TV, nor to deny the place of fans of high culture and anti-fans. The findings herein are representative of a very broad range of fannish production. As Turney points out (2009: 3), knitting culture is not monolithic. This book serves to illustrate the do-it-yourself nature of handicrafting and the ways in which handicrafters make their own material culture, as indeed they always have. One important aspect here is that because of this the cultural capital of fan handicrafting is largely set apart from other communities organized around fan production. As discussed in preceding chapters, handicrafting and fan fiction intersect, as does the handicrafting community and cosplayers, but overall the findings of this study indicate that the large majority of fan handicrafters exist by and large independent of established fan cultures (though they are clearly fans, self-define as fans, and follow the patterns of fan consumption recognized by the culture industries in the era of the social web). Fiske's notion of a shadow cultural capital—whereby fans define their own cultural capital separate from mainstream dominant culture—would seem to apply here too to the way in which handicrafting produces its own shadow cultural economy. Matt Hills's discussion of hierarchies within fandom is especially relevant here. The fan handicrafters are, by the fact that they form fan groups on Ravelry, a handicrafting-focused community, placed outside of organized fandom, yet clearly they have created their own fannish social groups (and they also consider themselves to be fans). In terms of change brought about by the social web and the culture industry's embrace of fannish behaviors, they illustrate the ways in which fandom itself is changing.

In his afterword to Grey, Sandvoss, and Harrington's collection in *Fandom* (2007), Henry Jenkins ponders the question of whether fandom will any longer exist in a world in which fan tastes are ruling the box office, dominating television, and gravitating toward the affinity spaces of the social web. Jenkins (2007: 361) concludes that fandom itself was transitional, a movement toward the ideal media consumer. Fandom now is everywhere, all the time. The fan handicrafting community explored in this account illustrates one way in which fans are no longer marginal. However, the concern that the culture industries are now commodifying fan cultural production in order to sell it back to fans (Jenkins 2007: 362) is problematized by fan handicrafters' investments in their own micro-economy. The do-it-yourself forms of prosumption at the heart of fan handicrafting is still to a large extent centered around shared fan interests and largely unconnected to the culture industry's commodification of fandom. At its heart, handicrafting itself is difficult to co-opt in this way, since for handicrafters generally handmade is always best. What is clear, on the other hand, is that the fan handicrafting community is one that crystallizes the idea that we are all fans now. Whether on Ravelry, on fan sites across the Internet, on personal blogs, or at fan conventions knitting groups, and craft fairs, we can all cast on our own fiber fan art.

NOTES

Introduction

1   While accepting that definitions of "popular culture" are complex and cannot be fixed, the term is used here and throughout the book in the loose sense of that part of culture that is of popular and widespread appeal. Similarly, the term "cult media" is employed to refer to those texts with high levels of fan appeal and which develop fan audiences who are active participants in production and performance organized around the text. Cult media texts and cult genres are not in this sense oppositional to popular culture. They are not necessarily of niche or cult interest, though they may be. Moreover, many of the examples of cult media referred to throughout this book can be considered as popular culture texts in their own right. However, my focus on films, TV series, and novels with large and active media fandoms locates these fan interests within the category "cult media."

2   In *Harry Potter and the Half-Blood Prince* (Rowling 2005), Dumbledore reveals that he likes to read *Muggle* knitting magazines in the toilet, though like the Doctor it is not revealed whether he regularly knits or not.

3   Available at http://www.craftyarncouncil.com/know.html (accessed September 3, 2014).

4   The Ravelry site gave the number as 5,123,341 on March 9, 2015, available at http://www.ravelry.com/statistics/users (accessed March 9, 2015).

5   The collective term used by the Pythons for any of their middle-aged female characters performed in drag.

6   Available at http://www.knitrowan.com/designs-and-patterns/patterns/time-travellers-scarf (accessed November 26, 2013).

7   Available at http://www.clivebanks.co.uk/Clangers/Makeclanger.htm (accessed October 7, 2014).

8   Available at http://www.bbc.co.uk/cbeebies/grownups/clangers-knitting-pattern (accessed June 7, 2015).

9   Available at http://www.thinkgeek.com/product/f108/ (accessed September 3, 2014).

10   Available at http://www.bbcshop.com/doctor-who-official-bbc-fourth-doctor-scarf-/invt/dw4scarf (accessed September 3, 2014).

11   Available at https://vampireknits.wordpress.com/2010/07/25/vampire-knits-at-comic-con (accessed March 16, 2013).

Chapter 1

1   Available at http://imadeathing.dreamwidth.org/ (accessed January 14, 2014).

2   In fanvids, short clips from the series are cut together to accompanying music tracks.

3   In Toffler's account (1980, 266), the term "prosumer" was coined to describe conditions in the pre-industrial age before the Industrial Revolution separated the two functions of production and consumption. Before this point in history, people were neither producers nor consumers in the accepted sense; people consumed what they themselves had produced.

4   *Steampunk Magazine* adopts a retro-futuristic approach privileging paper and ink which reference the Victorian world and to this end offers pdf downloads for readers to print out if they wish. There has also been a small contingent in recent years of *Doctor Who* fans still producing print-style fanzines (*Plaything of Sutekh*, *Fish Fingers and Custard*, *Wibbly Wobbly Timey Wimey*, *The Terrible Zodin*) that can again be downloaded as pdfs for optional printing. These follow traditional print layout and format; it is the mechanism of distribution that has changed rather than the design. *Vworp Vworp* sells traditional print copies of its comic strip-based 'zine. The Doctor Who Appreciation Society sends its members a monthly newsletter.

5   The discussion arises in a post by obsession_inc on her Dreamwidth blog, available at http://obsession-inc.dreamwidth.org/82589.html (accessed September 5, 2014).

6   Cosplayers also rework or transform costumes, as with the feminization of the Doctor's costume, and steampunk cosplays are often original and based on steampunks' invented steam personae.

7   Data extracted from http://www.ravelry.com/statistics/users (accessed December 14, 2014).

8   I use the term "social web" as proposed by Tapscott and Williams (2007) since it has relevance to audiences and fan activities online. Gauntlett uses "web 2.0," although this term is not uncontested—see O'Neill et al. (2013).

Chapter 2

1   Available at http://www.knittersreview.com/forum/ (accessed March 1, 2013).

2   Available at http://www.knittingparadise.com/ (accessed March 1, 2013).

3   Quote taken from http://www.ravelry.com/about (accessed June 23, 15). It should be noted that Ravelry is a member-only community. Accordingly, many projects are unavailable outside Ravelry (this is a setting at the discretion of the user), as are forum posts. Since access is restricted, direct links are not provided, but they can be found via Ravelry's search facility if so desired. The patterns stored in the Ravelry database that are mentioned in this book can be viewed externally.

4   Generally, Ravelry does not delete groups since this action would also delete posts that would then no longer be recorded either in the forum or the member's profile.

5   Available at https://www.keepflying.com/about.html (accessed June 18, 2015).

6   Available at https://www.pottermore.com/ (accessed June 18, 2015).

7   Available at http://gallifreybase.com/forum/index.php (accessed January 30, 2015).

8   Ravelry is designed to be an inclusive site and it displays a rainbow flag on its header logo to mark Stonewall every year. A large number of its members are supportive of LGBTI rights as evidenced by the defense of equal rights during the 2014 Winter Olympics in Russia.

9   Of the interviewees in this study, four were men. While this number is overrepresentative of the demographic grouping, it was felt important that they were given a voice. Two of the men were recruited from fan groups, one was a designer from a mathematics group, and the other was an organizer of a *Battlestar Galactica* crafting game.

Chapter 3

1   It is worth noting that this feature of Ravelry belies the stereotypical image of the knitter by having this as an optional field on the profile page, locating handicrafters in the category of craftivism and feminist art rather than domestic femininity.

2   Available at http://whogrooveson.tumblr.com/ (accessed September 4, 2014).

3   Fangirling refers to extreme obsessions and emotional reactions to an object of affection in the fandom (commonly a character/actor, though it could be a plot development). These reactions (squee) often spill over into excess and are expressed verbally (making high-pitched noises or whoops, screaming) or physically (bouncing up and down, raising arms and making fists as if cheering, clapping). This behavior is associated with female fans (hence the term "girling"), but it can be observed among male fans too.

4   Available at http://knitdowntoharry.blogspot.co.uk/2007/02/introduction.html (accessed March 12, 2010).

5   Available at http://hogwarts-sock-swap-two.blogspot.co.uk/ (accessed March 10, 2010).

6   They are quasi-competitive because although teams compete for points, the only prizes are digital art badges. Handicrafters are often only competing with themselves to meet challenges, learn new skills, and give themselves deadlines to complete projects. Moreover, teams often play just for fun and not with the intent of trying to win.

7   Available at https://www.pottermore.com/ (accessed April 21, 2015).

8   The teams that did not take part were the teams for which it was difficult to find connections to dragons (the teams for sitcoms, medical dramas, Gilmore Girls, and Psych). This does indicate that in some instances the focus on cult media (and fantasy, science fiction, and horror in particular) can work to exclude fans of mainstream media, though there were no expressions of negativity in this instance. Players of these teams enjoyed seeing all the dragon connections.

9   Available at http://www.goodyarnguide.com/2014/08/26/a-little-excursion-around-londontown/ (accessed September 14, 2014).

10 This was part of the Books About Town pop-up art series by the National Literacy Trust in 2014.

11 Seen, for example, in Cath Kidston prints, Oasis's line of Floral Frocks, Laura Ashley limited editions from the archive, predistressed reproduction furniture, and the Channel Four lifestyle program Kirsty's Vintage Home.

12 Available at http://cosyliving.info/?p=1838 (accessed May 28, 2013).

13 This should not be extrapolated widely across the crafting community of course. The handicrafters on Ravelry and in this study come from all classes and levels of affluence, and choose their projects, materials, and tools according to their budgets.

Chapter 4

1 Available at http://www.marknewportartist.com/work/real-heroes/ (accessed May 13, 2014).

2 See Keiyla's Blog, available at http://keiylasblog.blogspot.co.uk/2009/01/cunning-jayne-cobb-hat-revisted.html (accessed July 13, 2014).

3 The site http://wittylittleknitter.com (accessed June 3, 2014) is no longer available though an archive can be found on the Wayback Machine.

4 Available at http://www.ravelry.com/patterns/library/la-veste-de-starsky (accessed June 19, 2014).

5 Paul Michael Glaser-endorsed versions of the cardigan sold today are machine-knit in a mill. These are sold online at Paul Michael Glaser Signature Sweaters, available at http://www.starskysweater.com/ (accessed April 25, 2015).

6 Available at https://www.etsy.com/listing/32335134/wonder-woman-bodysuit-pattern-bodysuit (accessed July 12, 2015).

7 Available at http://www.ravelry.com/patterns/library/cogwheel (accessed December 4, 2014).

8 Available at http://www.illusionknitting.woollythoughts.com/ (accessed June 12, 2014).

9 Available at http://www.spoonflower.com/tags/sherlock (accessed May 12, 2015).

10 Available at http://knitceterawhatever.blogspot.co.uk/2012/12/the-wallpaper-had-it-coming-again-chart.html (accessed September 10, 2014).

11 This is a term used to refer to a shirt worn in the episode "The Great Game" (BBC, 2010) that the fandom finds particularly appealing. On thesherlockfandom Tumblr, available at http://thesherlockfandom.tumblr.com/post/11270319035/the-purple-shirt-of-sex (accessed November 10, 2014), the reason for the shirt's status is explained ": Its most exemplary moment comes when Sherlock is examining Carl Powers's shoes in the kitchen and is bustling about for a few precious moments with his sleeves rolled, his top two buttons undone, and his blazer off, allowing the audience to see the full slim-fit pectoral-hugging glory of the purple shirt. Though all his shirts are similarly fitted, the camera angles in this scene, the length of the scene, and the colour of the shirt make it appear particularly flattering."

Chapter 5

1   Drabbles are fics of 100 words, though length does vary. Crackfic are short stories depicting unlikely, intentionally funny, scenarios. Flashfics are written quickly in response to a prompt (in a similar way to creative writing exercises).

2   Available at http://redscharlach.tumblr.com/post/19565284869/otters-who-look-like-benedict-cumberbatch-a (accessed November 10, 2014).

3   Available at http://reapersun.tumblr.com/post/10473458482/butts-im-sorry-i-choose (accessed November 10, 2014).

4   Available at http://www.ravelry.com/patterns/library/rosies-firestarter-socks (accessed May 15, 2015).

5   Available at https://www.fanfiction.net/s/10093578/1/Knitting-is-Hard, (accessed February 17, 2015).

6   Available at https://www.fanfiction.net/s/9948248/1/To-Interlace (accessed February 19, 2015).

7   Available at https://www.fanfiction.net/s/8394714/1/In-Which-Sherlock-Knits-And-Other-Tales-of-221B (accessed February 12, 2015).

8   Available at https://www.fanfiction.net/s/6556915/1/Mrs-Hudson-s-knitting-circle-gets-a-fright (accessed February 20, 2015).

9   Available at https://www.fanfiction.net/s/9203117/1/You-re-Using-Four-Needles (accessed February 10, 2015).

10 Available at http://archiveofourown.org/works/774281 (accessed February 14, 2015).

11 Available at https://sites.google.com/site/blushingnewbsknittingportal/ (accessed March 10, 2015).

12 Available at http://archiveofourown.org/works/1111458 (accessed March 10, 2015).

13 See HiddenLacuna's Tumblr, available at http://hiddenlacuna.tumblr.com/post/75766929877/blushingnewbs-and-hiddenlacunas-warm-things (accessed February 17, 2015).

Chapter 6

1   In fact, needles of this size are used for extreme knitting—see textile artist Rachel John's work, available at http://www.megaknitz.com/ (accessed August 31, 2014).

2   This is not to say that some of those fans in this segment do not have high levels of education or knowledge in history or the development of crafting. They simply put less weight on this or make a conscious decision not to let it impinge of their viewing and crafting pleasures.

3   The *Outlander* shrug can be viewed at Inner Wild's Etsy shop, available at https://www.etsy.com/uk/listing/159997025/the-caledonia-shrug-in-nature-greens (accessed August 31, 2015).

4   Available at https://www.pinterest.com/entendante/team-brass-octopus-tie-ins/ (accessed June 14, 2014).

5   Captain Hammer is a character played by Nathan Fillion in Dr Horrible's Sing-along.

6   Available at www.brassneedles.com (accessed September 17, 2014).

7   The Dark Knit: available at http://thedarkknitpodcast.blogspot.co.uk/ (accessed September 12, 2014); Geeky Girls Knit: available at http://geekygirlsknit.blogspot.co.uk/ (accessed November 6, 2014).

8   The alien characters in the series were created by Jim Henson's Creature Shop.

9   See the limited edition bags of the month at Slipped Stitch Studios for example, available at http://www.slippedstitchstudios.com/ (accessed March 12, 2015).

10 Ravelry only allows yarn- and craft-related advertising.

11 Available at http://www.nerdgirlyarns.com/(accessed June 1, 2015).

12 Such commodification is not always unproblematic for micro-entrepreneurs or for their customers. One or two indie dyers (not necessarily fan dyers) have taken orders they cannot fulfill, and such cases often become notorious on the Ravelry forums, including one where a dyer faked her own death and another where a dyer "died for five minutes" (see also Humphreys 2008, para 28). Reputations within the community can be lost.

13 Available at http://www.welcometonightvale.com/ (accessed November 19, 2014).

14 Available at http://lattesandllamas.com/category/geek-a-long/ (accessed March 12, 2015).

BIBLIOGRAPHY

Abercrombie, N. and Longhurst, B. (1998), *Audiences: A Sociological Theory of Performance and Imagination*, London: Sage.

Bacon-Smith, C. (1992), *Enterprising Women: Television Fandom and the Creation 252of Popular Myth*, Philadelphia: University of Pennsylvania Press.

Bailey, C. (2000), "Feminist Art and (Post)Modern Anxieties," *Genders*, 32. Available: http://www.genders.org/g32/g32_bailey.html [Accessed September 18, 2012].

Bainbridge, J. and Norris, C. (2009), "Selling otaku? Mapping the relationship between industry and fandom in the Australian cosplay scene," *Intersections: Gender and Sexuality in Asia and the Pacific*, 20. Available: http://intersections.anu.edu.au/issue20/norris_bainbridge.htm [Accessed September 23, 2015].

Barber, E.W. (1994), *Women's Work: The First 20,000 Years — Women, Cloth and Society in Early Times*, London: W.W. Norton.

BBC (2008), "Dr Who Fan in Knitted Puppet Row," BBC News May 14, 2008. Available: http://news.bbc.co.uk/1/hi/entertainment/7400268.stm [Accessed May 18, 2015].

Bennett, L. and Booth, P.J. (2015), "Performance and Performativity in Fandom," Transformative Works and Cultures, 18. Available: http://dx.doi.org/10.3983/twc.2015.0675 [Accessed August 12, 2015].

Bley, R. (2009), "RL on LJ: Fandom and the Presentation of Self in Online Life," in M. Kirby-Diaz (ed.), *Buffy and Angel Conquer the Internet: Essays on Online Fandom*, 43–61. Jefferson, NC: McFarland.

Booth, P. (2010), *Digital Fandom: New Media Studies*, New York: Peter Lang Publishing.

Bourdieu, P. (1984), *Distinction: A Social Critique of the Judgement of Taste*, Cambridge, MA: Harvard University Press.

Brooks, M.M. (2010), "'The Flow of Action': Knitting, Making and Thinking," in J. Hemmings (ed.), *In the Loop: Knitting Now*, 34–39. London: Black Dog Publishing.

Brownie, B. (2015), "The Masculinisation of Dressing Up," *Clothing Cultures*, 2.2: 145–155.

Busse, K. (2006), "Fandom-is-a-Way-of-Life versus Watercooler Discussion; or, The Geek Hierarchy as Fannish Identity Politics," *Flow TV*, 5.13. Available: http://flowtv.org/2006/11/taste-and-fandom/ [Accessed October 10, 2009].

Busse, K. (2013), "Geek Hierarchies, Boundary Policing, and the Gendering of the Good Fan," *Participations: Journal of Audience and Reception Studies*, 10.1: 73–91.

Buszek, M.E. (2011), "Introduction," in M.E. Buszek (ed.), *Extra/Ordinary: Craft and Contemporary Art*, 1–22. Durham, NC: Duke University Press.

Carriger, G. (2009), *Blameless*, London: Orbit.

Carriger, G. (2009), *Heartless*, London: Orbit.

Carriger, G. (2009), *Soulless*, London: Orbit.

Carriger, G. (2009), *Timeless*, London: Orbit.

Carriger, G. (2010), *Changeless*, London: Orbit.

Carrott, J. and Johnson, B. (2013), *Vintage Tomorrows: A Historian And A Futurist Journey Through Steampunk Into The Future of Technology*, Sebastopol, CA: O'Reilly Media.

Chander, A. and Sunder, M. (2007), "Everyone's a Superhero: A Cultural Theory of 'Mary Sue' Fan Fiction as Fair Use," *California Law Review*, 95.2: 597–626.

Cherry, B. (2001), "Refusing to Refuse to Look: Female Viewers of the Horror Film," in M. Jancovich (ed.), *Horror: The Film Reader*, 169–178. Abingdon: Routledge.

Cherry, B. (2010), "Squee, Retcon, Fanwank, and the Not-We: Computer Mediated Discourses and Online Chat About NuWho," in C. Hanson (ed.), *Ruminations, Peregrinations, and Regenerations: A Critical Approach to Doctor Who*, 209–232. Newcastle upon Tyne: Cambridge Scholars.

Cherry, B. (2011), "Knit One, Bite One: Vampire Fandom, Fan Production and Feminine Handicrafts," in G. Schott and K. Moffat (eds), *Fanpires: Audience Consumption of the Modern Vampire*, 137–156. Washington, DC: New Academia.

Cherry, B. (2013), "Extermi…Knit!: Female Fans and Feminine Handicrafting," in P. Booth (ed.), *Doctor Who: Fan Phenomena*, 106–115. Bristol: Intellect.

Cherry, B. and Mellins, M. (2011), "Negotiating the Punk in Steampunk: Subculture, Fashion & Performative Identity," *Punk and Post-Punk Journal,* 1.1: 5–25.

Clarke, A. M. (2010) "Introduction: Approaching Twilight," in A.M. Clarke and M. Osborn (eds), *The Twilight Mystique: Critical Essays on the Novels and Films*, 3–14. Jefferson, NC: McFarland.

Classen, C. (1998), *The Colour of Angels: Cosmology, Gender and the Aesthetic Imagination*, Abingdon: Routledge.

Coppa, F. (2007), "Gender and Fan Culture (Wrapping Up, Part Four)," *Confessions of an Aca-Fan: The Official Weblog of Henry Jenkins*, November 28. Available: http://henryjenkins.org/2007/11/gender_and_fan_culture_wrappin_2.html [Accessed September 19, 2010].

Coppa, F. (2008), "Women, Star Trek, and the Early Development of Fannish Vidding," *Transformative Works and Cultures*, 1. Available: http://journal.transformativeworks.org/index.php/twc/article/view/44 [Accessed October 4, 2010].

Corkhill, B. and Riley, J. (2014), "Knitting for Well-being: Psychological and Social Benefits of Hand Knitting," *Textile*, 12.1: 36–43.

Crawford, S. and Waller, J. (2008), *A Stitch in Time: Vintage Knitting and Crochet Patterns 1920–1949*, Wigan: Arbour House Publishing.

Davisson, A. and Booth, P. (2007), "Reconceptualizing Communication and Agency in Fan Activity: A Proposal for a Projected Interactivity Model for Fan Studies," *Texas Speech Communication Journal*, 23.1: 33–43.

de Certeau, M. (1980/2011), *The Practice of Everyday Life*, Trans. Steven Rendall, Oakland: University of California Press.

Derecho, A. (2006), "Archontic Literature: A Definition, A History, and Several Theories of Fan Fiction," in K. Hellekson and K. Busse (eds), *Fan Fiction and Fan Communities in the Age of the Internet*, 61–78. Jefferson, NC: McFarland.

Dirix, E. (2014), "Stitched Up—Representations of Contemporary Vintage Style Media and the Dark Side of the Popular Knitting Revival," *Textiles*, 12.1, 86–99.

Doyle, J. and Karl, I. (2012), "Shame on You: Cosmetic Surgery and Class Transformation in *10 Years Younger*," in G. Palmer (ed.), *Exposing Lifestyle Television: The Big Reveal*, 83–100. Aldershot: Ashgate.

Falero, S.M. (2008), "Fanzines," in H. Sheumaker and S.T. Wajda (eds), *Material Culture in America: Understanding Everyday Life*, 187–188. Santa Barbara, CA: ABC-CLIO.

Fiske, J. (1992), "The Cultural Economy of Fandom," in L.A. Lewis (ed.), *The Adoring Audience: Fan Culture and Popular Media*, 30–49. Abingdon: Routledge.

Gabaldon, D. (1991), *Outlander*, London: Arrow Books.

Gammon, J. (1984), *The Doctor Who Pattern Book*, London: BBC.

Gauntlett, D. (2011), *Making is Connecting: The Social Meaning of Creativity, from DIY and Knitting to YouTube and Web 2.0*, Cambridge: Polity.

Gee, J. (2003), *What Video Games Have to Teach Us About Learning and Literacy*, New York: Palgrave Macmillan.

Geraghty, L. (2014), *Cult Collectors: Nostalgia, Fandom and Collecting Popular Culture*, Abingdon: Routledge.

Goffman, E. (1959), *The Presentation of Self in Everyday Life*, New York: Doubleday.

Goulding, C. (2015), "Corsets, Silk Stockings and Evening Suits: Retro Shops and Retro Junkies," in S. Brown and J.F. Sherry Jr (eds), *Time, Space and the Market: Retroscapes Rising*, 54–74. Abingdon: Routledge.

Hale, M. (2013), "Airship Captains, Pith Helmets and Other Assorted Brassy Bits: Steampunk Personas and Material-Semiotic Production," *New Directions in Folklore*, 11.1: 3–34.

Hall, E. (2013), "Firefly Hat Triggers Corporate Crackdown," *BuzzFeedNews*, April 10. Available: http://www.buzzfeed.com/ellievhall/firefly-hat-triggers-corporate-crackdown [Accessed May 20, 2015].

Halls, J. (2014), *Inventions That Didn't Change the World*, London: Thames and Hudson.

Halnon, K.B. (2009), "Poor Chic: The Rational Consumption of Poverty," *Current Sociology*, 50.4: 501–516.

Hansel, A. (2007), *Charmed Knits: Projects for Fans of Harry Potter*, Hoboken, NJ: Wiley Publishing.

Hatcher, E.P. (1999), *Art as Culture: An Introduction to the Anthropology of Art*, Santa Barbara: Greenwood Publishing Group

Hellekson, K. and Busse, K. (2006), *Fan Fiction and Fan Communities in the Age of the Internet*, Jefferson, NC: McFarland.

Hellekson, K. and Busse, K. (2014), *The Fan Fiction Studies Reader*, Iowa City: University of Iowa Press.

Hemmings, J. (2010), "Rethinking Knitting," in J. Hemmings (ed.), *In the Loop: Knitting Now*, 8–9. London: Black Dog Publishing.

Hills, M. (2004), *Fan Cultures*, Abingdon: Routledge.

Hills, M. (2006), "Not Just Another Powerless Elite?: When Media Fans Become Subcultural Celebrities," in S. Holmes and S. Redmond (eds), *Framing Celebrity: New Directions in Celebrity Culture*, 101–118. Abingdon: Routledge.

Hills, M. (2009), "Participatory Culture: Mobility, Interactivity and Identity," in G. Creeber and R. Martin (eds), *Digital Culture: Understanding New Media*, 107–121. Maidenhead: Open University Press.

Hills, M. (2010), "As Seen on Screen? Mimetic SF Fandom and the Crafting of Replica(nt)s," *In Media Res*, September. Available: http://mediacommons.futureofthebook.org/imr/2010/09/10/seen-screen-mimetic-sf-fandom-crafting-replicants [Accessed July 19, 2013].

Hills, M. (2013), "Fiske's 'Textual Productivity' and Digital Fandom: Web 2.0 Democratization versus Fan Distinction?," *Participations: Journal of Audience and Reception Studies*, 10.1: 130–153.

Hills, M. (2014), "From Dalek Half Balls to Daft Punk Helmets: Mimetic Fandom and the Crafting of Replicas," *Transformative Works and Cultures*, 16. Available: http://dx.doi. org/10.3983/twc.2014.0531 [Accessed January 14, 2015].

Horozewski, M. (2011), *Austentatious Crochet: 36 Contemporary Designs From the World of Jane Austen*, Philadelphia: Running Press.

Humphreys, S.M. (2008), "The Challenges of Intellectual Property for Users of Social Networking Sites: a Case Study of Ravelry," *Proceedings Mind Trek*. Available: http:// eprints.qut.edu.au/14858/ [Accessed November 19, 2011].

Jenkins, H. (1992/2013), Textual Poachers: Television Fans and Participatory Culture, Abingdon: Routledge.

Jenkins, H. (2007), "Afterword: The Future of Fandom," in J.A. Grey, C. Sandvoss and L. Harrington (eds), *Fandom: Identities and Communities in a Mediated World*, 357–364. New York: New York University Press.

Jenkins, H. (2010), "Fandom, Participatory Culture and Web 2.0," *Confessions of an Aca/Fan: The Official Weblog of Henry Jenkins*. Available: http://henryjenkins. org/2010/01/fandom_participatory_culture_a.html [Accessed March 9, 2011].

Jenkins, H. (2012), "Cultural acupuncture: Fan activism and the Harry Potter alliance" *Transformative Works and Cultures*. Available: http://dx.doi.org/10.3983/ twc.2012.0305 [Accessed January 22, 2015].

Jensen, J. (2002), *Is Art Good For Us?: Beliefs About High Culture in American Life*, Lanham, MD: Rowman & Littlefield.

Johnston, J.E. (2015), "Doctor Who—Themed Weddings and the Performance of Fandom, Transformative Works and Cultures," 18. Available: http://dx.doi. org/10.3983/twc.2015.0637 [Accessed August 23, 2015].

Jones, B. (2014), "Written on the Body: Experiencing Affect and Identity in My Fannish Tattoos," Transformative Works and Cultures, 16. Available: http://dx.doi. org/10.3983/twc.2013.0527 [Accessed May 17, 2015].

Kelly, M. (2008), "Knitting as a Feminist Project? Untangling the Contradictions of the 'New Knitting' Movement," *Proceedings of the American Sociological Association Annual Meeting*, July 31. Available: http://www.allacademic.com/meta/p241231_ index.html [Accessed August 26, 2012].

Kimmel, M.S. (1997), "The Power of Gender and the Gender of Power," K. Martinez and K.L. Ames (eds), *The Material Culture of Gender, the Gender of Material Culture*, 1–6. Winterthur: Henry Francis du Pont Winterthur Museum.

Kirby-Diaz, M. (2013), "Ficcers and Shippers: A Love Story," in J.K. Stuller (ed.), *Fan Phenomena: Buffy the Vampire Slayer*, 38–51. Bristol: Intellect Books.

Kokko, S. (2012), "Learning Crafts as Practices of Masculinity: Finnish Male Trainee Teachers' Reflections and Experiences," *Gender and Education*, 24.2: 177–193.

Kustritz, A. (2003), "Slashing the Romance Narrative," *Journal of American Culture*, 26: 371–386.

Lamerichs, N. (2011), "Stranger than Fiction: Fan Identity in Cosplay," *Transformative Works and Cultures*, 7. Available: doi:10.3983/twc.2011.0246 [Accessed May 19, 2012].

Lamerichs, N. (2014a), "Cosplay: Material and Transmedial Culture in Play," *DeFragging Game Studies*, 7. Available: http://www.digra.org/digital-library/ publications/cosplay-material-and-transmedial-culture-in-play/ [Accessed March 22, 2015].

Lamerichs, N. (2014b), "Costuming as Subculture: The Multiple Bodies in Cosplay," *Scene*, 2.1: 113–125.

Lamerichs, N. (2015), "Express Yourself: An Affective Analysis of Game Cosplayers," in J. Enevold and E. MacCallum-Stewart (eds), *Game Love: Essays on Play and Affection*, 97–114. Jefferson, NC: McFarland.

Larson, G.O. (1997), *American Canvas*, Washington, DC: NEA.

Lister, M., Dovey, J., Giddings, S., Grant, I. and Kelly, K. (2009), *New Media: A Critical Introduction*, Abingdon: Routledge.

M, S. (2008), *Lamia*, unknown: Smiling Goth.

Macheski, C. (1992), "'Some Classic Pattern': Pens and Needles on the Home Front," in M.P. Holsinger and M.A. Scholfield (eds), *Visions of War: World War II in Popular Literature and Culture*, 170–180. Madison: University of Wisconsin Press.

Manovich, L. (2009), "The Practice of Everyday (Media) Life: From Mass Consumption to Mass Cultural Production," *Critical Inquiry*, 35.2: 319–331.

Matchar, E. (2013), *Homeward Bound: Why Women are Embracing the New Domesticity*, New York: Simon & Schuster.

Mellins, M. (2013), *Vampire Culture*, London: Bloomsbury.

Meyer, S (2005), *Twilight*, London: Atom.

Miller, G. (2010), *Vampire Knits*, New York: Potter Crafts.

Minahan, S. and Wolfram Cox, J. (2007), "Stitch 'n Bitch: Cyberfeminism, a Third Place and the New Materiality," *Journal of Material Culture*, 12.1: 5–21.

Myzelev, A. (2009), "Whip Your Hobby into Shape: Knitting, Feminism and Construction of Gender," *Textile*, 7.2: 148–163.

Newington, L. (2010), "Knitting Has an Image Problem," in J. Hemmings (ed.), *In the Loop: Knitting Now*, 26–31. London: Black Dog Publishing.

Newport, M. (2010), "Alter Egos," in J. Hemmings (ed.), *In the Loop: Knitting Now*, 46–55. London: Black Dog Publishing.

O'Neill, B., Gallego, J.I. and Zeller, F. (2013), "New Perspectives on Audience Activity: 'Prosumption' and Media Activism as Audience Practices," in N. Carpentier, and L. Hallett (eds), *Audience Transformations: Shifting Audience Positions in Late Modernity*, 157–171. Abingdon: Routledge.

Olin-Scheller, C. (2011), "'I want Twilight information to grow in my head': Convergence Culture From a Fan Perspective," in M. Larsson and A. Steiner (eds), *Interdisciplinary Approaches to Twilight: Studies in Fiction, Media, and a Contemporary Cultural Experience*, 159–175. Lund, Sweden: Nordic Academic Press.

Ordover, H. (2013), *Grounded: The Seven*, Tucson: Crafting-a-life Books.

Padovani, C. and Whittaker, P. (2010), "Twists, Knots, and Holes: Collecting, the Gaze and Knitting the Impossible," in J. Hemmings (ed.), *In the Loop: Knitting Now*, 10–17. London: Black Dog Publishing.

Patch, R. (2007), *Contemporary Hobby Knitting: The Preservation and Reinvention of Traditional Craft*, St. John's Newfoundland: Memorial University Press.

Pearson, R. (2007), "Bachies, Bardies, Trekkies, and Sherlockians," in J.A. Grey, C. Sandvoss and L. Harrington (eds), *Fandom: Identities and Communities in a Mediated World*, 98–109. New York: New York University Press.

Pentney, B.A. (2008), "Feminism, Activism, and Knitting: Are the Fibre Arts a Viable Mode for Feminist Political Action?," *Thirdspace, a Journal of Feminist Theory and Culture* 8.1. Available: http://www.thirdspace.ca/journal/article/viewArticle/pentney/210 [Accessed November 12, 2012].

Peterson, K.E. (2011), "How the Ordinary Becomes Extraordinary: The Modern Eye and the Quilt as Art Form," in M.E. Buszek (ed.), *Extra/Ordinary: Craft and Contemporary Art*, 99–114. Durham, NC: Duke University Press.

Prown, J.D. (1982), "Mind in Matter: An Introduction to Material Culture Theory and Method," *Winterthur Portfolio*, 17.1: 1–19.

Rehak, B. (2014), "Materiality and Object-Oriented Fandom," *Transformative Works and Cultures*, 16. Available: http://dx.doi.org/10.3983/twc.2014.0622 [Accessed January 20, 2015].

Risatti, H. (2007), *A Theory of Craft: Function and Aesthetic Expression*, Chapel Hill, NC: University of North Carolina Press.

Robertson, K. (2010), "Embroidery Pirates and Fashion Victims: Textiles, Craft and Copyright," *Textiles*, 8.1: 86–111.

Robertson, K. (2011), "Rebellious Doilies and Subversive Stitches: Writing a Craftivist History," in M.E. Buszek (ed.), *Extra/Ordinary: Craft and Contemporary Art*, 184–203. Durham, NC: Duke University Press.

Rowling, J.K. (1997), *Harry Potter and the Philosopher's Stone*, London: Bloomsbury.

Rowling, J.K. (1998), *Harry Potter and the Chamber of Secrets*, London: Bloomsbury.

Rowling, J.K. (1999), *Harry Potter and the Prisoner of Azkaban*, London: Bloomsbury.

Rowling, J.K. (2000), *Harry Potter and the Goblet of Fire*, London: Bloomsbury.

Rowling, J.K. (2001), *Quidditch Through the Ages*, London: Bloomsbury.

Rowling, J.K. (2003), *Harry Potter and the Order of the Phoenix*, London: Bloomsbury.

Rowling, J.K. (2005), *Harry Potter and the Half-Blood Prince*, London: Bloomsbury.

Rowling, J.K. (2007), *Harry Potter and the Deathly Hallows*, London: Bloomsbury.

Rowling, J.K. (2009), *Fantastic Beasts and Where To Find Them*, London: Bloomsbury.

Sandvoss, C. (2005), *Fans: The Mirror of Consumption*, Cambridge: Polity.

Schor, J. B. (1991), *The Overworked American*, New York: Basic Books.

Schwabach, A. (2011), *Fan Fiction and Copyright: Outside Works and Intellectual Property Protection*, London: Ashgate.

Scodari, C. (2003), "Resistance Re-examined: Gender, Fan Practices, and Science Fiction Television," *Popular Communication*, 1.11: 1–30.

Scott, S. (2009), "Repackaging Fan Culture: The Regifting Economy of Ancillary Content Models," *Transformative Works and Cultures*, 3. Available: http://dx.doi.org/10.3983/twc.2009.0150 [Accessed June 2, 2012].

Scott, S. (2013), "Battlestar Galactica: Fans and Ancillary Content," in J. Mittell (ed.), *How To Watch Television*, 320–329. New York: New York University Press.

Sheumaker, H. and Wajda, S.T. (2008), "Introduction," in H. Sheumaker and S.T. Wajda (eds), *Material Culture in America: Understanding Everyday Life*, xi–xvii. Santa Barbara, CA: ABC-CLIO.

Skeggs, B. (1974), *Formations of Class and Gender*, London: Sage.

Stacey, J. (1994), *Star Gazing: Hollywood Cinema and Female Spectatorship*, Abingdon: Routledge.

Stoller, D. (2003), *Stitch 'n Bitch: The Knitter's Handbook*, New York: Workman Publishing.

Stoller, D. (2005), *Stitch 'n Bitch Nation*, New York: Workman Publishing.

Stoller, D. (2006), *Stitch 'n Bitch Crochet: The Happy Hooker*, New York: Workman Publishing.

Strawn, S. M. (2007), *Knitting America: A Glorious Heritage From Warm Socks to High Art*, Minneapolis: Voyageur Press.

Sullivan, J. L. (2013), *Media Audiences: Effects, Users, Institutions, and Power*, London: Sage.

Tapscott, D. and Williams, A.D. (2007), *Wikinomics: How Mass Collaboration Changes Everything*, London: Atlantic Books.

Thornton, S. (1996), *Club Cultures: Music, Media and Subcultural Capital*, Cambridge: Polity.

Toffler, A. (1989), *The Third Wave*, New York: Bantam.

Turney, J. (2009), *The Culture of Knitting*, London: Bloomsbury.

Turney, J. (2010), "Knit Lit," in J. Hemmings (ed.), *In the Loop: Knitting Now*, 40–45. London: Black Dog Publishing.

Voigts-Virchow, E. (2012), "Pride and Promiscuity and Zombies, or: Miss Austen Mashed Up in the Affinity Spaces of Participatory Culture," in P. Nicklas and O. Lindner (eds), *Adaptation and Cultural Appropriation: Literature, Film, and the Arts*, 34–56. Berlin: Walter de Gruyter.

Walker, B. (1998), *A Treasury of Knitting Patterns*, Pittsville, WI: Schoolhouse.

Weldon and Company (1974), *Victorian Crochet*, Mineola, NY: Dover Publications.

Williamson, M. (2005), *The Lure of the Vampire: Gender, Fiction and Fandom from Bram Stoker to Buffy*, Brighton: Wallflower.

Willis, I. (2006), "Keeping Promises to Queer Children: Making Space (For Mary Sue) at Hogwarts," in K. Hellekson and K. Busse (eds), *Fan Fiction and Fan Communities in the Age of the Internet*, Jefferson, NC: McFarland.

Wills, K. (2007), *The Close-Knit Circle: American Knitters Today*, 153–170. Westport, CT: Praeger.

Woerner, M. (2013), "Fox Bans the Sale of Unlicensed Jayne Hats from Firefly," *iO9*, September 4. Available: http://io9.com/fox-bans-the-sale-of-unlicensed-jayne-hats-from-firefly-471820413 [Accessed May 20, 2015].

Woo, B. (2014), "A Pragmatics of Things: Materiality and Constraint in Fan Practices," *Transformative Works and Cultures*, 16. Available: http://dx.doi.org/10.3983/twc.2014.0495 [Accessed November 19, 2015].

Woodward, I. (2007), *Understanding Material Culture*, Thousand Oaks, CA: Sage.

Videography

Ballykissangel (1996–2001), UK, BBC.

Battlestar Galactica (2004–2009), USA, NBC Universal.

Being Human (2008–2013), UK, BBC.

The Big Bang Theory (2007–), USA, CBS.

Boardwalk Empire (2010–2014), USA, HBO.

Bob the Builder (1998–2005), UK, HIT Entertainment.

Bones (2005–), USA, Fox.

Buffy the Vampire the Slayer (1997–2003), USA, Mutant Enemy.

Call the Midwife (BBC 2012–), UK, BBC.

The Clangers (1969–74), UK, BBC.

Columbo (1971–2003), USA, NBC.

CSI (2000–2015), USA, CBS.

Despicable Me (2010), directed by Pierre Coffin and Chris Renaud, USA, Universal.

Doctor Who (1963–), UK, BBC.

Downton Abbey (2010–), UK, Carnival Film & Television.

Farscape (1999–2003), Australia/USA, Jim Henson Productions.

Firefly (2003), USA, 20th Century Fox.

Forbrydelsen/The Killing (2007–12), Denmark, Denmarks Radio.

Game of Thrones (2011–), USA, HBO.

A Grand Day Out (1990), directed by Nick Park, UK, Aardman Animations.

Harry Potter and the Philosopher's Stone (2001), directed by Chris Columbus, UK/USA, Warner Brothers.

Harry Potter and the Chamber of Secrets film (2002), directed by Chris Columbus, UK/USA, Warner Brothers.

Harry Potter and the Deathly Hallows Part 2 (2011), directed by David Yates, UK/USA, Warner Brothers.

The Hobbit: An Unexpected Journey (2012), directed by Peter Jackson, USA/New Zealand, New Line.

The Hobbit: The Desolation of Smaug (2013), directed by Peter Jackson, USA/New Zealand, New Line.

The Hobbit: The Battle of the Five Armies (2014), directed by Peter Jackson, USA/New Zealand, New Line.

The Hunger Games: Catching Fire (2013), directed by Francis Lawrence, USA, Centralmovies.

Into the Woods (2015), directed by Rob Marshall, USA/UK, Disney.

Kick-Ass (2010), directed by Matthew Vaughn, UK/USA, Lionsgate.

Lark Rise to Candleford (2008–2011), UK, BBC.

Mad Men (2007–2015), USA, AMC.

Magic Roundabout (1964–1971), UK, BBC.

Marvel Avengers Assemble (2012), directed by Joss Whedon, USA, Marvel Studios.

Mary Poppins (1964), directed by Robert Stevenson, USA, Disney.

Misfits (2009–2013), UK, E4.

Monty Python's Flying Circus (1969–74), UK, BBC.

My Little Pony: Friendship is Magic (2010–), USA/Canada, Discovery.

NCIS (2003–), USA, CBS.

Orange is the New Black (2013–), USA, Tilted Productions.

Outlander (2014–), USA, Tall Ship Productions.

Pushing Daisies (2007–2009), USA, ABC.

Sailor Moon (1995–2000), Japan/Canada, Cloverway International.

Sanctuary (2007–2011), Canada, SyFy Channel.

Shaun the Sheep (2007–2014), UK, BBC.

Sherlock (2010–), UK, Hartswood Films.

Star Trek (1966–), USA, CBS.

Star Wars (1977–), USA, Lucasfilm.

Starsky and Hutch (1975–79), USA, Spelling-Goldberg

Supernatural (2005–), USA, Warner Brothers.

True Blood (2008–2014), USA, HBO.

Twilight movies (2008–2012)

Vampire Diaries (2009–), USA, Alloy Productions.

The Walking Dead (2010–), USA, AMC.

Warehouse 13 (2009–2014), Universal.

Wartime Farm (2012), UK, BBC.

The West Wing (1999–2006), USA, NBC.

INDEX